A TREASURED LANDSCAPE

the HERITAGE *of* BELVOIR PARK

Edited by Ben Simon

2005

THE FOREST OF
BELFAST

Cover Picture. Belvoir Park from Malone by Jonathan Fisher. Private collection. Photograph: photographic survey, Courtauld Institute of Art.

The former entrance to Belvoir Park.

ISBN–10. 0-9551583-0-3
ISBN–13. 978-0-9551583-0-8

Text © The authors, 2005. Photographs © as indicated in the Acknowledgments

Published by The Forest of Belfast,
4-10 Linenhall Street, Belfast BT2 8BP.
In partnership with Belfast City Council and Environment and Heritage Service
In association with Forest Service and the Northern Ireland Housing Executive

Design by designhouse

Printed by W & G Baird, Greystone Road, Antrim BT41 2RS

Contents

Foreword

BELVOIR IS WITHOUT DOUBT one of the finest examples of urban woodland on these islands. Its natural history, cultural heritage, landscape value and recreational uses make it a huge asset to the people of Belfast. But how many of those who drive past it daily, walk through it, play golf in it or even live on its fringes, recognise this value and understand the history which has led to its development? We tend to see an area's obvious assets, but not look deeper to discover why, or how, or when, these have developed.

Although the brainchild and labour of love of Ben Simon, this book could not have been written by any one person. By combining the efforts of numerous experts in their fields we have a much more comprehensive view of Belvoir which provides insights into many aspects of the area. Of particular interest are the firsthand reports from those who lived there in times past, giving us a unique insight into a long lost way of life.

This book is a partnership, and demonstrates well the value of this approach – by building on the expertise, knowledge, enthusiasm and abilities of many, working together for a common goal, something new and innovative has been produced that is greater than the sum of its parts. Indeed without partnership it would not exist at all. Partnership is a key theme for government, and is now enshrined in policy; it is something that the Forest of Belfast and Northern Ireland Environment Link have been promoting and demonstrating for many years. Few people or organisations dispute the value of partnerships in theory. However, when it actually comes to co-operating and overcoming the difficulties inherent in working to a common agenda, things do not always run smoothly. But, again as demonstrated by this book, persevering in the effort does eventually pay off to the benefit of all.

The value of Belvoir is great – as wildlife site, recreational amenity area, 'green lungs' for the city, landscape feature and open space, as an aid to the physical and mental health of the city's residents and visitors – but can we put a cash value on these? Its potential value to developers is also high, and that is much easier to attach a pound sign to. We must all ensure that those in whose hands Belvoir's future lies – the politicians, the civil servants, the Council officers; ultimately all of us as voters – recognise the intrinsic and unquantifiable asset that it provides for all residents, whether we visit on a regular basis or only breathe the air it helps to purify. This book helps to make those connections and highlight the importance of Belvoir Park.

This study raises a number of issues. We need to adopt an integrated approach to the management of habitats that are within the ownership of more than one organisation (e.g. there are ancient oaks in Forest Service, Housing Executive and golf course land). We need open discussion of key management objectives. For example, should there be a scheme to restore the ancient woodland, with extensive removal of conifer plantations and the planting of oaks from acorns collected from the Belvoir oaks? Should elements of the old gardens like the fish ponds be restored and the gardens recreated? If so, to what style and period? Even more challenging, should a large building such as a hotel be constructed at the site of the mansion house to form a new focal point for the demesne? Would such a development add to the attractiveness and usefulness of the site, bringing new people to appreciate its value, or would it destroy the peace and tranquillity current visitors

value? How can we decide if the benefits of a public transport route through Belvoir would outweigh its negative impact on the historic landscape, on wildlife and on the amenity of the area? How do we ensure that the Belvoir of the 21st century is a vibrant contributor to the city within which it resides while retaining its historic and natural value?

Sustainable development is now an accepted concept – Northern Ireland should have its own Sustainable Development Strategy early in 2006. But will it, like so many of Northern Ireland's other strategies, simply sit on the shelf? Or will it become a fundamental and accepted part of all of our lives? How we deal with the complex issues posed by managing Belvoir will be a test of whether we really do want a sustainable Northern Ireland. This can only be achieved by all sectors working together to ensure the best possible future for the citizens and their environment.

For all those who have visited Belvoir Park the book provides a valuable insight into what they have seen. For those who haven't yet been there it provides a great incentive for a day of discovery. For those who drive by but have never stopped – next time

you're in the area, why not come in for a few minutes or hours to experience this fascinating site on your doorstep?

Professor Sue Christie
Director
Northern Ireland Environment Link

Editor's Acknowledgments

THIS STUDY WAS UNDERTAKEN as a contribution to the Forest of Belfast, the partnership to promote trees throughout greater Belfast. The Forest of Belfast encourages tree planting and tree care and increases awareness of the value of trees, for example by commissioning sculptures that reflect the local environment and by undertaking research into tree folklore and heritage. This project grew out of an initial study of the veteran trees of Belvoir Park and a realisation of the immense importance of this site.

I would wish to thank the members of the Forest of Belfast committee for their support and commitment to this project over a period of four years. I would like to thank the contributors who have brought a wide range of skills and expertise to this study of Belvoir Park. I am also grateful to the many local residents who kindly contributed information about Belvoir Park, stories they recalled, family history and childhood memories.

This publication has been enhanced with many illustrations provided by local residents, individuals with a connection to Belvoir Park, the Forest Service, Ulster Museum, private collections and archives. I wish to thank all these individuals and organisations for permitting their photographs to be used. Acknowledgements are given at the end of the publication, but I would like to make special mention of the beautiful line drawings by Carol Baird which appear throughout the publication.

The development of this project has benefited greatly from the assistance given by friends and colleagues who very kindly spent long hours discussing the contents and reading drafts of text. I would like to sincerely thank all of these people including Roy Anderson, Dorin Bell, Sue and Peter Christie, Peter Cush, Fiona Holdsworth, Maurice Parkinson, Dick Schaible, Robert Scott and Martin Walsh.

Field data collected in this project will be of use as baseline information for future studies. To assist research into local history, a number of documents about Belvoir Park were copied with the kind permission of Lord Deramore and have been deposited in the archives of Built Heritage of the Environment and Heritage Service and in the Public Records Office of Northern Ireland. Copies of photographs of the mansion house, including the very important colour photographs of Belvoir Park by Douglas Deane, have also been deposited in these archives.

Two people mentioned in various chapters of this book played a vital role in raising awareness of the importance of Belvoir Park. Douglas Deane and Norman Taylor deserve our sincere thanks.

Contributors

Roy Anderson is a soil chemist and environmentalist working for the Department of Agriculture and Rural Development at Newforge Lane, Belfast. He was educated at Annadale Grammar School Belfast (now Wellington College) and went on to receive a 2:1 Honours degree in Chemistry at Queen's University before completing a PhD in Animal Nutrition with the Faculty of Agriculture and Food Science at Queen's in 1973. He has always retained a fervent interest in the environment and has written over 150 papers on invertebrate and fungal ecology, biogeography and taxonomy. He lives with his wife and two children in Newtownbreda village close to Belvoir Park and spends much of his spare time studying the local fauna and flora.

Ernie Andrews. Ernie has always lived close to Belvoir Park. He was a motor mechanic and raced motorbikes; his other interests are shooting and fishing. Ernie loved going to Belvoir as a child, fishing in the Lagan and walking in the forest. Now he is retired and lives in Newtownbreda. Still passionate about the countryside, Ernie is often up in the Belvoir woods with his dog early in the morning, which he enjoys as much today as in his youth.

Mike Baillie is Professor of Palaeoecology in the School of Archaeology and Palaeoecology at Queen's University, Belfast. He was one of the main players in the construction of the Belfast Long Oak Chronology and has published widely in the fields of dendrochronology and abrupt environmental change. His books include *Tree-ring dating and archaeology*, Croom-Helm, London 1982, *A Slice Through Time: dendrochronology and precision dating*, Routledge 1995, and *Exodus to Arthur: catastrophic encounters with comets*, Batsford, London 1999.

David Brown is an experimental officer in the School of Archaeology and Palaeoecology at Queen's University Belfast. He provides a commercial dendrochronogical or tree-ring dating service for archaeologists, building historians and environmentalists. He has helped in the construction of two of the world's longest tree-ring chronologies.

Dorin Bell. Born in Belfast, Dorin (Doreen) grew up in Donaghadee where, during visits from her grandmother, Dorin first heard of Belvoir Park Estate. Her family emigrated to Ontario, Canada, when she was ten, but Nannie Seabrooke (Lily Dobbin) visited the family several times before Dorin graduated from McMaster University, Hamilton. Dorin began her career as a secondary school English teacher, eventually moving to Calgary, Alberta. Here she raised two sons and taught from 1968 until her retirement in 2002.

Stephen Clarke studied for his PhD in the Department of Applied Plant Science, Queen's University of Belfast. His project involved the genetic characterisation of oak and ash populations within the British Isles and identified a number of distinct ash and oak gene pools within Ireland.

Sue Christie has been Director of Northern Ireland Environment Link since 1993 and before that was the first Director of the Ulster Wildlife Trust and Project Manager of NI2000. She has been involved in a number of voluntary organisations and government committees and working groups on environmental issues, including The Forest of Belfast. She is Visiting Professor at the Department of Environmental Sciences at the University of Ulster, Coleraine.

David Coburn. David was born in 1925 and grew up in Gosford Street off McClure Street on Ormeau Road. Gosford Street has gone now. When he was 14 he left school to start work at Lewers Carrol electrical contractors in College Square East. During the War they did a lot of wiring work for the army and after the War David was employed for a while wiring buses. David then worked with his brother in the electrical business before becoming a self-employed electrician. He has been retired for a good few years.

Peter Cush was born in Bangor Co. Down. He moved to Holywood when he was nine, where he developed his interest in natural history exploring the shoreline, wetlands and grasslands of North Down from Kinnegar to the fringes of the shipyard and roaming the length and breadth of the Holywood hills. He worked for many years in the Veterinary Research Laboratories at Stormont and then moved to the Environment and Heritage Service of the Department of the Environment, where he is a Senior Scientific Officer in the Biodiversity Unit. Married with four children, he has lived in South Belfast now for near on 25 years and has continued his roaming habits by exploring the Lagan Valley Regional Park as time permits.

Colin Fleming. Colin is a Principal Scientific Officer in the Department of Agriculture and Rural Development for Northern Ireland and Lecturer in Applied Plant Science, Queen's University of Belfast. As Programme Leader for Molecular Biology and Biotechnology he is responsible for plant health diagnostics and the genetic analysis of agricultural, forestry and amenity plants. He has supervised a team of undergraduate and postgraduate students who have been assessing the genetic diversity in woodland tree species and is particularly interested in the genetic characterisation of native tree species.

Dermot Hughes. As a naturalist, Dermot fits into that 'generalist' category of people who know a little about everything, though he knows most about birds and plants. Married with four children, Dermot is originally from Dublin but has lived in Galwally Park for over 22 years. Belvoir is on the doorstep and most of his observations come from casual though frequent visits through all the year. He works as Director of Programs for the Ulster Wildlife Trust, which includes responsibility for conservation. This gives him added insights into the Trust Nature Reserves which include the Lagan Meadows.

Chris Murphy. A freelance ecologist and tour leader, through 'Murphy's Wildlife' Chris organises trips throughout the British Isles with occasional sorties to places like Nepal, Poland and Morocco. Originally from Liverpool, he has been bird watching for over 40 years and has lived in Northern Ireland since 1984. Chris is a member of the Northern Ireland Bird Records Committee and regularly writes articles about birds. Married with two children, he is active in campaigning on planning and environmental issues.

Ben Simon. Born in Belfast, Ben has always enjoyed being out of doors, going for walks in the town, in the hills or by the sea. He received a degree in Environmental Science and Ecology at the University of Ulster and then studied for a PhD in Earth Science at Glasgow University, followed by three years' research at Trinity College, Dublin. Ben has been back in Belfast since 1987 and was employed as Manager of the Ulster Wildlife Trust until 1995 when he became Forest Officer with the Forest of Belfast, the urban forestry initiative.

John Witchell. Brought up on the family farm in Gloucestershire, John graduated from Trinity Hall in 1976 having read Geography and Land Economy. He did a post-graduate course in Advanced Farm Management before moving to Northern Ireland in 1978 to join Blakiston Houston Estates for whom he still works. He completed an MBA in Construction and Real Estate in 2000 and was chairman of the Royal Institution of Chartered Surveyors, Northern Ireland, in 2004.

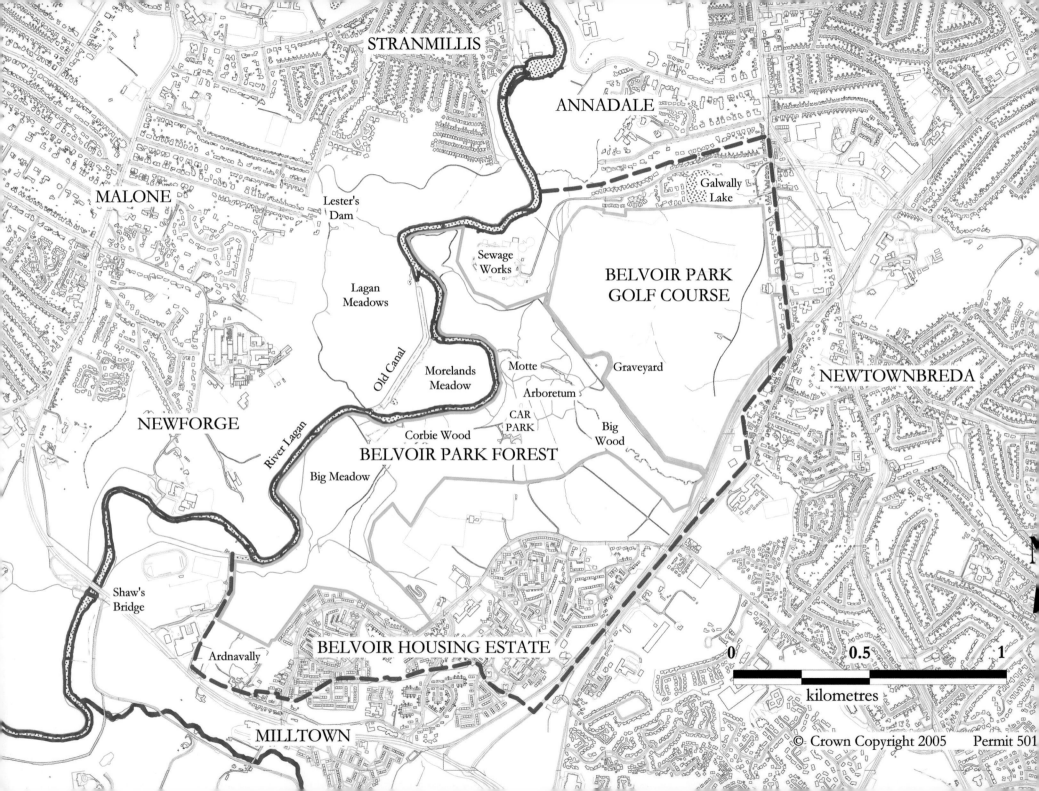

STRANMILLIS

ANNADALE

MALONE

Lester's Dam

Galwally Lake

Sewage Works

BELVOIR PARK GOLF COURSE

Lagan Meadows

Old Canal

Morelands Meadow

Motte

Graveyard

NEWTOWNBREDA

Arboretum

NEWFORGE

River Lagan

CAR PARK

Corbie Wood

Big Wood

BELVOIR PARK FOREST

Big Meadow

Shaw's Bridge

Ardnavally

BELVOIR HOUSING ESTATE

MILLTOWN

0   0.5   1

kilometres

© Crown Copyright 2005   Permit 501

CHAPTER *One-* *discovering* BELVOIR PARK   **Sue Christie and Ben Simon**

Above: A shoot at Belvoir Park

Opposite page: Map of Belvoir Park. The location of the demesne wall is shown by the red dotted line. The boundary of the forest and golf course are shown by the green and yellow lines. Sites mentioned in the book are highlighted.

Map based upon MapInfo image with the permission of the Controller of Her Majesty's Stationery Office © Crown Copyright 2005.

THIS PUBLICATION CHARTS the heritage of a small area of land by the bank of the River Lagan near Belfast. Belvoir Park. It is a fascinating story, there is much that will surprise and delight. Come along on a voyage of discovery with a number of experts; it is a study of plants and animals and the influence that people have had on this landscape over the last 350 years. Each chapter examines Belvoir Park from a different perspective: together they help us to understand how the land has come to be as it is today.

Perhaps the most surprising discovery has come from examining tree rings of some of the larger fallen oak trees. A number of these trees started to grow in the 17th century, with the oldest oak tested dating from 1641. It is likely that many of the oaks that are still growing at Belvoir are several hundred years old, a living heritage and record of our past that had not been previously suspected. Today the biggest of the veteran trees at Belvoir has a circumference of nearly nine metres just above ground and is one of the largest girthed native oaks so far discovered in Ireland.

The Belvoir estate was founded in the early 18th century by Arthur Hill, a descendant of Moyses Hill who had amassed a huge landholding in Counties Antrim and Down. The mansion house was constructed on an imposing site overlooking the River Lagan and a wall 5km in length was built to surround the grounds. The walled grounds (demesne) remained an oasis of woodland during the 18th and 19th centuries, when timber was an extremely valuable resource. During this period most trees in Ireland were felled before they had grown to maturity and today, outside of Belvoir Park, there are few native trees with a girth of over 3m in the northern Lagan Valley.

The woods and parkland formed an attractive setting for the mansion house. They also provided valuable cover for game birds and some of the earliest references to the estate concern the protection of pheasant, turkey and wild duck. Like many other estates in Ireland, the owners of Belvoir Park were interested in agricultural improvement, and farmland within the demesne was laid out in enclosures. Near the house there was a walled garden with glasshouses and pleasure gardens with walks. In this area exotic trees were planted in the 19th century to create an arboretum.

In Victorian times there were over 7,000 houses with associated parks of four hectares or more in

Morelands Meadow

The history of many of the estates in Ireland was heavily influenced by events such as the 1798 Rebellion, the Famine and the agricultural depression and land wars of the latter part of the 19th century. Acts to promote land distribution in the late 19th and early 20th centuries also had a major impact. The First World War was, however, the watershed in the life of the big houses of Ireland.[2] It heralded changes in society and politics and increased taxation including death duties. The big house was no longer a dominant part of community life and in the following years, during the period of unrest that resulted in the partition of Ireland, nearly 300 Irish mansions were burnt.[2]

After the First World War, the upkeep of Belvoir house with its 20-plus bedrooms and the cost of managing the woods, pleasure gardens and the estate buildings became increasingly unaffordable. An attempt to develop the demesne farm as a Model Dairy did not succeed. In the early 1920s, there were proposals by the newly created Government of Northern Ireland to acquire Belvoir Park, but these failed and the future of the house became a cause for concern. By 1925 the house was empty and the grounds unmanaged, though there were still large

Ireland.[1] In many respects Belvoir Park developed as a typical Irish demesne. However, the extent of the walled grounds, at over 600 acres (245ha), made it the largest demesne near Belfast and larger than most in Ulster.

Fascinating details about the estate and a way of life that is long gone are provided by the recollections of people associated with Belvoir. These stories, together with information from old newspapers and other sources, help us understand the history of Belvoir Park

and its owners. In the 18th century Belvoir was the residence of the Hill-Trevor family. In the 19th century it was acquired by the Bateson (Deramore) family. The last residents of the big house were Walter Wilson of Harland and Wolff and Sir James Johnston, a former Mayor of Belfast. Equally interesting are the glimpses we have of those who worked in the estate and made life in the big house possible.

Above and below right: The Arboretum at Belvoir.

areas of farmland outside of the demesne in Newtownbreda and Malone that were leased to farmers.

During the 20th century the way of life associated with the big houses in Ireland largely disappeared. Many of the remaining mansions were abandoned or demolished, the gardens turned into agricultural land and the woods clear-felled for timber.[2,3] At Belvoir part of the demesne was used to create an 18-hole golf course. Suburban development could easily have resulted in the obliteration of the remainder of the demesne landscape when, in 1934, the mansion house and remaining estate lands totalling 823 acres (300 ha) were acquired by a building company. However, the Depression, the Second World War (when Belvoir House, like all of the big houses around Belfast, was taken over by the military), and the introduction of planning controls in 1945 prevented any significant development within the estate. By remarkable good fortune, the old oak trees in Belvoir demesne were not felled and sold.

The history of Belvoir Park and the northern Lagan Valley from 1945 provides a case study for the successful development and implementation of planning control. Although proposals to retain Belvoir Park demesne as a public park were unsuccessful, only limited housing development was permitted. The Belvoir housing estate was planned to retain as much open space as possible and housing was kept away from the woodland and scenic riverside area. Although in the early 1960s there was often little appreciation of the importance of the natural environment in Northern Ireland, at Belvoir attention was paid to retaining existing trees, and new areas of woodland were planted in the housing estate. Demesne land near the housing estate was used for playing fields and the Forest Service planted a commercial conifer woodland on much of the remainder of the site. Riverside land was protected and has since been managed by Belfast City Council as parkland with low level grazing by cattle. In subsequent years paths overgrown for decades were reopened and bridges over the old canal and River Lagan provided enhanced access to Belvoir. With the development of the Lagan Valley Regional Park, Belvoir has become an important part of a much larger area managed for amenity and wildlife. However, although some elements of the built heritage of Belvoir have survived, unfortunately the mansion house, the focal point of the estate, was demolished in 1961.

Some wildlife has probably gone forever from Belvoir. For example, hares and pine martens no longer live there and red squirrels are under severe threat. A heronry that existed at the Belvoir woods for over 100 years was last occupied in the late 1950s. However, today some species not generally associated with the urban fringe are seen in the area. Otters are sometimes glimpsed. Kingfishers and long-eared owls can be seen. Occasionally rare and completely unexpected species are recorded, including on at least one occasion a seal that swam up the tidal Lagan and climbed the fish ladder at Stranmillis! The most important elements of the flora are the veteran trees: the woodlands at Belvoir include 270 single stem trees with a girth of 3m or more. Some invertebrate and plant species associated with long-established

woodland occur, reinforcing the view that Belvoir is an ancient woodland site. A study of the genetic signature of the Belvoir oaks also shows that they have a close genetic affinity to Northern Irish semi-natural woods. The best flora is seen in areas that have been least disturbed, though interesting plants occur throughout much of the demesne.

The future management of the woods, meadows and wetlands at Belvoir requires careful consideration to ensure that the most important elements of biodiversity are retained and, where possible, enhanced. The first step in managing habitats is to discover what species are present, their status and requirements. This study takes a big step in that direction, and also highlights some of the complex issues to be considered in managing habitats. For example, the coniferous woodlands are of little value for herbaceous plants and in several places are heavily shading veteran oaks. However, the conifer plantations are important for the red squirrels and the larch plantation is teeming with birdlife. Some conifer trees are also important for individual species, such as the Monterey cypress in the Arboretum, under which earth star fungi have been found.

The management and future development of Belvoir Park must take account not only of flora and fauna, but also of the many other, occasionally conflicting, uses of the park. It is an important recreation area and the interests and requirements of golfers, walkers and other visitors need to be included in any plans. A large section of Belvoir Park is a commercial forest which introduces additional financial and management considerations. Belvoir Park is also an historic landscape, the most important element of which is the mature parkland trees, a priority habitat in the *Northern Ireland Biodiversity Strategy*.[4]

Housing spreading out from Belfast now almost completely surrounds Belvoir Park. Belvoir lies between Belfast and Lisburn, a growing conurbation recently designated as a city. This urban setting brings pressures for development and in the 1960s three roads, including two motorways, were proposed to cut through Belvoir. Although these plans have now been shelved, a public transport route is still being considered which would pass through Belvoir Park close to the boundary between the forest and golf course. Key current policies that will help to influence the future of Belvoir Park include the *Biodiversity Strategy for Northern Ireland, Planning Policy Statement 6* (which refers to the importance of historic parks, gardens and demesnes[5]) and the *Belfast Metropolitan Area Plan* (BMAP) which was published in draft form in late 2004.[6] Will these policies, which largely promote protection, be followed when there is such pressure for highly profitable development? This will happen only if the politicians and civil servants are convinced that the people do truly value this land.

There are some intriguing questions which have been highlighted by this study. You would think that identifying the species of oak tree would be fairly straightforward, but the field botanists did not agree with geneticists about which of the veteran oaks are *Quercus robur* and which are *Quercus petraea*. Dating more of the oaks would add to our understanding of the early history of the region. More detailed studies of the flora and fauna of other areas in the Lagan Valley would enable us to more fully appreciate the regional value of Belvoir Park. It would also be rewarding to discover more about the mansion house and gardens and to learn about the early history of the site from archaeologists. This study is certainly not the last word about Belvoir.

Belvoir Park is one of many old walled demesnes in Ireland, large areas of land where there was often a continuity of management for generations. These are historic landscapes, rich in built heritage and sites which often contain old trees, extensive gardens, woods and wetlands as well as agricultural land.[7] It is highly likely that Belvoir Park is not the only demesne where there has been long established woodland or where veteran trees remain. For example, demesnes such as Charleville Forest in County Offaly, Curraghmore in County Waterford, Abbeyleix in County Laois, Coolattin in County Wicklow and Crom in County Fermanagh would be prime sites to explore for species indicative of ancient woodland.[8] Some of these sites may well include veteran trees; at Charleville oaks over 300 years old have been reported.[9]

Although there is an increasing realisation of the importance of biodiversity and heritage in Ireland there is also a growing pace of change and development. A number of the remaining demesnes are the subject of proposed development – for housing, recreation or even business. This book demonstrates the potential of multi-disciplinary studies in understanding the value of these landscapes, and is an approach that should be helpful in gaining a better understanding of other demesnes. The survival of much of Belvoir Park is a reminder of the critical importance of planning control, partnerships and the determination of individuals and organisations in protecting treasured landscapes. If Belvoir is to remain, its value must be recognised and accepted by all those who will have a role in deciding its future.

16

Early history

The Belvoir motte

*Opposite page: A dramatic view of Belvoir
from the River Lagan by Hugh Frazer.*

ONE OF THE FIRST SIGHTS to attract the eye of visitors arriving at the car park at Belvoir Park Forest is a prominent mound close to the steep eastern bank of the River Lagan. This is believed to be a Norman motte,[1,2] dating to the 12th-14th century. A short walk from the motte, across a small river valley, leads to the old graveyard of Breda at the boundary between Belvoir Park Forest and the more open ground that is now Belvoir Park Golf Club. The church of Breda was referred to in 1442 and was said to have been ruined in 1622.[3,4]

Although little is known about the appearance of the Lagan Valley during this period, it is generally thought to have been wooded.[5-7] A map dated about 1570 that shows the area around Belfast as woodland also includes an annotation 'Alonge this river by ye space of 26 miles groweth much woodes as well Okes for Tymber...'.[8]

From the 16th century northwest County Down was known as South Clandeboye and was under the control of the O'Neills, though in the early 17th century the increasing influence of England forced Con O'Neill to hand over most of this land. Documents relating to the transfer of townlands include some references to trees and woods; for example two leases mention that Con O'Neill sought to retain timber rights when he disposed of townlands around Castlereagh.[9] One lease concerning Ballynafeigh, now a suburb of southeast Belfast, refers to woodland management. The lessor reserved wood for firing, hedging and fencing and the lessees, a tanner and carpenter, had to maintain the 'springs' of the woods and 'coppyis' (young trees and coppice trees?). Timber was not to be used to fire bricks or tiles without the lessor's licence and no trees thought fit for barking (oak bark was used for tanning) were to be felled before 1 May. [9]

With the break up of the O'Neill lands Breda and Galwally passed to others, first through a lease to Michael White of Carrickfergus. The townland south of Breda, Ballylenaghan, (also referred to as Donnedegane or Dunreagin) was for a while given as the residence of Con O'Neill, though this land was also transferred. At the end of a complex series of agreements, in 1616 Moyses Hill and James Hamilton were granted extensive lands in County Down by Con O'Neill including Breda and adjacent townlands.[9]

Creation of the demesne

Moyses Hill built forts by the western bank of the River Lagan at Malone and Stranmillis and later the family residences were at Hill Hall, near Lisburn, and Hillsborough.[10-12] In 1690, Michael Hill, a descendant of Moyses, married a rich heiress, Anne Trevor. Their eldest son, Trevor Hill, inherited Hill properties and became Viscount Hillsborough; his descendants built the present mansion house in Hillsborough. The second son of Michael Hill and Anne Trevor, Arthur Hill, inherited Trevor estates.[13] For Arthur Hill a new house and demesne were created and the site chosen was on the eastern bank of the River Lagan in the area around Breda.

THE EARLIEST EVIDENCE of the creation of Belvoir Park dates from 1722 when Arthur Hill acquired 475 acres at Ballylenaghan for the sum of £2,000.[14,15] In 1731 he acquired the adjacent townland of Breda[16] and two years later he obtained an interest in the next townland to the north, Galwally.[17] Parts of these three townlands were used to create the grounds for his house. In the earliest legal documents referring to Arthur Hill his address was given as Dublin but by 1731 documents start to use Bellvoir or Belvoir, County Down, suggesting that by this time he had moved to the new estate.

Some of the early 18th century documents regarding this transfer of land are of particular interest as they provide the earliest description of the townlands.[15, 18] Most of the area was described as arable land, meadow and pasture. Other land was referred to as wood and scrub, heath, moor and marsh. These documents also give information about buildings. For example, in Ballylenaghan there were stated to be 30 messuages (a messuage was a term for a dwelling house, its outbuildings and adjoining land), 100 cottages, 100 tofts (former house sites), along with 100 gardens and 2 orchards. The list for

Ballylesson, Edenderry and Breda comprised 2 castles, 100 messuages, 150 cottages, 50 tofts, 100 gardens, 10 orchards and 4 mills. It is not known how accurate this information is, though the picture it provides agrees with that given by Richard Dobbs who, in his 1683 account of County Antrim, noted that the road from Lisburn to Belfast '…is all along for the most part furnished with houses, little orchards, and gardens…'.[19]

The new mansion house was constructed at an imposing location on a ridge overlooking the Lagan. This was a significant undertaking and involved the construction of tall retaining walls on the western and eastern side of the buildings to create a large level site. In the valley by the house formal gardens were developed and slightly over 600 acres (245ha) of land extending to the bank of the River Lagan were enclosed by a wall 5km in length. A further 10ha of land at Morelands Meadow, on the western bank of the river, are also generally considered to form part of the demesne. The enclosed land included the graveyard of Breda and existing settlements, and a new church and village were located just outside the wall. The replacement church, which was for the combined parishes of Knock and Breda, was built in

1737 and named Knockbreda, and the new village became known as Newtownbreda.[20-22]

There are no known accounts of the building of Belvoir House though it is said to have had a shingled roof that was blown off in a storm, and the first greenhouse in Belfast is supposed to have been built here.[23] The earliest depiction of a house at Belvoir is a tiny sketch on the 1739 map of County Down by Oliver Sloane.[24] Although Arthur Hill is named in all of the early legal documents about Belvoir, it is interesting to note that his mother (who after the death of her first husband remarried and became Viscountess Middleton) paid for the construction of Knockbreda church.[25] In her will she mentioned that for many years Arthur Hill had managed her affairs[26] and it seems likely that mother and son worked together to create Belvoir Park. The walled demesne was developed for game and notices placed in the Belfast News-Letter refer to the grounds being stocked with pheasant and wild turkey (Appendix 1). The latter might be a reference to capercaillie, a large game bird that occurs in Scotland, though there is evidence that American wild turkeys had been introduced into the nearby Portmore Estate in the 18th century.[27] Exotic birds would have been a remarkable sight in Belfast and from the News-Letter of 1753 we also learn that a grey parrot with red tail feathers was lost at Belvoir.[28] A half guinea reward was offered for its return.

The early Belfast News-Letter advertisements about Belvoir Park provide additional insights into the difficulties of managing a large estate on the edge of what was the growing town of Belfast, with references to trespass, theft and poaching (Appendix 1).

We are fortunate to have three early and informative accounts of the grounds of Belvoir Park. These were by Walter Harris, Mrs Delany and Edward Willes.

> *'Belvoir, an agreeable Seat of the Honourable Arthur Hill Esq;, stands about two Miles south of Belfast, pleasantly seated on the River Lagan, which by the Help of the Tide is navigable for Boats to the Foot of the Garden, the Water there being from two to three Feet and a half deep. The Avenue is large, handsome, and well planted; the Gardens are formed out of an irregular Glyn into regular Walks, beautified with Canals, Slopes, Terraces and other Ornaments. The Demesne is judiciously disposed, planted and formed into proper Inclosures, round a Variety of Meadow and Tillage Ground. The Produce of Wheat here by the Means of Lime Manure has been considerable, and the Lands thereby highly advanced in Value; although Limestone is not the Produce of the Soil, but is conveyed six Miles by Water to it'.* Walter Harris, 1744.[25]

'This place is much more finished than Hillsborough, and in a finer country, and much enriched with bleach yards, farm-houses and pretty dwellings. On Friday we went in a boat on the river, which runs round the improvements almost, and several turnings of it can be seen from the house. The grounds are laid out in enclosures, which with the hedge-rows and woods on the sides of some of the hills make the prospect very rich. The town of Belfast, Cave-Hill, and the bridge of 22 arches over the river, in a very clear day can be seen from the windows'.

Mrs Delany, 1758 [29]

'I went by Mr Hill's (now Trevor's) house and plantations which are very fine. Few people can brag of larger plantations which are of their own rising. He has a most noble demesne, wall'd in with a stone wall I believe about 500 acres. 'Tis not in a park but contains many inclosures, and I observed a great stock of horned cattle and sheep. If I mistake not, he is one that can boast of fatting bullocks on his own ground. For to say the truth what fat beef you do see at table is very little of it fatted so far north'.

Edward Willes, 1759 [30]

Above: A second painting of Belvoir House by Jonathan Fisher, showing the northern and eastern façade. The grounds are illustrated somewhat imaginatively; this view of the house could not be seen from the river. The painting does, however, show two interesting structures – a small summerhouse in the woodland and a remarkable ecclesiastical-looking gothic building on top of the hill. The latter building, which is not described in any literature about Belvoir, is also shown in the view Fisher painted of Belfast from Belvoir. It may have stood at Bowling Green Hill. Private collection. Photograph: photographic survey, Courtauld Institute of Art.

Above: View of Belfast from Belvoir by Jonathan Fisher. The well-wooded grounds of Belvoir demesne in the foreground are bounded by the demesne wall, shown where it terminates at the river edge. The Lagan Valley, with fields and few tall trees, are in sharp contrast to the woods of Belvoir. In the distance is Belfast and the bridge over the Lagan. On the right hand side of the painting the mysterious gothic building is again seen. Private collection. Photograph: photographic survey, Courtauld Institute of Art.

The main area of farmland was the gently undulating ground in the northeast of the demesne, land which two centuries after the creation of the demesne would become a golf course. The boundary between this land and the woodland surrounding the house is marked by a prominent ditch which can still be seen, running parallel to the wide track that passes Breda graveyard. This ditch was probably a feature known as a ha-ha, a boundary used to keep farm animals out of the woods without restricting views over the grounds.

By far the best impression of Belvoir Park in the 18th century is given in beautiful paintings of the house and grounds by Jonathan Fisher. These paintings were probably commissioned by Arthur Hill and date from around 1770. The house at this time had two stories with, on the northern façade, a prominent portico with a pediment that extended above the roof line. Surrounding the house are mature woodlands and meadows with sheep and cattle. The paintings also clearly depict the contrast between the well wooded demesne and the surrounding farmland in the Lagan Valley and Castlereagh hills with neat hedgerows and only occasional tall trees.

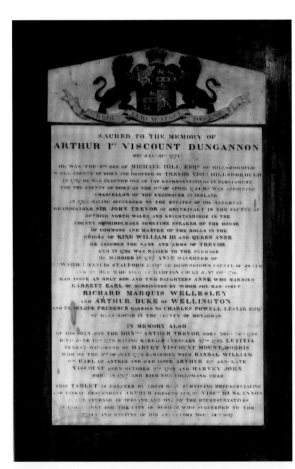

Above: The Dungannon plaque in Knockbreda Church. The text is given in reference 35.

Of the people who worked in the estate in the 18th century we have the names and professions of a few people, with Kenneth Sutherland described as gardener at Belvoir,[31] and John Lomas was for many years steward.[32] The family history of Arthur Hill and his descendants is given in a plaque in Knockbreda Church. He married twice and had children by his second wife, Anne Stafford. In 1758 Mrs Delany wrote of her impressions of Arthur Hill on a visit to Belvoir. 'A fine gentleman is the character he aims at, but in reality he is a very honest, hospitable, friendly, good man, with a little pepper in his composition…but he has the advantage of seeing his own peevishness and making a joke of it himself'.[29]

Mrs Delany also noted that Arthur Hill had a fine fortune and a year later this was enhanced when he received an inheritance on the death of his uncle, Sir John Trevor. Arthur Hill took on the Trevor family name, becoming Arthur Hill-Trevor and was later made Viscount Dungannon, a title that had previously been used by the Trevor family. He was an active politician, a member of many committees and for a year he was Chancellor of the Exchequer.[33,34] He died in 1771 and was buried in the family vault

at Belvoir.[35] Today he is perhaps best remembered because one of his daughters, Anne Hill, was the mother of Arthur Wellesley, the Duke of Wellington. According to local tradition the future Iron Duke played at Belvoir when a child and later in life Anne is said to have lived at Annadale Hall, a house just north of Belvoir.[36-38]

A year before the death of the first Viscount Dungannon his son, also called Arthur Hill-Trevor, had died and been buried at Newtownbreda.[39] He was the only son of the first Viscount and the estate passed to the next generation, the grandson of the first Viscount (who confusingly was again given the name Arthur Hill-Trevor) who was only eight years old at the time. He became the second Viscount Dungannon.

Notices placed in the newspapers indicate that trespass and vandalism became a problem at Belvoir over the following few years, with pheasants being killed, melon beds vandalised, fruit trees torn down from walls and fruit stolen. On one occasion even the mansion house was broken into (Appendix 1). It seems that the young Viscount and his family were only resident intermittently at Belvoir. Other newspaper notices of the period refer to the sale of timber at Belvoir in December of 1772 and 1783.[40,41] The first was for '…between twenty and thirty elm and ash trees, some of them large', the second for a quantity of ash and other timber '…fit for various uses in husbandry'. The latter reference is probably for branches and small trees, thinnings taken out in woodland management.

At some time before the end of the 18th century an additional floor was added to the mansion house. This is shown in a painting of Belvoir from this period that was published in a paper by Francis Bigger[42] and in drawings of Belvoir by Lord Mark Kerr.

By 1788, when the second Viscount Dungannon was 25 years old, he was reported to be at Belvoir living in a princely style[43] and on Twelfth Night, early in 1796, he hosted an extraordinary ball at Belvoir –

Upwards of 150 Masques assembled, for whose reception three Rooms were opened, fitted up in an elegant manner, being decorated with natural Holly, and a variety of Evergreens, intermixed with artificial flowers, and coloured lamps, under the immediate direction of Lady Dungannon, who presided in the character of a SULTANA – her dress was superb and costly – Among a variety of characters, the most

Above: Belvoir House with added third storey. Drawn by Lord Mark Kerr, probably around 1800.

Above: Hill-Trevor boundary marker incorporating a reindeer's head and wyvern, symbols of the Downshire and Dungannon families.

grotesque and laughable figures were, a corpulent man as LEONORA in the Padlock, singing 'Sweet Robin' with a Turkey Cock perched on his finger; and a Taylor, apparently sitting cross'd leg'd on his shop board, while he was in reality at liberty to walk with it'. [44]

The Belfast News-Letter noted that festivity and humanity went hand in hand and that the poor of the neighbourhood had also been entertained and given presents at Christmas. The ball must have been the social event of the year and the paper could not resist continuing its account in the next issue. The sultana, it reported, had been attended by three captivating female slaves. There was also a plump mother abbess, a sailor, a clown and a well dressed hermit. Other costumed guests included a vendor of trifles, a Scotch woman who excelled in the highland reel, a vigilant watchman with the north Briton dialect and a group of shepherds and shepherdesses, described as being as innocent as their flocks. [45]

This event, however, seems to have been a finale to the grand life of the Dungannon family at Belvoir. Not long afterwards they left Belfast and later developed the Trevor ancestral home at Brynkinalt in north Wales as their residence. [46,47] In the summer of 1796 Edward Kingsmill, agent to Viscount Dungannon (and the Marquis of Donegall), died and his son-in-law, Cortland Skinner, was appointed as the new agent to Viscount Dungannon. His duties included collecting rents and he doubtless also looked after the Dungannon properties during this period of growing social unrest. Cortland Skinner resided at Belvoir and with the assistance of his employer he was made

Magistrate of County Down. [48-50] He became an officer during the 1798 Rebellion. [51]

The Dungannon family never again lived in Ireland though they retained land and an interest in the area. Their property included the impressive earthworks southwest of Belvoir known as the Giant's Ring which attracted the attention of the third and last Viscount Dungannon. He paid for the erection of a circular wall to protect the monument and a plaque in which he '...earnestly recommends it to the care of his successors'. [52]

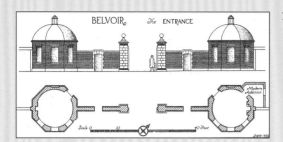

BELVOIR   The ENTRANCE

The 'ink-pot' entrance gates of Belvoir Park.

Belvoir and the Batesons

NO REFERENCE HAS BEEN FOUND of Belvoir having been a target during the 1798 Rebellion, though the estate did become neglected[53] and a number of people considered acquiring Belvoir including David Ker of Portavo, one of the largest landowners in County Down.[54] A letter of 1808 from David Ker to his son, who was involved in the negotiations, gives a vivid description of the condition of the buildings and grounds at the time. –

'Ask Lord Dungannon if he knows that all the timber outside of the wall towards S. field is cut down – ask him if he knows all the hothouses are in perfect ruin and the gardens wild, that all the roads and walks are out of order, that the outhouses except the Stables and Coach Houses are in a demolished state. Ask him if he knows the walls are very much injured, the village in a state of ruin, ask him if a house from which he has been absent about 12 or 14 years can be in such a state as he left it…'. [55]

The reference to the felling of timber outside of the wall is of interest. This probably refers to the several hundreds of oak, ash, elm and beech trees on Dungannon land described as being in the wood between Newtownbreda and Purdysburn that were

advertised for sale in the Belfast News-Letter of January 1800.[56]

During 1808 there were auctions at Belvoir of crops, cattle, brewery equipment, furniture and the library of 3,000 books, suggesting that the estate was being made ready for disposal.[57-60] In the following year the mansion house and the surrounding land were sold, though not to Mr Ker but to three Belfast businessmen; John Gilles, William Blacker and Robert Davis. The final ending of the Hill family's interest in Belvoir was marked by the inclusion in the sale of '…the pew or seat belonging to Arthur Viscount Dungannon in the church of Newtown Bredagh'.[61-63]

In 1810 Belvoir was mentioned in a court case concerning an attempt to steal a tree valued at 40 shillings from the estate. The published account gives some indication of the importance of timber at the time and the extent to which the estate owners tried to protect their investment. The culprits were discovered by the steward and manager of the demesne of Belvoir, Mr Hugh Crosbie. 'When going his rounds as usual to prevent depredations, particularly of the timber in said demesne, with a double-barrelled gun, loaded, his attention was

attracted by a noise near the edge of the River Lagan – he stopped, and in some minutes after, he heard a great splashing in the river, and on looking farther, he perceived that a tree had been thrown into the river from the demesne side thereof'. There followed a fight in which an attempt was made to shoot the steward who in turn shot one man and beat another. The accused were later apprehended by Cortland Skinner in their homes, where they were recovering from their wounds. They were sentenced to transportation for seven years.[64]

Gilles, Blacker and Davis probably acquired Belvoir as a short term investment and they soon entered into negotiations to sell the property to Robert Bateson of Orangefield. The discussions were complicated when John Gilles became a bankrupt, but this was resolved during 1811. In April of this year a notice of a sale by auction of the rights of John Gilles in the house, demesne and lands of Belvoir was advertised[65] and his share was purchased by Blacker and Davis, who quickly completed the sale (which

Robert Bateson

again included the Dungannon pew at Knockbreda church!) to Robert Bateson for £39,000.[66]

Before the end of May 1811 Robert Bateson was advertising to let land at Belvoir,[67] signalling the start of the association of the Bateson family with the estate that was to last to the end of the century.[68] They were originally from the north of England and had been active in banking and commerce in Belfast. The family had already acquired the Salters estate at Magherafelt in County Derry and the Moira estate near Lisburn in County Down.[50] The initial purchase at Belvoir had been for the mansion house and part of the demesne, though during the 19th century the family continued to acquire land in the area to make this their main property.[69]

With these acquisitions the Bateson family became the principal landlords of Moira and Newtownbreda, settlements that developed on the edge of their two County Down demesnes. These villages became prosperous and well presented[70-72] and the village by Belvoir impressed many Victorian visitors –

'…Newtownbreda, belonging to Sir Robert Bateson, is another pleasant specimen of what a country village ought to be, the houses being substantial, neat, and clean, having trim flower and garden plots attached, the former imparting a cheerful appearance at all seasons, but rendering it particularly gay during the summer and autumn months'.[73]

Robert Bateson was a politician and a member of committees that contributed to Belfast life[74] and he had a particular interest in agricultural improvement. He introduced short horn cattle to his land as early as 1820 and kept up a herd until his death,[75,76] exhibited at agricultural shows and was a member of the societies that promoted new ideas in farming.[77] His gardener, Samuel Millikin, exhibited at the Belfast Horticultural Society.[78]

A glimpse of the estate at this time is given by the Ordnance Survey Memoirs of 1832 which refer to pleasure grounds laid out with a good deal of taste and judgement.[79] The accompanying Ordnance Survey six inch map of 1834 shows rows of trees, the distribution of woods, the mansion house and the gardens bordering the stream between the house and

Breda graveyard. The writers of the Ordnance Survey Memoir also give us an impression of the interior of the house, noting that it was neat and in good order with a good library and a collection of paintings, some modern and a few ancient, that crowded almost every room. A catalogue of over 50 paintings at Belvoir House dating from 1865 has been preserved. This includes family portraits, still life, landscape and classical scenes, a number of which are attributed to great masters like Titian, Caravaggio, Rubens and Gainsborough.[80] Some are specifically referred to as being copies, but it is interesting to speculate if some might perhaps have been original.

The estate was affected by the Great Wind, a storm of quite exceptional ferocity that hit Ireland and parts of Britain on the night of the 6th January, 1839. The News-Letter of the 8th January and 15 January gave details of the damage –

'In the country districts surrounding Belfast, the destruction of trees, even of the oldest growth, has been immense, and furnishes impressive evidence as to the violence of the storm. We understand that at Belvoir, the residence of Sir R. Bateson, Bart. M.P. much damage of this kind has been done, and even the castle itself has

Left: Belvoir House and lock keeper's cottage from the River Lagan. Painted by Hugh Frazer in the mid 19th century. Despite the newspaper reports of damage by the Great Wind, this painting suggests that much of the woodland survived.

Below right: Robert Bateson memorial at Knockbreda Church.

suffered. At Annadale, the oldest oaks were torn up by the roots, and strewed about...'.[81]

'At Belvoir Park...above 1,000 of the largest elms, Spanish chestnuts, firs, larches and beech trees, some of them from 100 to 200 years old, and one remarkably large pinaster, were blown down. Two stacks of chimneys fell into a room where two men-servants slept'.[82]

The historian Colin Johnston Robb in an article about Belvoir referred to replacement tree planting in 1841-1846,[83] though unfortunately the source of this information was not given. Some records of trees planted in parts of the Belvoir estate during the 19th century have been located in registers that list planting by tenants under acts to encourage afforestation (Appendix 2). These provide an insight into the scale of planting in the Belvoir area and the surprisingly wide range of coniferous and broadleaved species planted. Many Victorian estate owners were fascinated with growing the exotic and unusual and it was almost certainly Robert Bateson who created the Arboretum in the valley to the east of the mansion house. Non-native trees were also planted at prominent locations around the demesne and an interesting account dating from 1854 of a visit to an estate near Stranmillis, which

from the description must have been Belvoir, noted evergreen oaks, arbutus, bay, rhododendron, Irish yew, pines, cedars and redwood in the lawns along the drive to the house.[84]

Robert Bateson died in 1863 and was buried at the church in Moira. The funeral procession was headed by members of the family and staff of the Belvoir and Moira estates. The entourage included the bailiff and agent for each estate and also two valets, two footmen, a coachman and groom, a farm steward, gardener and butler. Twelve estate labourers, in groups of four, carried the coffin.[85-86]

Robert Bateson's eldest son (also called Robert) had died in 1843 and so it was the second son, Thomas, who inherited the Bateson properties. Around this period additional work was undertaken at the mansion house, including the construction of a sandstone entrance porch and balustrades to surmount the walls. The alterations were the creation of W. J. Barre,[87] who was one of the best known Irish architects of the mid 19th century. It seems likely that this work was undertaken for Thomas Bateson.

The father and both of the sons were at times Conservative MPs for County Londonderry, though Thomas later became MP for Devizes in Wiltshire

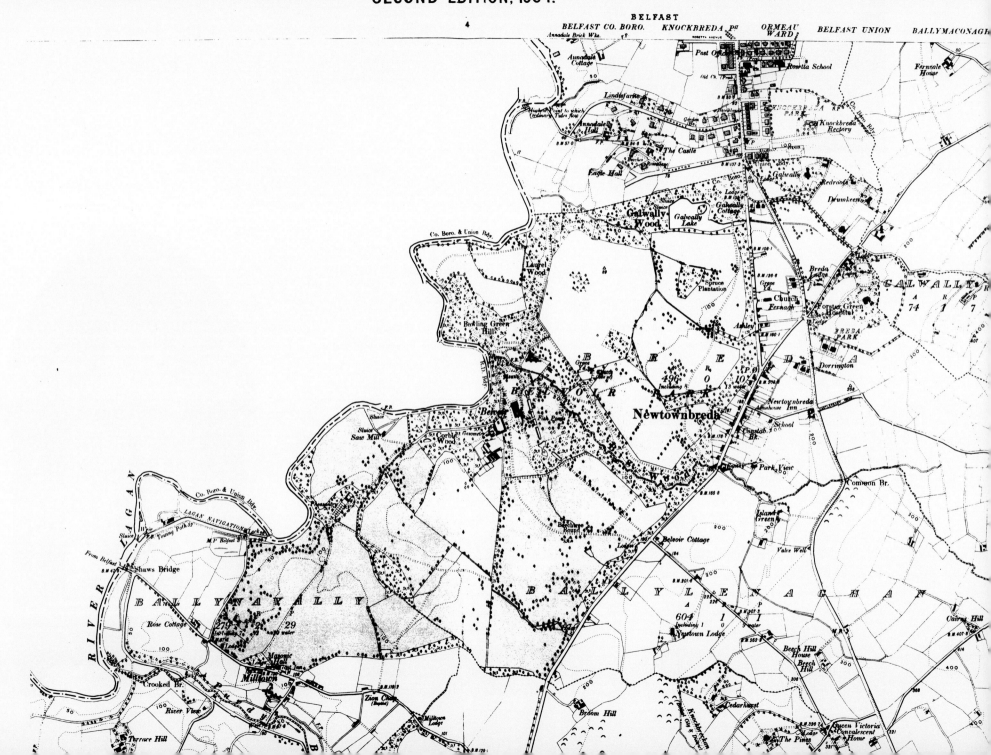

BELFAST

BELFAST CO. BORO.   KNOCKBREDA P.H   ORMEAU WARD   BELFAST UNION   BALLYMACONAGH

Annadale Brick Wks.

Rosetta Avenue

Annadale Cottage

Post Office

Fernnale House

Rosetta School

Lindisfarine

Old Ch. 79 Feet

Annadale Hall

Knockbreda Park

The Castle

Knockbreda Rectory

Eagle Hall

Union Bay   Galwally

Galwally Wood

Galwally Lake   Galwally Cottage

Redroofs

Drumkeen

Co. Boro. & Union Bdy.

Laurel Wood

Spruce Plantation

GALWALLY

74

Breda Lodge

Church Fernagh

Forster Green Hospital

BREDA PARK

Battling Green Hill

BELVOIR PARK

496   Dorrington

Belvoir

Newtownbreda

Newtownbreda Almshouse Inn

Sluice Saw Mill

Corbel Wood   Gasometer   School

Constab. Br.

Park View

Common Br.

RIVER LAGAN

Co. Boro. & Union Bdy.

LAGAN NAVIGATION Lock

Beechers Mound

Island Green

Sluice   Towing Path 32

From Belfast   M.P Belfast

Shaws Bridge

Belvoir Cottage

Valve Well

BALLYNAVALLY

BALLYLENAGHAN

604

Rose Cottage

279   29   Newtown Lodge

Masonic Hall

Cairns Hill

Milltown

Beech Hill House   Beech Hill

Crooked Br.

Zion Ch (Baptist)

Cedarhurst

River View

Milltown Lodge

Broom Hill

Queen Victoria Convalescent Home

Terrace Hill

The Pines

Left: The Bateson crest with bat's wings were prominently displayed on the northern façade of the mansion. The bat's wings were a symbol apparently derived from their name (Bateson, son of bat) and their motto was also inspired by bats – Nocte Volamus, We fly by night!

site page: Second
n Ordnance Survey
f Belvoir Park.

(a position formerly occupied by his brother-in-law). The involvement of the family in politics made Belvoir Park a popular destination for visiting dignitaries[88-90] and the visit by the Earl of Carnarvon, Lord Lieutenant of Ireland, in 1885 was described in particular detail in the newspapers. He arrived at Newtownbreda in the evening and was greeted at an event superintended by Sir Thomas Bateson's land steward, James Hill. There were cheering crowds, bonfires on the adjacent hills, the firing of 21 charges of dynamite, triumphal arches and flags. The windows of every house in the village were illuminated with candles and outlined with laurel and flowers.[91] The reception at Belvoir was also a colourful event and was reported in glowing terms –

'The beautiful apartments and halls of Belvoir were brilliantly illuminated, and presented a scene seldom equalled for its brightness and animation. The handsome suite of rooms on the ground floor were all thrown open to the guests, who began to arrive shortly after ten o'clock….The continuous hum of conversation received a harmonious accompaniment from the band of the Royal Inniskiling Fusiliers, who were stationed in the gallery of the large central hall. The conductor, Mr. M'Laren, with his customary discretion had chosen several excellent selections of chamber music, and the performance of the band was, as usual, of a highly interesting character. Supper was served in the large dining hall, and everything that could be done to add to the comfort and convenience of the guests was carried out'.[92]

Thomas Bateson seems to have been appreciated by his tenants who, on the occasion of the marriage of his younger daughter, praised him on his 'live and let live' approach, noted that injustice was alien to the management of his estates and acknowledged his interest in agricultural improvement.[93,94] When, towards the end of 1885, he was created Lord Deramore, the news was celebrated in Newtownbreda where most people observed a holiday. A deputation arrived at Belvoir House to read an address, signed by 200 tenants, to Lord and Lady Deramore. That evening the new Lord and his wife visited Newtownbreda. The local newspaper described the scene. The village was crowded, a triumphal arch had been erected, there were fireworks and, the writer added, salutes were fired at intervals from ordnance on the castle grounds.[95,96]

However, Lord Deramore was in poor health, withdrew from political life and within five years he had died. On the announcement of his death, all business was suspended in Newtownbreda and shops and schools were closed.[97] The title of Lord Deramore passed to his brother George, who had married the eldest daughter of John Yarburgh of Yorkshire. The family no longer resided at Belvoir and the Deramore name became associated with that of Yarburgh and their family home, Heslington Hall in York.[97,98]

No descriptions have been found of the grounds during this period, though we do have the name of the head gardener, William M'Laren.[98] A poignant relic of the Batesons' legacy at Belvoir was an oak tree that was known as the Great Oak or Deramore Oak (from the Irish for big oak). It was said that Lord Deramore took his title from the name of this tree. Unfortunately the tree is long gone though the title of 'The Deramore Oak' has been kept alive by writers who have since bestowed the honour to another very impressive oak, a multi-stemmed tree growing near the motte.[99-101]

The last residents

Above: The Farr family was one of many families who worked at Belvoir Park. Robert Farr (right) came from Wiltshire about 1860 and was shepherd for Thomas Bateson. He died in 1906 aged 83. His second wife Elizabeth Parker (beside him) died in 1892. His younger son George is pictured with Anne Symons (left) from Cornwall, a lady's maid to Lady Deramore, whom he married in 1891. The photograph was taken at Beechill Cottage around 1891, a house demolished in the late 1980s to make way for apartments.

IN OCTOBER 1900 there was a sale of the contents of the mansion house[102] and in the next month Walter Wilson, one of the partners of the Harland and Wolff shipyard, moved with his family to Belvoir house on his retirement. His lease for Belvoir Park is of interest as it included a number of conditions regarding the grounds. Lord Deramore retained the rights to all of the trees and timber. The lessee had to ensure that the trees and woods were preserved and the gardens had to be '…well cropped and manured and in proper order and condition and the fruit trees pruned'. The importance of the game shoots at this time is also apparent from the lease; at the termination of their tenure the Wilson family had to leave a stock of game '…equivalent to one thousand pheasant eggs, one hundred and eighty pheasants and forty hares'.[103]

The 1901 census of every household in Ireland provides fascinating insights into the management of the Belvoir estate. For the mansion house at Belvoir the census lists no less than 17 members of staff who occupied the building with the Wilson family. These were a governess, housekeeper, under butler, 1st footman, 2nd footman, page, lady's maid, cook, children's maid, stillroom maid, four house maids, kitchen maid, scullery maid and dairy maid. The census also lists either Walter Wilson or Lord Deramore as landlord for around 35 other properties in

Above: The four partners of the shipyard: Wolff, Wilson, Pirrie and Harland. Walter Wilson, who hated publicity and was rarely photographed, is standing, dividers in hand, second from the left.

Breda; many of the residents of these houses most likely worked in the estate. They included a land steward, coachman, carpenter, painter, dairyman, shepherd, two gate keepers, three laundresses, three gamekeepers, several gardeners, servants and agricultural labourers.[104]

At Belvoir Park Walter Wilson could indulge his interests in the outdoor life, including shooting, fishing and growing fruit and flowers. However, after enjoying only a few years of retirement, Walter Wilson died.[105] Subsequently the family handed back to Lord Deramore the north-eastern part of the demesne, including the area around Galwally Lake, in return for halving the rent.[106] Alec, the only son of Walter Wilson, attempted to develop the demesne by creating a Model Dairy at Belvoir with up-to-date buildings, milking machines and a strong emphasis on hygiene. The enterprise was enthusiastically described in the press, but appears to have only lasted for a few years.[107, 108] The Wilson family continued to lease Belvoir during the Great War and finally left in 1918.

In 1919 Sir James Johnston (Lord Mayor of Belfast from 1917-18) moved to Belvoir house with his family; they became its last occupants.[109] Staff employed at this time included David Agnew who lived with his family in the outbuildings of Belvoir house and looked after cattle, Johnny Skates who was gateman at the delightful but tiny pair of octagonal 'ink-pot' gate lodges and James Wishart, a carpenter by trade, who worked the water-powered saw mill by the weir on the River Lagan. James lived with his wife and 10 children in a two storey estate house at the Milltown demesne gate.[110, 111]

In 1921 Belvoir, along with Belfast Castle and Orangefield, were considered by the recently created Northern Ireland Cabinet as possible locations for the new parliament. Initially Belvoir was preferred as it could have accommodated the parliament buildings, speaker's house, courts of justice and other government buildings, with the remainder of the site used as a park. However, Belvoir Park was subsequently rejected in favour of Stormont. The main difficulties had been that the site was larger than needed, the negotiations had become protracted and the cost of acquiring the demesne was high. Although discussion with Lord Deramore had indicated his willingness to sell for a reasonable figure, the sitting tenant, Sir James Johnston, wanted an additional £8,500 to surrender his lease.[112] A few years later, Belvoir was again examined by the Northern Ireland Government, this time as a possible residency for the Governor.[113] At one stage Lord Deramore was made an offer of £60,000 for the house and demesne, with the expectation that land surplus to requirements could later be sold by the Government for housing.[114] Again, for many of the same reasons as before, the negotiations came to nothing. Although a property near Belfast was desired for the Governor's residence, the mansion at Hillsborough was eventually chosen. An outcome of these discussions about Belvoir Park was, however, the creation of an archive of material about Belvoir house that is of considerable interest. The files include a copy of the 20 year lease signed by Sir James Johnston (the conditions were similar to those arranged with Walter Wilson), detailed plans and some photographs of the mansion and an annotated map of the farm buildings.[115]

The plans show that the house had six main function rooms on the ground floor. The first floor accommodation included five large bedrooms, some with attached dressing rooms. There were also bathrooms and a sitting room. On the top floor there were five more large bedrooms, bathrooms and servants' quarters.

Opposite page: The hall and staircase, probably at the time of the Wilson family.

Right and below: The hall, drawing room and dining room at the time of the Johnston family.

Around the quadrangle of two-storey buildings attached to the house were more rooms for staff, kitchens and store rooms. From other documents in the archive we learn that there was no electricity supply, that acetylene was used for lighting in the house and that communication within the house was by a system of mechanically operated bells.

Photographs of the interior of the house taken around this time provide a wonderful glimpse into the lifestyle of the families. The style of the furnishings can also be appreciated from the auction lists when these families left Belvoir. For example, the 1918 sale included a richly carved oak high backed suite of 21 pieces upholstered in crocodile leather, a massive carved oak dining table, olive wood and walnut bedroom suites, brass bedsteads, richly carved Chippendale palm stands and tables, brass ware, antique armour, gilt mirrors and oak and walnut overmantles.[116]

The changed times following the First World War must have made it difficult to obtain staff to manage the house and the top floor was not furnished in the time of Sir James Johnston.[115] Sir James was also in poor health but held out for compensation in the discussions about the future of the house and finally moved from Belvoir Park in the autumn of 1923.[117] He died in April of the following year and was buried in Knockbreda churchyard.[118] For a while the family continued the lease but a garden party hosted by his son, William Johnston, in July 1925 appears to have been the last public function held at Belvoir.[119]

Break-up of the demesne and plans for development

WITH THE MANSION HOUSE VACANT the gardens were soon overgrown.[120] The future of the demesne must have become uncertain and in an article in 1926 the Belfast historian Francis Bigger expressed his concern – 'Such a place as Belvoir Park is a great heritage to a city like Belfast, and one can only hope and trust that it will not be ravished and despoiled but maintained for some great public use much as it has remained for so many varying generations'.[42] However, the huge empty house must have become a liability and the agent of Lord Deramore, Mr Burke-Murphy J.P., looked for new uses for the estate. Some relatively small areas of land were disposed of, including the southwestern corner of the walled demesne where a private house was constructed in woodland and named Ardnavally. This house was later to become the residence of the American Consul.[121] In a far more important development, 163 acres in the northeast of the walled demesne were leased to create the 18 hole Belvoir Park Golf Club, which opened in June 1929.[122]

The onset of the great depression must have affected plans for the demesne and in 1934 all of the remaining Deramore landholdings were leased to J. and W. Stewart (London and Belfast) Limited. This was a company headed by Mr W. J. Stewart who was the MP for South Belfast and principal of the building company Stewart and Partners. It was a very significant land acquisition comprising the mansion house and 430 acres remaining in the demesne of Belvoir Park, 99 acres in Malone and 294 acres near Newtownbreda.[123] A Belfast Telegraph article of the time indicated that the grounds would be developed as a 'park estate' to be designed by Sir Arnold Thornley, the architect for the parliamentary buildings at Stormont,[124] and in another article it was suggested that Belvoir would become the site for the greatest building development ever undertaken in Ireland.[125] These grand plans however came to nothing and the only work was limited housing on the fringes of the estate. The reason why there was no

major development is not clear. At that time there was a campaign to considerably extend the boundaries of the city and there may have been an expectation that Belvoir would become incorporated into Belfast and developed as a new suburb. However, the city boundaries were not extended and Belvoir Park remained a rural area.

There appears to have been little activity in Belvoir demesne in the 1930s. A local resident could only recall that cattle were rested at Belvoir for a few days when they were being brought from the countryside before being herded down the Ormeau Road to the docks for export.[126] Another local person mentioned that before the War he was a member the local Newtownbreda scout group that was permitted to use the Belvoir grounds for activities, but that at this time the house had been unused and nothing much happened in the demesne.[127]

Mr Tommy Chesney was employed as caretaker of the house and grounds by Stewarts in 1937, a job

he was to hold for over 20 years. At first Mr Chesney cycled from his house in Ballycoan to Belvoir but later in the year moved into the courtyard buildings where he lived with his wife and seven children. For a time his parents and also two cousins lived in the pair of ink pot gate lodges; one was the day room, the other the night room.[128]

It was during this period, when the estate was not actively managed, that the old graveyard of Breda, which lies within the demesne, started to suffer from vandalism. A few burials had taken place as recently as the 1920s[129] and a photograph published in 1925 shows a number of standing gravestones.[130] However, an article a decade later mentioned that many had for some unknown reason been removed.[131] More recently, other gravestones were smashed and the vault of the Dungannon family was broken into and the lead coffins stolen.[101,132]

The War years – more plans and more decay

AT THE START of the Second World War the army took over most the grounds around the house and subsequently the Admiralty developed the demesne as a temporary armaments depot. The house was used by army and navy personnel and a total of 131 buildings were erected in the grounds, mostly Nissen and elephant huts. Armaments, including torpedoes and large shells for battleships, were brought up by barge from the Belfast docks and unloaded at a wharf that still stands on the Lagan by the Big Meadow.[2] The Chesney family were allowed to remain in their accommodation and were even invited to attend concerts, shows with singing and dancing organised by the military in the mansion house. The people who lived on the road from Newtownbreda to Purdysburn, along the side of the demesne, were less fortunate. The road was shut, there were barricades and sentries at each end and they had to leave. The golf club was largely unaffected except that the fifth fairway was dug up and cultivated. Belvoir was not attacked during the War though Tilly, the third daughter of Mr Chesney, remembers the family sheltering in the entrance to the old ice house, by the motte, during air raids over Belfast.[133-136]

In 1945 the Interim Report of the Planning Commission, the first planning strategy for Belfast, was published. Although the report recognised the urgent housing problems of Belfast, the area around Belvoir was zoned for agriculture. Belvoir appears not to have been considered for housing because the Planning Commission sought to control haphazard suburban growth and because the Lagan Valley was recognised as being an area of great beauty used by increasing numbers of walkers and holiday-makers. The report stressed in the strongest terms that the riverside should be protected and development controlled.[137]

The new planning framework soon started to have an impact on proposals for Belvoir. When in 1946 Belfast Corporation considered the compulsory acquisition of the Belvoir demesne for a cemetery, park and other municipal purposes, this was rejected by the County Council because of the open space zoning.[138,139] Similarly, although Stewart and Partners were able to build on some of the Deramore land in Newtownbreda, proposals for a major development at Belvoir were rejected[140] and after they took back the estate from the Admiralty in 1950, the only productive use that this building company made of Belvoir was as a site to manufacture concrete blocks.[141] Fields were let to local farmers who grew flax and other crops and the woodlands and old gardens remained unmanaged and became a popular place for youngsters to explore.[142-144] The mansion house was used as a store and was described by Douglas Deane as being '…shuttered and cluttered with cement and cranes and sewer pipes and tin shacks'.[145]

The possibility of large-scale tree felling at Belvoir during this period was suggested in one newspaper article[146] though it has not been possible to confirm this statement. The only felling that is known to have taken place at this time was the removal of some big conifer and beech trees in the southern part of the demesne.[147]

There were renewed calls for Belvoir Park to be developed as a public park[148,149] but no detailed proposals appear to have been put forward. There was probably growing pressure on the planners for development from both Stewarts and the councils and, when the Second Report of the Planning Commission was published in 1952, the zoning for part of Belvoir Park was changed. The southern part of the estate was now designated for housing and only the area around the house, the Big Wood and Bowling Green Hill zoned for public open space.[150]

Left and below: Belvoir House in its final years, empty and decaying.

A new approach –
integrating housing, conservation and recreation

In the early 1950s, Hillsborough Rural District Council considered acquiring Belvoir Park demesne for a mixed development of housing and open space. It was proposed to construct 3,000 houses on 200 acres of land with an additional 226 acres set aside for playing fields and other recreational and educational purposes.[151,152] However, as the proposal was to help reduce the housing problems of people in Belfast who lived outside of the Hillsborough Rural District Council area, financial assistance for the housing scheme was required. As this assistance was not forthcoming, the proposal came to nothing.

Belvoir housing estate

Eventually, in 1955, the Northern Ireland Housing Trust, which had been set up to address the need for public housing throughout Northern Ireland, acquired all of Stewarts' land within the demesne wall.[153-155] Plans for housing were quickly developed and by 1959 construction of Belvoir housing estate in the southeastern part of the demesne was well under way.[156] Stewarts continued to be involved in the area; the purchase of the site included an unusual clause that they could build 250 of the houses at a price equivalent to the lowest tender submitted.[157] Initially the development was promoted as a success, and by 1963 facilities including shops, churches and a school were being constructed.[158,159] However, house building slowed and in 1964 Stewart and Partners laid off all of their staff and the company closed.[160,161] Many houses at Belvoir were left half built and abandoned and it was only when Unit Construction took over the contract that work was resumed. By the late 1960s Unit Construction had completed most of the rest of the housing estate. The only Housing Trust properties

that they did not build were the single storey bungalows by Belvoir Drive and the two tower blocks, which were constructed by Farrans.[162]

The design of the Belvoir housing estate had been addressed by the Housing Trust in a very thoughtful and imaginative way, realising the vision of Belvoir Park being retained as predominantly amenity open space with public access. From the outset it was decided to keep the housing away from the river corridor, to retain a large area of land for playing fields and to leave the scenic land towards the River Lagan untouched. The scale of the housing development was kept to a manageable 1,000 dwellings and the area of open space was maximised by constructing a mixture of tower blocks, maisonettes and terraces, even though this was more expensive than traditional two storey dwellings.[156, 163-165]

Discussions were held with the Association of Boys' Clubs and subsequently with the Boys' Brigade that resulted in the latter organisation taking over 22 acres of land on the edge of the housing estate for playing fields.[166,167]

Left: Tower blocks and trees at Belvoir.

Right: An early sign for the forest.

In a pioneering move to integrate housing with woodland, the Trust approached the Ministry of Agriculture with a request to take over and plant blocks of forestry within the housing estate. Although the Ministry considered it impractical to take responsibility for these small areas, assistance in planting woodland in the estate was given by Forestry Division.[156,168] The estate was also laid out to ensure that few large trees were disturbed; a newspaper article of April 1960 that celebrated the Trust taking over the first six completed houses noted that –

'The Housing Trust's declared intention of preserving as much of the natural beauty of the park as possible has been strictly followed. The plans have, in one instance, been altered to avoid removing a tree. Trees are almost sacred; none can be cut down without the permission of the architect, and the lopping off of branches is regarded as a last extremity. A Ministry of Agriculture plantation on the site is treated with the respect once accorded to the Druidic grove'.[169]

Belvoir Park Forest

The Housing Trust approached the Ministry of Agriculture with the offer of a large area of land north of the housing estate for the planting of a commercial forest with public access. This suggestion quickly developed into a plan for the creation of Belvoir Park Forest on about 170 acres (68 hectares) of land.[170] Some trees were taken out to facilitate new planting and, for safety reasons, some tall trees by paths were removed and left where they fell, as there was no suitable lifting gear available.[171,172] In an unusual arrangement, prisoners from Crumlin Road Prison were brought by van to Belvoir to get fresh air, a change of scene and, under the supervision of Warders, cut up logs with cross-cut saws.[173] Large-scale planting started in 1961 and continued until 1969 in areas of former parkland and farmland. The main species planted were conifers and as early as 1966 the forest was starting to take shape, with plantations of trees 3-4 feet high. Poplars were also established at the northern end of the forest, near the river, and were considered to grow with excellent vigour and health.[174,175] An interesting discovery made at Belvoir at this time was a small seedling of an unusual hybrid conifer.[176] This is now

known as Robinson Gold, and the original tree can still be seen at Belvoir (see Chapter 4).

The first large-scale felling in the forest took place around 1988 when the poplar plantation was sold for timber and replanted with oak.[177] Belvoir Park, a unique commercial forest in a city, has proved to be of very high amenity value and attracts thousands of visitors every year. There have been few problems apart from occasional instances of damage to trees and issues relating to mountain-biking and motor-biking.[178,179]

Concern about heritage

Unfortunately, a viable future could not be found for Belvoir House. One newspaper article of 1953 indicated that it was being considered as a community centre for the proposed new housing estate.[146] In 1955 it was examined to see if it might be suitable as a site for the planned Folk Museum, but it was found to be too decayed, it had been left in poor condition by the Admiralty and Stewart and Partners.[180-182] As no use could be found for the building, the Ministry of Agriculture considered the possibility of gutting the house and retaining the shell, and three firms were asked to quote for this work, but the responses indicated that the work would be difficult and dangerous and would cost more than the value of the salvage. A decision was made to ask the Territorial Army to demolish the house, as they had done a similar task at Langford Lodge in County Antrim and there would be no cost to the Ministry. Some material was to be salvaged and Lord Deramore visited the site and requested a few items, but the bulk of the material was destined for building paths and the car park at Belvoir.[183,184] Mr Chesney finally ended his job as caretaker and on 18th February 1961 the demolition, code named 'Operation Lusty', took place. It took two attempts to demolish the house and all of the local papers published photographs of the end of this historic building.[185] Today all that remains is the courtyard, the block of outbuildings that were kept for use as stores and offices. The rooms in the courtyard formerly occupied by the Chesney family became the accommodation for the foreman.

Concern about the loss of the house was, however, overshadowed by a number of planned and projected schemes that put the future of the forestry project in serious jeopardy.[186] High voltage electric cables crossed the southern part of the site limiting the development of woodland in this area. A new sewage works was built at the northern end of Belvoir Park, with large diameter pipes being run across the forest site, necessitating tree felling and impacting on the amenity of the Arboretum.[187] A new dual carriageway was constructed along the eastern margin of the estate from Belvoir to Newtownbreda; it was this scheme that necessitated the removal of the ink pot gate lodges in the early 1960s.[188] Even worse were proposals for road projects that would have cut the former demesne into fragments. The first was a motorway (to have been called the M4) for traffic from the southeast of Belfast that would go through the recently planted forest and Arboretum, roughly paralleling the boundary with the golf course. The second was to be a Lagan Valley motorway (to be called the M8) that would pass close to Milltown,

---

OPERATION LUSTY

PROGRAMME

18 FEB 1961

1000 - 1430   Preparation of building for demolition.

1400   Perimeter Sentries in position. Sweep of Wooded Area carried out by Asslt. Pnrs. 6 RUR.

1430   Visitors report to Report Centre.

1430 - 1500   Tour of Project and explanation.

1500   All visitors checked through Report Centre and into Safety Area. Final Inspection by OIC Demolition.

1530   Demolition.

1545   All Clear, followed by inspection by Visitors, and dispersal.

1.   The time for the actual demolition is given as 1530 hrs and it is hoped to adhere to this schedule, but it is possible that the demolition may be delayed for various reasons.

2.   Visitors are asked to check in at the Report Centre on arrival, on entering the Danger Area, and on leaving the Danger Area. Particular emphasis is placed on this last check as considerable time may be lost in searching for the person, if this is omitted.

3.   Visiting Officers in charge of parties are responsible for ensuring that all of their party are in the Safety Area, and for reporting this to the Report Centre

4.   Visitors are requested not to ask questions of, or impede, those officers and ORs working on the project. A Conducting Officer will be available to answer questions.

5.   When the actual demolition occurs, all present should look up so that any flying debris may be avoided.

6.   The entrance to Deramore House is MR Sheet 314, 341697 and the route will be signed from the junction CHURCH ROAD - ORMEAU ROAD.

DISTRIBUTION:-   107(Ulster)Indep Inf Bde Gp (TA)
                  24 Engr Gp (TA)
                  SORE II N.I.C. (2)
                  146(Antrim Artillery)Fd Engr Regt RE (TA)
                  Civil Defence Officer
                  6 Bn RUR (TA) (2)
                  All Other Units 107 Bde (1 each)
                  13 Flight A.A.C.
                  R.U.C.
                  File 591/8/G
                  Spare (6)

R. McMullan esq. Unis of Agr. Forestry Div.

Preparing Belvoir House for demolition, February 1961.

traverse the forest near the River Lagan to reach Annadale, where the two motorways would converge and head towards the city centre along the Annadale Embankment. A third road (the A7 Belvoir Link) was proposed to cross the River Lagan from Malone and Newforge to the main Belvoir-Newtownbreda dual carriageway. This would have required a new bridge over the River Lagan at the southern end of Morelands Meadow and would have cut through the open space between the Belvoir housing estate and the forestry plantations.[189]

Most of these road proposals were subsequently seen to be excessive and were withdrawn by the Roads Service in 1977.[190,191] However, when the Belfast Urban Area Plan was published in 1987, one route through Belvoir Park was retained, a road for the southern approaches to the city that would be constructed along the boundary between the forest and golf course and connect with the Annadale Embankment to take traffic to the Ormeau Bridge.[192] Increasing awareness of the importance of

Belvoir Park and growing concern about environmental issues resulted in widespread opposition to this road scheme and the Belfast Telegraph ran a high profile 'Save Belvoir Forest' campaign.[193-196] In 1991, the Friends of Belvoir group, chaired by Norman Taylor, was formed to oppose the proposed road and to increase community involvement in the area by developing a new broadleaved woodland on Housing Executive open space between the housing estate and forest.[197] These campaigns resulted in a re-appraisal of the road scheme which was subsequently shelved.[198]

The development of a wonderful resource

At about the same time that proposals for major roads were being developed for the Belvoir area, the importance of protecting the Lagan Valley was stressed in the Belfast Regional Survey and Plan, published in 1963. This followed earlier planning documents in highlighting the amenity value of the Lagan between Belfast and Lisburn, but also made an important recommendation that the area should be

planned and administered for public amenity.[199] In 1965, the Lagan Valley became the first Area of Outstanding Natural Beauty to be declared in Northern Ireland[200] and shortly afterwards a report commissioned by the government proposed that the area should become a Country Park.[201] An advisory committee was set up in 1969[202] and by the mid 1970s the riverside lands from Belfast to Lisburn, including the woods, grassland and golf course at Belvoir Park, were being promoted as The Lagan Valley Regional Park.[203]

The Regional Park was envisaged as comprising both public and private land, though key areas were acquired where possible. This included Lagan Meadows and Morelands Meadow, parts of the former Belvoir Park estate by the River Lagan which are of very high landscape and ecological value. The Lagan Meadows had been sold to 'The Trustees for the Better Equipment Fund of Queen's University' in 1913, but, with the development of the Regional Park, was acquired by the government and in 1986 transferred to Belfast City Council.[204,205]

Another area of conservation importance is Galwally Lake which lay within the walled demesne near the northern boundary. After the creation of the

Above and below left: Tree Fair at Belvoir.

golf course and building of houses in Galwally, the lake became isolated and its future must have been questioned. A cast iron sign that still stands by the lake states that it was declared a Bird Sanctuary by the Ministry of Home Affairs, N. Ireland.[206] This declaration was made in 1951 under The Wildbird Protection Act of 1931 though protection was lost when the Act was superseded by The Wildlife Order of 1985.[207]

With the development of the Regional Park, public access along the River Lagan towpath was encouraged and links were developed, including new footbridges from Belvoir Park Forest to Morelands Meadow and from Morelands Meadow across the old canal to the towpath. Belfast City Council developed the meadows as a nature park grazed by cattle. Over 50 widely spaced standard oak trees were planted in Morelands Meadow to maintain the parkland landscape and a nature trail was created at Lagan

Meadows. In 1988 the Ulster Wildlife Trust leased the wetlands on the Malone side of the river from the Council to manage as a Nature Reserve.

The courtyard at Belvoir Park Forest became a focus for environmental activity. This started in 1978 when rooms formerly used to house the Forest Service foreman were let to the Royal Society for the Protection of Birds as their regional headquarters. The Forest Service developed an educational programme with the appointment of forest guides and creation of a display room in part of the upper floor of the courtyard. A new education/lecture room and offices were also constructed on the western side of the courtyard and officially opened in 1982.[208] In the same year office space was provided for the recently created position of Lagan Valley Regional Park Officer.[209] To improve the amenity and wildlife of the area, the Arboretum was enhanced and the Big Wood was developed as a Forest Nature Reserve. The forest was also the venue for two highly successful 'Tree Fairs' organised by The Forest of Belfast, the urban forestry partnership, in 1993 and 1996, and this organisation commissioned a number of timber sculptures reflecting the local environment for the forest and Morelands Meadow.[210]

In 1993 the Lagan Valley Regional Park Local Plan was published and three years later a management strategy and action programme were developed.[211-213] These documents and subsequent plans have provided a framework for enhancing habitats, developing the landscape and improving access. Much of the work is promoted by the Park Officer and two Rangers, who liaise with landowners and organise an annual programme of events and activities. Voluntary organisations are also playing a major role. For example, in 2000 the Woodland Trust became involved in the area, managing the Friends of Belvoir Nature Reserve and planting adjacent areas of grassland to create a broadleaved wood of 9.2ha. In the same year the Grassroots Conservation Group started a programme of work around Morelands Meadow, clearing vegetation

Left: Kingfisher sculpture commissioned by the Forest of Belfast in 1994 for Belvoir. Designed as a temporary work, it was made from soft beech timber and slowly decayed and returned to the earth.

Left: Ulster Wildlife Trust staff in 2004 clearing vegetation at Lester's Dam.

and laying gravel to reopen the former path to the east of the old canal and putting up fencing to keep cattle from sensitive wetlands. In 2004, the Ulster Wildlife Trust employed a Warden based at Lagan Meadows Nature Reserve to facilitate habitat management and enhancement work. Projects have included path maintenance, clearance of invasive species, scrub control, grassland management, fencing and pond clearance. The local community is encouraged to get involved through volunteering and events.

Given the long and varied history of the estate and its proximity to Belfast, it is remarkable that so much remains of the demesne. Sections of the old boundary wall still stand, many huge old trees continue to grow at Belvoir, parts of the old parkland landscape remain to impress the visitor and, although the mansion house has gone, some of the built heritage and remnants of the landscaped gardens can still be seen.

Perhaps most importantly, Belvoir Park is still a beautiful and attractive landscape, a place of tranquillity that attracts regular walkers and many visitors. The future of Belvoir Park is to some extent secured by its popularity as an amenity area and much loved landscape within the Lagan Valley Regional Park. The biodiversity value of the long established habitats and heritage value of the demesne should also help safeguard the site. However, this open space is too close to the city of Belfast to ever be free from the risks of development, pollution and over-use. Suburbs now almost entirely surround Belvoir Park. It is an ancient wooded landscape within a developing city, and the protection and management of this important resource will be an ever growing challenge.

Visitors on a public walk at Belvoir in 2003 under the huge oak by the car park

Acknowledgments

I am very grateful to Sue Christie and Martin Walsh for commenting on a draft of the text.

Terence Reeves-Smyth of Environment and Heritage Service Built Heritage was supportive of this research and kindly informed me of the early paintings of Belvoir house.

I am very grateful to past staff of organisations that have been involved in the Belvoir area who provided information, in particular Mr Cecil Kilpatrick, former Chief Forest Officer and Mr Douglas MacAnally, former Education Officer with the Forest Service. I am particularly grateful for the assistance given by many local residents including Albert Allen, Jack Agnew, Berkley Farr, Clifford Fairweather, Dr C. Field, Mrs McMinn, Mrs Martin, Andy McFall, the Wishart family and Frances Weir. The recollections of these people have helped to bring to life the history of Belvoir Park.

Lord Deramore made a major contribution to this project in providing access to legal documents concerning Belvoir held by Crawford and Lockheart solicitors. Lord Deramore has also been very supportive of the project and I am extremely grateful

to him for kindly permitting key documents concerning Belvoir to be copied and placed in the Public Records Office of Northern Ireland. Patrick White of Crawford and Lockheart provided every possible assistance in this work.

The owners of the 18th century paintings of Belvoir Park by Fisher are sincerely thanked for permitting these beautiful images to be published. Hector McDonnell very kindly permitted the painting by Lord Mark Kerr to be reproduced in this publication.

I would also wish to express my thanks to the staff of the Ulster Museum, Linenhall Library, Central Library, Queen's University Library, the Public Record Office of Northern Ireland, British Library and Courtauld Institute for their assistance.

CHAPTER *Three* — MEMORIES

Life in the big house
The Wilson family at Belvoir Park

John Witchell

O N THAT AUGUST MORNING in 1963 I was an excited ten-year old with no need for an alarm clock. My two brothers and I slid out of our berths and raced up the stairways of the Heysham ferry to witness our arrival in my mother's hometown of Belfast. She was already on deck, circled by calling gulls, the varnished surfaces wet and glistening in the early morning sunshine. She proudly pointed out the famous building docks and slipways and filmed us with her cine camera as the Harland & Wolff quay slipped past in the background.

A short ride in a black taxi took us past the evocatively tessellated gable of the TGWU building, bumped us over the tram tracks at Castle Junction and deposited us at the tradesmen's door of Anderson & McAuley's.

Our cousins the Andersons sent us on a tour of the famous family department store and then took us to see the building works for their exciting new venture, Supermac. The detour through the houses of nearby Belvoir Park seemed purely incidental in comparison with the fascination of seeing the country's first out of town supermarket under construction, with the now familiar rows of freezers and food shelving.

Little could I have guessed that 15 years later I would return to Northern Ireland as a trainee Chartered Surveyor to learn the business of estate management with the Blakiston Houston family, who were once neighbours of Belvoir Park on the Orangefield Estate. Both estates are now all but subsumed into the city of Belfast, but there are still echoes of the days when cows grazed the fields of Castlereagh in demesnes surrounded by high walls penetrated by ink pot gate lodges.

In 1900 my great grandfather, Walter Wilson, took a 20 year lease of Belvoir Park from Lord Deramore. Aged 61, he was nearing the end of a remarkable career spanning the phenomenal growth of Harland & Wolff from its inception in 1858 to being the world's greatest shipyard with some 12,000 employees. He left school in 1857 at the age of 17. He had a keen interest in engineering and joined the firm of Hickson & Co, iron ship builders, as a gentleman or premium apprentice. A year later the manager, Edward Harland, bought out the works and Walter was one of about 50 of the 100 strong workforce whom he asked to stay on to complete the work of the old firm. Harland's assistant, Gustav Wolff, became a partner in 1862 and thus Harland & Wolff was created.

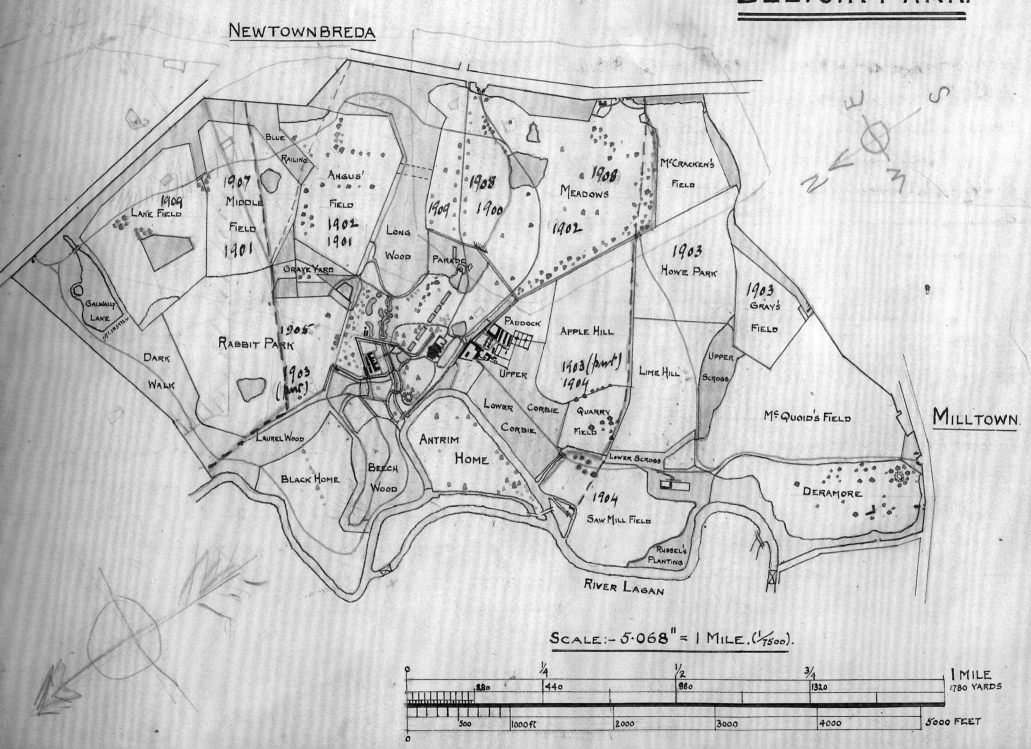

BELVOIR PARK.

NEWTOWNBREDA

MILLTOWN.

Lake Field
1909

1907
MIDDLE
FIELD
1901

Blue
Railing

Angus'
Field
1902
1901

Long
Wood

1908
1909

1900

1908
MEADOWS
1902

McCracken's
Field

1903
Howe Park

1903
Gray's
Field

Graye Yard

Parade

Galwally
Lake

1905

Rabbit Park

1903
(part)

Paddock

Apple Hill

1903 (part)
1904

Upper

Lime Hill

Upper
Scrogs

Dark
Walk

McQuoid's Field

Laurel Wood

Black Home

Beech
Wood

ANTRIM
HOME

Lower
Corbie

Corbie

Quarry
Field

Lower Scrogs

Deramore

1904
Saw Mill Field

Russel's
Planting

RIVER LAGAN

SCALE:- 5.068" = 1 MILE. (1/7500).

0   1/4   1/2   3/4   1 MILE
880   440   880   1320   1780 YARDS

500   1000ft   2000   3000   4000   5000 FEET

Walter continued to apply his engineering skills and ingenuity, introducing many innovations to the business. By 1868 he had been promoted to manager of the yard, but his greatest reward came in 1874 when he and William Pirrie, who had also joined the firm as a gentleman apprentice, were invited to become partners. The famous partnership was now complete and during the next 21 years these four men made a unique team: they were the owners of the firm, the sole shareholders, as well as designers and experts in naval architecture. Although trained as a naval engineer and draftsman, he was respected at all levels for his management skills and was affectionately known throughout the yard as 'Watty'.

In 1875 Walter married Sarah Wynne, known by all as 'Lil'. They first lived in 1 Botanic Avenue before renting Stranmillis House, now Stranmillis College, where they had more room for entertaining. The move across the River Lagan to Belvoir House, surrounded by over 600 acres of land, was an even greater step.

They had one son, Alec, and four daughters; Marion (known as May), Florence, Dorothy (my grandmother) and Kitty. It was a privileged life for the five children, but by no means an easy one, with a strong emphasis on education. Alec went to Cheam School and then to Harrow whilst the girls stayed at home and were taught by governesses; a German Fraulein from Potsdam followed by a French Mademoiselle. No English was spoken until teatime, so they all became fluent in both languages. They also spent time in the 'still room' learning to bake simple cakes, soda bread and make up butter into decorations for the table centre. They were all taught to play the piano and Kitty also studied the violin, which she continued to play throughout her life. They learned to paint with water colours, but only May continued in earnest. They were taught to knit, sew and darn, to dance in ballroom etiquette with dance cards and to ride and swim, maybe at Portrush where my mother was later given lessons in the icy cold Blue Pool. They were all interested in wildflowers and Alec gave Dorothy a copy of Bentham and Hooker's *British Flora* which we still have. She and my mother marked the date and place where they found specimens of different flowers and carefully coloured in the book's illustrations.

The family was obviously very caring. During his time at the shipyard Walter had purchased an ambulance exclusively for the workers – an indication of the dangers involved in shipbuilding. At Belvoir the family were concerned about the lack of nursing care for the community and campaigned for the appointment of a district nurse for the Milltown area. With the agreement of Lord Deramore, they provided land just inside the estate wall for a single storey house to provide accommodation for a nurse. It had one large room suitable for use as a waiting room or for running first aid classes.[1] This attractive building still stands, largely unaltered but now a private residence, and is one of the few remaining buildings from the original estate.

Sadly, nearly all the family records of my great grandfather's time at Belvoir Park have been lost. However, we are fortunate that the game book has been handed down through the family. This gives a wonderful insight into the Wilsons' love of field sports and contains details of the bag from shoots spanning the entire period that the family lived at Belvoir. There are also some intriguing press cuttings about poaching, together with a few photographs and a detailed map of the estate with all the woods and fields individually named.

Walter, and later Alec, loved the Antrim Hills and must have spent many invigorating winter's days criss-crossing them with their friends. They walked up snipe and woodcock in much the same way as I do today, as guests of the same families. He also invited his friends and neighbours to shoot at Belvoir where the bag included wild duck, pheasant, hare and rabbit. However the shoot did not preclude other activities from the estate and, as president of the Cross-Country Association, he allowed championships to be held in the grounds.

Walter was also a keen fisherman and president of the Belfast Anglers' Association. My mother remembers seeing a photograph of two Belvoir footmen holding up a large salmon caught by him. It would be nice to think it was caught on the Lagan, but it is more likely that it came from the Bush or the Bann which were his favourite rivers. One problem he had was that he could only get away to fish at the weekends, but did not wish to break the Sabbath. He overcame this by fishing without a gillie on Sundays, which also gave the fish a better sporting chance as he had to rely on landing a fish with no net.

It is said that Walter took on the lease of Belvoir Park so that he could entertain visitors to the shipyard in more style than was possible at his home

in Stranmillis. But his love of country sports, together with his interest in gardening, may well have been the real reason why he took it on. He had a particular interest in growing orchids and would have relished the use of the Belvoir greenhouses. He also had a fascination with ferns and purchased Cranmore House, next to Maryville, the house on the Malone Road where he had lived as a boy, to create a fernery by replacing the old roof with glass.

Tragedy however struck in May 1904 when, at the age of only 65, Walter died quite unexpectedly on the short train ride between Kilrea and Portrush. He had been in Kilrea fishing on a stretch of the Bann he rented with Gustav Wolff and was travelling to Portrush on business as a member of the Northern Counties Committee of the Midland Railway, of which he was a shareholder. His death was so sudden that when the train arrived at Portrush it appeared as though he was asleep in his seat and there was even a cigarette still burning between his lips.

He left Lil with the burden of the remainder of the lease but it was Alec, then aged 28, who took over the management of Belvoir Park for his mother. He later suggested that it may have been a mistake for his father to have rented the demesne and that, if

so, it was certainly an expensive one. Not long after Walter's death Alec took Lil on a round the world trip and appears to have become particularly interested in Japanese culture and art. His collection of Japanese art was lent to the then recently opened Ulster Museum for an exhibition in 1908.[2]

It is a pity that Walter did not have the opportunity to fully enjoy the benefit of his successful career but Lil was obviously determined to carry on the Belvoir lifestyle. She continued to organise house parties and would sometimes invite Percy French to come and entertain her guests. He would draw, recite and sing songs such as 'Phil the Fluter's Ball' and 'The Mountains of Mourne'. She once asked him to do a watercolour painting of her rock garden and stream. It is very different from the usual Percy French landscapes, giving a fine impression of the romantic informal garden of the day.

But times were changing at Belvoir as the children grew up and became more independent. May was the first of the five to leave. She married Colonel Dooner, a divorcee, and they moved to Dunmurry to start up a small boarding school. She was later widowed and moved to 'Saltpans' in

Above: Wedding of Alex and Mab at Knockbreda Church and the reception at Belvoir, 1915. Convalescents at Belvoir with Alec Wilson and Lil.
The family cars at Belvoir. (R-L) Florence Wilson, Dorothy Wilson, Lil, Robert Noel Anderson, Alec Wilson, Kitty Wilson.

47

Portballantrae where she supplemented the income from Harland & Wolff dividends with the sale of her watercolours.

Alec was next. He married Mab Bloomer, a governess, in July 1915 and they made their new home at Ballyaughlis, on the Hillhall Road near Drumbeg. He named the house Croglin after the Dumfriesshire home of his Stewart antecedents. However he seemed to enjoy the Belvoir lifestyle and continued to manage it for his mother. He had a keen interest in the latest agricultural techniques and at Belvoir installed one of the first in-bucket mechanised milking machines in Ireland, selling milk to the public at 4d per quart. The dairy maid, Katy Daley, supervised and worked long hours to separate the cream and make butter in an up and over barrel churn. She later joined them as cook at Ballyaughlis.

Alec had wide ranging interests. He was a member of the Belfast Literary Society and published articles on many topics including the dairy industry, town planning, proportional representation, political reform and the history of Harland and Wolff. Belvoir provided him with the opportunity to share his interests with friends and colleagues from the literary world and Cathal O'Byrne, in his book *As I roved out* [3] gives a wonderful description of an open air theatre performance hosted by Alec and performed on the grass at the foot of the motte. He also pursued his love of nature, history and archaeology as a member of the Belfast Naturalists' Field Club.

He and Mab loved the company of children and my mother has fond memories of visits with her sister Wynne to Croglin. Here Alec and his wife bred sealyham and cairn terriers and kept poultry; ratting under the chicken coups with the terriers was considered to be great sport. Sadly they had no children of their own and so the family name was to die out. They later moved to London where Alec became a part of an even larger family in the form of the League of Nations, for which he worked enthusiastically. They eventually retired to Rye in Sussex where they lived out their days.

My grandmother, Dorothy, was sixteen when her father died and was a bit of a rebel. Her mother sent her to Alexandra College in Dublin in an attempt to bring her into line. This ploy obviously failed as, on her return, she decided that the genteel Belvoir lifestyle was not for her and she rented a cottage on Sketrick Island in Strangford Lough. She employed Willie and Sarah Duff to help out with the house-work and cooking, sailing in summer and hunting in winter. Willie was crew when she sailed her Jewel Class yacht Ruby and groom when she hunted with the County Down Stag Hounds, where she met her husband Robert Anderson. They were married in January 1916 at Knockbreda Church and went to live in Greenisland, Co Antrim.

Then there were only two girls left at Belvoir with their mother. The large house is said to have had 22 bedrooms, so the family were able to help the war effort by taking in convalescing soldiers. At about this time the last two girls left home. Florence met Horace Aychbourn from New Zealand. He was separated from his wife and had a daughter. The law relating to re-marriage meant a shorter period of waiting in New Zealand, so they went to New Plymouth, married, but had no children. Kitty was also a rebel who rode a motor bike and hunted. She married Jim Stewart-Thompson and they went to live near Coleraine. He was a farmer and they had commercial poultry and soft fruit.

So in 1918 Lil finally gave up the lease, auctioned off much of the fine furniture and works of art, and moved to the family's holiday cottage at the Limekiln, overlooking the Whiterock Strand near Portrush. She restored and enlarged it and, perhaps in memory of the family links with Harland and Wolff, gave it a maritime style, complete with bedrooms that had portholes looking out to sea across a veranda which was built like a deck, with ships railings. A stream in the garden powered a water wheel that provided electricity to the house. The Park Hotel stands on the site today; the views are still inspirational but I'm afraid that the fine Edwardian style has long gone. Some years later she moved in with May in Portballantrae, where she died in May 1939 aged 85.

Thus did the Wilson family, through the endeavours of Walter the shipbuilder, come and go from Belvoir Park. But, as Alec wrote in his book *Fragments that Remain* [4]

'*...looking back from 1950 it is easy enough to find fault with a way of life that has now 'gone with the wind.' But I for one have no criticism for a man who worked as hard as my father did for forty-odd years, and at the end still had heart and spirit to spend some of what he had earned upon good cheer for himself and his friends'.*

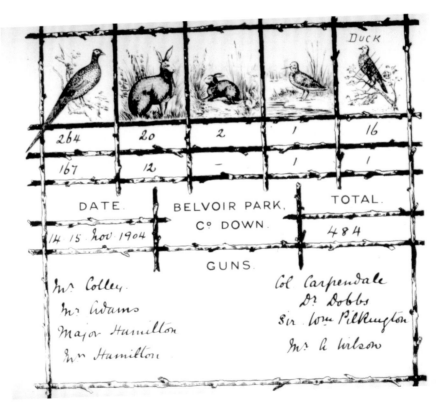

Record of a shoot at Belvoir in 1904.

Lily Dobbin in 1908 aged 13.

A child at the gate
Lily Dobbin's recollections

introduced by Dorin Bell

My Nannie Seabrooke (Lily Dobbin) was born in 1894 in the gamekeeper's lodge on the Phelps' Estate in Broadford, County Clare. Her mother died when Lily was only three years old, shortly after giving birth to two boys, neither of which survived infancy. When Lily herself died in 1972, her ashes were buried, at her request, in Broadford's now derelict Church of Ireland graveyard in her own mother's grave. For most of her adult life, Lily lived in Belfast where, after being widowed in 1926, she raised her three daughters and ran small boarding houses, first in Delhi Street and years later in Abercorn Street.

My mother was Lily's second daughter and, when I was about five and recovering from a bout of glandular fever, I spent six weeks living with my Nannie in a white-washed cottage in Ballylimp. It was there I first heard of her growing up at Belvoir. As she trimmed oil lamps, boiled jam, baked soda and treacle bread, or tucked me into bed at night to the sound of foxes baying across the fields, she told me of her childhood at Belvoir. She had drawn faces on stones which became her dolls, lined up as if in their desks at school, and stirring with a big stick, she washed her uncle's and father's clothes in a large pot set over a fire just outside the door of their gate-lodge. On Sundays she loved to walk to Shaw's Bridge or the Giant's Ring.

At heart, Lily remained a child of the countryside. I remember her rose-filled garden in her last home in Bangor, where in 1965 I asked her to write down for me the story of her early life. In 1967, Nannie sent me a little blue jotter full of her memories, including newspaper clippings she had saved about Milltown, 'my village' as she called it, and Belvoir.

Belvoir has always held a fascination for me, but it wasn't until September 2003 that I, now also a grandmother, at last walked in Belvoir, greatly changed of course, but as beautiful as it must have been when Lily left it 90 years ago. I treasure Lily's story and know she would have been surprised and delighted that it would be valued by others.

Could this have been Lily's home? This attractive, symmetrical gate lodge just inside the demesne wall at Milltown was probably originally built for a house known as Derramore which stood in the southern part of the demesne. When Derramore was demolished, the gate lodge marked one of the entrances to Belvoir. It had two front doors that originally opened into two separate rooms, one the bedroom, the other the living room. At some time in the early 20th century it was lived in by 'Granny Mackie'. When this corner of the demesne was sold to Miss Duffin in the 1920s and Ardnavally was built, it became the gate lodge to this property. An extension was built at the rear and it was lived in by Mr Christie, chauffeur to Miss Duffin, with his wife and three children. They left in 1961 and Patsy Downey lived in it for a short while, before it was demolished around 1963.

FROM EARLY IN 1900 when I was five until December 1913, just after I turned nineteen, I lived in a gate-lodge at Belvoir Park with my paternal grandmother and her bachelor son, Uncle Tommy, who was rather deaf. He was my father's elder brother and had gone deaf during a bout of scarlet fever when he was 14. He was always kind to me. It was a nice lodge, I wish I could draw a design of it. Belvoir Park was a walled in estate, so we lived behind the wall with big double wooden gates about 15 feet high and painted red. We could not see the road or anyone passing unless we stood up on a big tree trunk to look over the wall. Needless to say I spent a lot of time looking over the wall, and so got the nickname of Jack-in-the-Box by the village boys.

It was a beautiful place to live. Such a big park where I could wander for miles, and always alone. I could leave my home inside the park and follow the driveway between each of four big fields, each separated by big white wooden gates with a big latch that a man on horseback could open with his whip. I would eventually come out at the other lodge at Newtownbreda where my father's sister Aunt Mary Dickson lived. She had five daughters.

Lily two years my junior, Ellie, May, Winnie and Meta. So they were real red letter days for me when I was allowed to visit them. There were always cows, horses and sheep in the fields. I was afraid of them and would have to find gates and holes in the hedges to get past some of the beasts on the driveways. When coming back home, Lily and Ellie were allowed to lead me along about half a mile to the front gate lodge of the park, after that I was on my own through the jungle. Sometimes it would be almost dark before I got home. I used to keep my eyes on the clouds and imagine they were fairy castles and wonder and long for my dear little mother. My father always referred to her as his dear little wife. I had read lots of stories about children who had lost their mothers who were now angels in heaven and were allowed to protect their children on earth and that was a great comfort to me when lonely or afraid.

During school days we enjoyed the simple pleasures of gathering water cress and flowers in spring and blackberries and crab apples in autumn. In winter once it got dark at 4pm we were in for the night. The lamp was lit and a good fire. Learn your lessons and do your exercise and to bed early by candle light.

We had barrels for rain water but spring water for cooking was a problem. It was quite a way to the well and if I did not get there before dark Uncle Tom had to go when he came home from work. On a dark night I had to go with him and carry the lantern. He would take two big quart cans and that was called a 'go' of water and was used only for drinking, making tea and cooking. Granny used to say it was as precious as gold dust and had to last two days.

When I came North first I used to sleep with my granny but as I got bigger I got a tiny room and bed of my own. I put up a little shelf by hammering two very long nails in the wall and setting a narrow piece of wood on them. I had a chair, my own mother's trunk, also an old wooden sink set on end nails hammered in and a thick piece of cardboard for a shelf. Our floors were all flagged. A hot water bottle was unheard of, so I thought of warming the flat iron and putting it in for a little while before getting into bed.

The Wilson family who had Belvoir Park rented from Lord Deramore had a son, then two grown up daughters and two very pretty, haughty looking, young ones called Miss Dorothy and Miss Kitty who used to come in at our lodge gate which we had to

Lily Dobbin Seabrooke in 1916 aged 22 with her father John Dobbin aged 46 and her first daughter, Kathleen.

open and curtsy to them. They always had their governess looking after them. Miss Florence and Miss May had a Sunday school class every Sunday morning for the children on the estate. I had much further to go to the big house than the others. I loved going. Miss Florence taught us in the Gun Room and we sat on two hard forms. She read to us first the Peep of Day and Line upon Line for the older ones. Mr Ireland the foreman had seven children, six were girls. Mr Anderson the coachman had five girls. Mr Lindsay the gardener had five girls and poor little me was only one. Lessons over, we were all given a sweet each and taken along passages to the big hall where Miss May taught us to sing the hymn that we had learned. Some of the Ireland children used to lead me part of the way home through the park, down the quarry hill and past a dark lake under trees where we used to watch to see an otter appear. Past that was a grassy glen at the side of the road which in spring was covered with primroses. We usually gathered a bunch and we called it primrose land. The Ireland children would turn back home up the quarry hill and I would wend my way home past the gamekeeper's house and sawmill with the River Lagan in the distance through two gates. I usually

climbed over them just for a thrill. Then along the side of Tommy Gray's field (100 acres). If there were horses or cows on the avenue, I usually got over the hedge into the next field and back to the avenue further on past the beasts.

Our Lodge was at the back and longest way into Belvoir so we never saw any of the Quality arriving for parties. The milk cart came night and morning and a bread cart three times a week. An odd time Mr Wilson came through on horseback. Once he asked me if I would run in front and open the gates between the fields. I could run like a hare. I was not expecting anything from him but he really gave me a 6d.

My father came home two years after the Boer War ended. He stayed in Africa digging for gold but did not find any. He got work on the estate and stayed at home for a while. I dearly loved him and we used to go on long walks together and he would tell me about my mother and we would talk about Broadford and he was always amazed how much I remembered. At this time I would have been about 10 or 11. Although we did not have much traffic at our Lodge someone always had to be on call. So when granny went to Belfast on a Friday – one and a

half miles to walk to the tram and same home from the tram with a bag of groceries – I was kept home from school to mind the gate and lose my schooling but what did the Gentry care.

That summer granny got fed up at home and decided to visit her son Stewart who was principal of a school in Winsford, Cheshire, England. I expect she thought it was time my father looked after me. Well, she went for two or three months, part of the time was school holidays but still I missed school and loved learning. My father and uncle left the house at 6am. I had to make them lunches, do the washing and have their supper ready when they returned at

6pm and all had to be done on an open fire. One day I was standing looking over the wall as usual when two women passed and I overheard them say. 'Poor child. Her own mother would never have left her like that.' Well, I nearly broke my heart crying that day. Sometimes when I look back I do really think my mother's spirit has been near me and helped me down the years. Eventually I wrote to granny to please come home and I would be so good. Well, she did come and I was glad to see her.

My father went to Canada eventually and I did not see him again for seven years when he came to England during the 1st World War.

I was through sixth grade in July and should have gone back to school in August but granny said I was through the books so better not go back. I was not 14 until the December and did not go to work until the following Easter and all that time I could have been at school. (How lucky children are who have both parents). Granny spoke to our clergyman and he recommended me to a linen firm, John S. Brown. They did very high class work for the American trade but made their money by sweated labour. I was put on a new type of machine for machine embroidery. Five shillings per week. All the work had to be kept clean but sometimes after the machine was oiled it would drop on the work. Well, one day after two weeks Miss Ross sent for me and told me I was not being paid five shillings a week for sitting looking about me. Fresh in from the country and 100 girls and machines of different kinds going. I suppose I was interested in all the girls. However I went on to a plain machine like the one I've been using this 50 years and made plain pillowcases for 6d a dozen and 9d if they had frills. We started at 8:30 and if you got there at 8:40 the door was locked and you could go back home. We finished at 6 pm and an hour for lunch which usually consisted of a sandwich and a cup of tea in a cafe. We were off at 1:30 on Sat and by the time I got home it was 3pm. We had two days at Christmas two days at Easter and two days July 12 and 13 so you could go and see the Orangemen, but we were on our own time, holidays were not paid for. It was like a prison to me and I got married to get out of it. I had such freedom in woods and open air surroundings both in Clare and Belvoir Park that I just felt clamped down.

I earned about 15 shillings a week and gave granny 10 shillings and bought my own clothes. I was 17 when I met Willie Seabrooke and he was so kind and understanding and loved me so much. Well I thought I was in heaven. He was too young and we were so immature and no experience of life. Just two youngsters up in the clouds. Then war came in 1914 which altered everyone's way of just jogging along.

We were 13 stormy years married when Willie died and during the short spells we were together were ideally happy. I had my three little girls aged three, seven and ten and they were my whole life and living dolls to make pretty clothes for. They all married young and then I had the love of all my grandchildren.

As if it was yesterday
David Coburn's stories

I NOW LIVE IN BELVOIR PARK ESTATE. Previously I lived further down the Ormeau Road and as a school child would have come to Belvoir Park along the Lagan towpath. Of course everything is always better on the other side so I would have climbed over the wall into Belvoir. As children we were always terrified because the story was there was a gamekeeper there, and he had a shotgun. In those days children were frightened of authority so we very often had to scuttle, even though we never really ever saw anyone. We were frightened to come near the house, we would have just gone over the wall, down beside the Lagan River. That would have been 1937-38.

When war broke out I was just starting to serve my time as an apprentice electrician and after about two years, in about 1942-43 when I was about 16, I was sent with a number of men in a small car up to Belvoir Park. I remember going through Newtownbreda village which seemed in those days to be well out in the country, and we turned in at a gate which I would say would be opposite Beechill Road. Coming down the path with fields to each side of us there were various haystacks about the place. The grass had been cut and I presumed that these were just haystacks and then as I passed one I happened to look

up and I saw a door open in it! This army chap came out, to my amazement. Apparently that was where they stored a lot of their stuff, and this was their camouflage for it.

Then there was a man, Chesney, who was supposed to be the caretaker but he acted as if he owned the place! I believe he worked for Stewart and Partners, I think they owned this area. He was sort of looking after their interests. He was a man who walked about, trying to watch everything that was going on. He seemed to take a big interest in the place and I would have looked at him as a boss-man. He lived in the stable yard, over where the RSPB are now.

We had a number of different men on the job, some of them were working inside the house. I was with the men that were actually working outside; we were putting in poles to take an electric supply over to the stables. While we were working on the outside, at various times, perhaps once a week, they would warn you that there was going to be a bit of an explosion, down towards the Lagan. One of the army fellows said they were just testing explosives to see what sort of condition they were in. One day I was what we called dressing a pole, fitting the insulators while it was still on the ground, and I saw a kind of a mist come over, and I started to cough for no apparent reason and the cough got worse and then an ambulance came up and another one and another one! A lot of the army that were there were Pioneer Corps doing more or less labouring work, these were men who were not 100% fit, men used in supply depots and things like that. Quite a few of them, I think at least 12 of them, had to be taken to hospital, but it cleared away and everything seemed to go all right.

Another thing I do remember was what one of the army chaps said about the old graveyard. He was quite angry because he said some of the army had broken into the tomb. How true it was I don't know, but he seemed a genuine fellow who was annoyed that someone would have desecrated it. That would have been around 1942-3 but I didn't see the tomb then, only afterwards, in the 1950s. There were still quite a few of the headstones standing then.

The house itself was a beautiful old building. We were working from the main supply, so we weren't up through the house to the same extent as some of the other fellows would have been. I do remember there was like a courtyard at one side of the house and part of it was covered in with glass, like a walkway right around the square, and there were a couple of stables

in there. We had been told that when people in the house were going out somewhere a carriage could be brought in there and they would have had shelter. It was at the back of the main house, attached onto it. I remember going into the house. I do remember seeing the main staircase of the house. In my mind, the hallway had black and white tiles. There was a back staircase and there was an alcove on it and I wondered why there was this very narrow stairway. Someone said it was from the kitchens and the idea of the alcove was that if someone was coming up and someone was coming down it was a place to pass, you could step into it. The rooms were used for offices and some for sleeping accommodation. There were bare floorboards and the army was using trestle tables and such like things that they had brought in. There were a few huts further away, to the right of the building.

I was away from Belvoir in the '50s but I remember when in later years it was decided the house was going to be blown up. Already in Belvoir Park there were quite a number of Housing Trust houses built. I believe it was a Saturday at noon it was to be blown up and we all gathered at the top of Belvoir Drive to watch this. Sure enough, just after

12 there was a terrific explosion, dust everywhere, and when the dust all settled the house was just sitting as we all remembered it! It took them the next week or so to get rid of it.

Stewart and Partners built Belvoir Estate from the Newtownbreda side down to about the school and then I think they went bankrupt. Unit Construction took over and built all of the other houses. We moved here to this house in Crevenish Walk in 1964. If you wanted a house in Belvoir they sort of vetted you for it. There was a Miss Frazer who was in charge from the Housing Trust and she lived in a flat on the main drive and the assistant manageress was a Miss Ferris. The girl came round and collected the rent and if you had had any repairs done they would have a look and ask if you were satisfied. They had their office just where the wine store is in Drumart Square. Men were employed for cutting grass and things like that, practically every morning they would come from the top of Belvoir Drive and lift paper and rubbish. If you didn't keep your grass cut Miss Frazer would have been round to see you about it and she would threaten you with, well, having to move out. She was very, very strict. Mind you I would have said at the time she was fair. No doubt about it, when you lose someone like that or you are not able to enforce these things, people get more careless.

When we first moved out here we felt we were really in the country. It took about a year to get used to the place, the open space, the forest being so close. We had a dog at that time and took it out quite often around the forest. Then I got interested in a number of organisations here that were looking for help. I started taking boys for football. In those days they didn't have their own football pitch, we made our own and I think the boys appreciated this all the more. We spent many, many happy years here. It's just hard to put into words, it is just that comfortable feeling, good neighbours, everyone helped each other. My wife was very keen on voluntary work, any excuse and she would have B-B-Qs and things for the children here about, it was a very happy time.

As the years went on, my wife had a stroke and eventually died. The family said to me would I not think of moving. I said no, because no matter where I went in Belvoir I always met someone I knew. Shops were convenient. Everything was quiet and peaceful, we were well out of the Troubles, except when I was working in Belfast where there were many explosions.

One night in September 1992 it all changed. I remember my son was sitting in the chair near the window and I was facing him, there had been a football match on the TV and it was just coming to half-time, when the blind sort of lit up and there was an unearthly roar and crashing of glass. The pair of us bumped into each other trying to get out through the door to see what had happened. We couldn't find the key to the back door and in the pitch darkness we got to the front door and got it opened and we both fell out into the garden! The whole front door had moved out and broken the concrete step, it was taken right out.

We heard people calling. Two elderly ladies lived in apartments just across from us. They were panicking because they had turned the key the wrong way and were trying to get out. We got their door opened and went round the corner. The lady round there was obviously in shock and the bird cage had been blown across the room and the canary was flying about. I got her into the front room thinking it would be warmer for her, I tried to pacify her, and then suddenly realised there was no glass in the windows! Its only afterwards you think of some of the stupid things that you did.

Outside you couldn't see a thing, I had been through the blackout but it never seemed to be as dark as it was that night, no moon, no lights. The phones were off then as well. We were lucky, really. There was a girl who did some work for me who had a house nearer the bomb and the gable wall of her house had moved about four inches, all her kitchen cupboards had come off the wall. The Church of Ireland was wiped out and the Presbyterian Church had to be pulled down. The Methodist Church was badly damaged also. The bomb had been at the Forensic Science Laboratory. It was very lucky that two policemen had spotted the van, there had been no warning. They got the people out of the church hall. There was no one killed but one girl needed a lot of stitches and there were a lot of people suffering from shock.

It was like during the Blitz, people that you didn't really speak to spoke to you. It seemed that, if anything, it brought people together. However, there was hardship. Today there is no sign of it, everything is back to normal, as if it had never happened, the place grew up again, the churches and houses were rebuilt.

Up and over the wall
Ernie Andrews' stories

The Big House. Illustration by Deirdre Crone

I WAS BORN IN SUNNYSIDE STREET. Belvoir Park was a big attraction for all us kids because we were told not to go there. That was where we went in the 1950s. To get to it we used to go down Sunnyside Street and across the old Sunnyside Brickworks; there was a brickworks there with two big quarries and two magic ponds. Across from there, up Annadale Avenue, across the old Council dump by the bend in the river, up near the weir, and over the wall into Belvoir. Usually about half a dozen kids would all have been there but the big danger was the old game keeper, Chesney, and he did fire at us, he did take a shot and we were led to believe that they were salt pellets he fired out of the shot gun but in later years we found out it wasn't, it was the real thing! He was there, but once we got to know his movements we could avoid him, we became very good at camouflaging ourselves in the rhododendrons and bushes.

Certainly the military had been there during the War, all the traces were there, there were parts of a small railway that we found, running from the landing stage down at the river right up what we always used to know as Pigeon Hill. In those days we still could find bits and pieces. We used to find old 303 bullets, the old cordite bullets, and torpedo heads, the casings. We thought they were welding bottles at first but then we saw that they came apart and welding bottles don't unscrew the way these things did! The bullets were still live and went pop when you put them in a fire! I suppose it was dangerous, but you know the way kids are with things like that.

Over in the orchard there was a strange building that looked like a toilet - it was grey concrete, like reinforced concrete, and you zigzagged going into it, you went right and then left to get into it and then it opened out into just a plain room, nothing in it, but the same zigzag way out on the other side. This was where bombs would have been armed or disarmed or any work was done on them and we found mortar bombs lying about it, we recognised them from the black and white war movies we watched at the Curzon! But they had red tips on them; I would say they were practice bombs which was probably why they were left. We tried to set them off, but they didn't explode, which is why I am here today to tell you about it! If you were at the big house and you were looking down into the orchard it was to the extreme left, it was on the orchard side of the wall, on the steep slope down from the path to the graveyard. It's all overgrown and gone now, it was bulldozed when the Forest Service came, they knocked a lot of stuff down. If we had thought in those days we would have looked a lot closer for things than we did, but being kids we were more than happy to be up there climbing trees, lighting fires and catching fish in the river and one thing and another.

The other military buildings were not all that far from the old sawmill, on Pigeon Hill. If you took a direct line from the landing stage into the forest it was the big hill straight in front of you. Not on the Lagan side of the hill but on the other side, where the path runs.

I remember we found an owl one day, it had flown into the barbed wire fence that used to run near the river, it was dead as a doornail, hanging in the wire. We saw otters in the river, you can still see otters, I saw one near the landing stage a few days ago. There were never squirrels in Belvoir when I was young – I am sure I would have seen them. More recently there were red squirrels but the greys are now ousting them.

There was barbed wire round the house and what we would call hard stands for vehicles with a pit underneath them, I remember two of them at the front of the house. I remember here was one of the close encounters with Mr Chesney. He was in the big house and came running out, a couple of quick shots in the air and we were gone, we were long, long, gone!

We got into the house, obviously barbed wire wasn't a problem for a load of kids from Sunnyside Street! Massive rooms, we really had never been in a place as big, and a beautiful big staircase. The ceilings were very high, all done with plaster work, really beautifully done. We were able to get right down into the basements. They were flooded; a lot of water lying about them, obviously the house had not been looked after. The army guys had Mickey Mouse, Pluto, Donald Duck, all the Disney characters on the walls, some of them maybe six foot high. I am sure they would still be there because when they went to blow the house up it took them two goes and I would say that not all of the basements collapsed in. We would get in through windows that had been boarded up, and just weren't boarded all that well. We were everywhere, even up on the roof. We stayed overnight, or we tried to, one night, but there was a cat or something came in and we were terrified! We heard two squeaks of the floor boards and off we went! We did it just to prove that we could do it, I suppose for boasts, but we couldn't, it was too much for us. One torch among six of us, it wasn't enough!

If it had been now, the National Trust would have taken that house and restored it because it really was something. When you see some of the dilapidated houses that they have got and done them up, Belvoir would not have been as big a challenge to them. But the army got the job of blowing it up and that was it. It broke our hearts when we saw it.

I never saw cattle or sheep grazing in Belvoir Park, there was nothing in my time. The only cattle were across the river. There was open ground towards Milltown. We knew this as the pastures but I never remember cattle on it, just open ground. In the orchard towards the old graveyard there were apple trees, plums, cherries, there were a lot of pear trees in it and a vine along the wall. The bird sanctuary lake, Galwally, was a favourite haunt of mine. Well the big thing everyone wanted was a shot gun, because we used to see guys up along the Lagan, in those days you could shoot all over, because there were no houses or anything up there. I eventually became the age and

I got a shot gun. I used to go with these other guys that had been shooting for a year or two. We used to track where the duck would come out at night from the bird sanctuary and on a wet night or windy night they went such a way and on a dry night maybe with a bit of moon they came a different way, so we had it well planned. They used to come out over the golf course in their hundreds. Really, you didn't have to be a great shot to get a couple of them!

I remember the tombs were broken into, that must have been in the 1950s, and we heard about it, word came round the street and up we went, all the usual suspects went up to have a look. The police and all had been there and we found bones scattered, they were kind of green and everyone said if you touched them you would die and all the rest of it, so we didn't like the look of them. There were some quite long bones, ribs and stuff like that scattered on the path. They must have carried the coffins out and they must have tried to break them up. Being lead, they must have been quite a weight, and when they broke them open they would have just emptied the bones out. I always heard that someone was caught trying to sell them, that the police actually got them, but the word was that there was jewellery, a lot of jewellery in the coffins, which was never heard of again, it was spirited away. The bones lay about for quite a while up there.

There were two ponds in the forest, one of which the Forest Service filled in. It was by the path that takes you down from where the house used to be going towards Shaw's Bridge, before you get to where the army huts used to be, down a bit from where there is now a concrete platform in the woods. There were fish in it, we used to sit very quietly and watch them, I think they were either rudd or roach. It was very, very deep, there was a stone quarry face on the far side of it. It was a great wee spot, but they filled it in, they said it was dangerous but I was raging, I said why not put a fence round it, but no. There was another pond over at the side of forest, towards the housing estate, up towards the dual carriageway. I think it was a duck pond.

We couldn't get to Morelands Meadow in those days, there was a weir at the lock keeper's house at the end of Morelands Meadow, but it was fortified. It's all gone now and there is an ordinary wee foot bridge across and no weir anymore. I remember the lock keeper, a boy Rowan, he was every bit as bad as Chesney! The Rowans were famous lock keepers; they lived at the Stranmillis lock, the first lock. I actually worked with one of them in a place at Stranmillis, Campbell Browns. It was he who told me about fishing in the canal, I used to go up there, it was full of rudd in those days. You could have drunk the water it was so clean and we used to go about seven nights a week and fish it, just catch them and throw them back in. The Rowans also had the second lock house, at Morelands Meadow. They were supposed to be able to spend the rest of their days in it, but it was burnt down, you can still see the foundations. This would have been in the late '50s or maybe early '60s.

When the Forest Service first came they took over the old stables and made their headquarters there. The big house was blown up of course. They brought in heavy machinery and they levelled out a lot of places to make more ground for planting. They had very few staff at the start, guys that I had knocked about with as kids got jobs in it. Then that big sewage place was built. All we could see from the distance were these big silos; it looked like a rocket site when they were building it. I remember Belvoir housing estate going up. I thought this all was desperate; it had been a magic place in my young days!

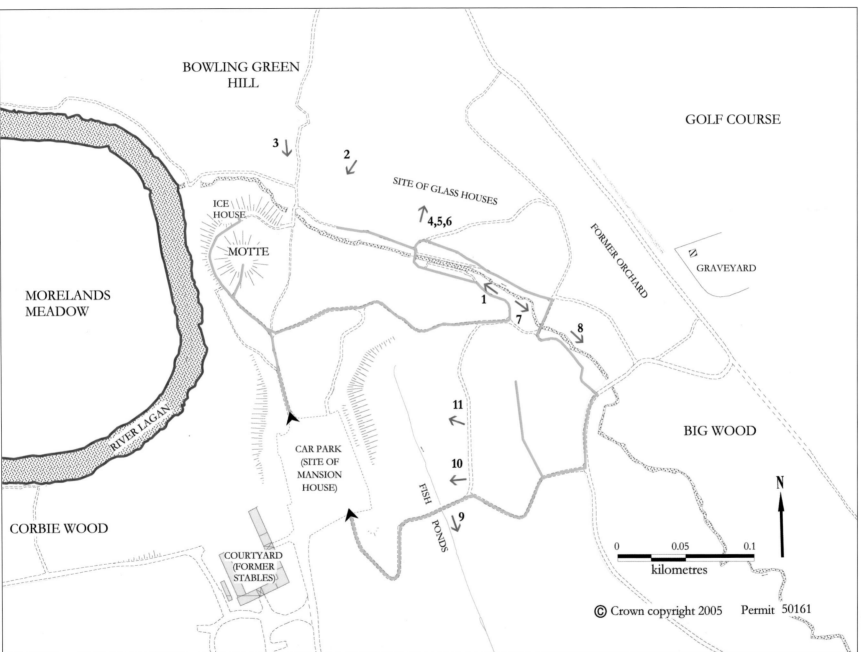

BOWLING GREEN
HILL

GOLF COURSE

Map of the gardens. The walk described is shown in green, red numbered arrows indicate the views of the former gardens shown in the old photographs.

3 ↓

2 ↓

SITE OF GLASS HOUSES

ICE
HOUSE

↑ 4,5,6

MOTTE

FORMER ORCHARD

GRAVEYARD

1

7 ↓

8 ↓

MORELANDS
MEADOW

RIVER LAGAN

BIG WOOD

11
←

CAR PARK
(SITE OF
MANSION
HOUSE)

10
←

CORBIE WOOD

FISH PONDS

9 ↓

COURTYARD
(FORMER
STABLES)

N

0   0.05   0.1

kilometres

© Crown copyright 2005   Permit 50161

CHAPTER *Four* – a brief *tour* of the *old* GARDENS   **Ben Simon**

The old sundail from Belvoir gardens.

THE BEST PLACE TO START a visit to the gardens and Arboretum is at the main car park at Belvoir. This is at the centre of the old estate, the site of the mansion house. The car park is built over the cellars of the house and the two-storey stone buildings and courtyard on the western side of the car park were the old stables. Walking to the far end of the car park there is a magnificent view with glimpses of the River Lagan in the foreground, the flat expanse of Morelands Meadow with its stately trees and, further in the distance, the fields and wooded slopes that lead up to Stranmillis. The Belfast Hills provide an impressive backdrop to this view. There is little to make the visitor suspect that it is only four kilometres to Belfast city centre.

A short distance from the viewing point overlooking Morelands Meadow at the end of the car park a path leads to the motte, an ancient conical, flat-topped mound. It is worth a walk up the wooden steps to the top of the motte. Although views are obscured by tall trees, here you can get a feel for the landscape of the demesne. Standing with your back to the car park, to the left (west) is Morelands Meadow and the River Lagan, straight ahead (north)

is quite a narrow valley with a Scots pine plantation on the far side, on Bowling Green Hill. Towards the right (east), the valley widens and here the gardens were developed. Behind the tree line on the horizon to the right is the golf course. After descending from the motte, before visiting the gardens, follow the path to the right, going round the base of the motte to find the remains of a short brick tunnel which leads to a metal gate through which can be seen a deep, dark cavern. This was an ice house which would have been packed with ice and used to store food in the days before refrigerators. The sloping sides of the motte in this area support a wide variety of wild flowers (see Chapter 5) though the presence of a few patches of the dark green, prickly shrub, butcher's broom, suggests that this area was at one time planted.

Retracing your steps back up the path towards the car park, towards the right you will see an old beech tree and on the left a remarkable ancient oak tree with three huge boughs that grow from ground level. The low, spreading boughs form an ideal seat, a place to contemplate the beauty of this age-old tree where generations of lords and ladies may have sat. This oak is also unusual in that it keeps its leaves

*Photograph 1:
Rustic bridge over
the stream (early
20th century)*

later into the autumn than any of the other native oaks at Belvoir. Walk along the gently sloping path in front of the old oak (the path between the oak and the car park, not the path between the oak and the motte!) and into woodland. There is a small plantation of mixed conifers dating from the early 1960s on your left, and on your right a small area of grey alder of similar age. A short distance further on is a group of four interesting old trees.

Just to the right of the path is a grafted beech tree. Some branches have an unusual narrow, pointed leaf with a serrated edge, though others have typical beech leaves.[1] Behind the beech are two oak trees with large trunks which have thick yellowish bark and keep some leaves all winter. These are Lucombe oak, a cross between Turkey oak and cork oak, and are again grafted trees; the line of the graft is clearly visible just above ground level. A little bit further along the path, on the left, is a lovely old oak which has dense, dark evergreen foliage and almost black bark. It is a holm oak, a species which originates from the western Mediterranean. Although one large bough fell in 2004, it is still an impressive tree.

Slightly further along the path, going down the slope, the dark green foliage of two yew trees is noticeable to the right and left of the path. Continuing along the path, passing a group of snowy mespil (*Amelanchier)* bushes on the left, notice that the path crosses over the line of an old brick wall, the remains of which can be seen through a tangle of brambles, grass and ivy on the right. Here there would probably have been a gateway. We are now in the area of the old gardens where attractive walks were created and fruit, flowers and vegetables would have been grown for the house. Exotic conifer and broadleaved trees have been a feature of this area since the time of the Bateson (Deramore) family in the 19th century. This wealthy family probably also embellished the gardens with many ornaments, though we only know of one, a slate sundial engraved 'Belvoir Garden' made by Richard Melville, Belfast, 1838. It is now sited, on a modern plinth, by the club house at Belvoir Park Golf Club. After the Belvoir gardens became derelict in the mid 1920s, there was no more planting and the area became a jungle of weeds, bramble and undergrowth until the Forest Service cleared the area in the 1970s and made new paths and planted specimen trees to create what is now a very attractive and interesting Arboretum.

Walking along the path through this area, on the left notice a silver fir tree with beautiful dark violet blue young cones in spring.[2] Also on the left are an alder, a young cedar and Lawson cypress.[3] By the path on the right is an incense cedar with a tight columnar shape[4] and an upright golden variety of Monterey cypress. All of these trees are fairly young, though on the lawn on the right there is a much older yew with a large trunk and long, rather pendulous branches that sweep to the ground. Continuing straight along the path you cannot miss a magnificent huge atlas cedar which stands on the edge of the path on the left. Pause here and look for a very tall old variegated Lawson cypress[5] next to the path on the right. It is difficult to see this tree because an old rose has grown round the tree and upwards to a remarkable height – it is perhaps the tallest rose in Ireland![6] Straight ahead is a second massive atlas cedar but rather than continuing along this route turn sharp left just before the big clump of bamboo and follow the path along the stream bank, going downstream.

Photograph 2: View of the motte from the pleasure garden (early 20th century)

Ahead are rows of closely planted yew trees on either side of the stream. Today the yews are a very visible feature from this location. However, the view in this area used to be very different. An old photograph taken from this position shows that just upstream from the yews a brick wall used to cut across the valley, dividing the gardens in half. The wall was embellished with brick pillars covered with climbers that were trained along chains that hung from pillar to pillar. By the wall, a bridge crossed the stream. This was designed to appear as though hewn from stone and was planted with alpines (photograph 1).

Continue along the path and, if it is early summer, you will notice an interesting tree on your left with leaves similar to a horse chestnut and yellow flowers tinged with pink. This tree, planted in the 1970s, is a sweet buckeye, a North American species. Walk along the path to the footbridge at the end of the avenue of yews and stop to search out some of the remains of the old gardens. If you stand on the bridge and look upstream, the original design of this part of the gardens can be appreciated. The yews would have been kept clipped to form parallel hedges on either side of the stream, which is confined within two parallel stone walls, the water cascading over a little

stone waterfall. This seems to be an example of the 'canals' which were mentioned in a description of the gardens published in 1744 (see Chapter 2). Turning around and looking downstream, the remains of some of the old brick walls that used to enclose the formal gardens can be seen. Near the bridge there are large rhododendron bushes (on the left) and a beautiful old Japanese maple with lime-green leaves that appear early in spring (on the right). These are more relics of the old garden planting. Go over the bridge and walk along the path downstream a short distance to where an old garden wall crosses the stream and the path. Beyond this wall, the level ground near the stream used to be planted as a pleasure garden with gravel walks, seasonal bedding in a manicured lawn and roses and other climbers trained over metal arches (photograph 2). The stream was contained within stone-faced banks with little waterfalls over which the water tumbled. Between the trees you would also have had glimpses of the impressive northern façade of the mansion house (photograph 3). Today the former pleasure garden is an impenetrable tangle of vegetation. A high level sewer pipe unfortunately cuts across this area and further downstream the river area is now dominated

by a mass of bamboo and a young alder plantation. The views to the motte and Morelands Meadow have been lost, though the lack of access and disturbance to these areas of scrub and woodland make it important for wildlife.

Returning to the footbridge over the stream, stay on the northern bank and walk upstream along the path by the water, with the yews on your right. On the left are young deciduous trees, mainly rowan, cotoneaster, maple and sycamore, behind which is a

Photograph 3: The northern façade of the house from the gardens (early 20th century)

Photograph 5: A second view of the glass houses. Some of the glass has been painted to provide shade (early 20th century)

Photograph 6: Ivy basket. This can also be seen in photograph 4 (early 20th century)

Photograph 4: The glass houses with clipped trees, hedges and roses (early 20th century)

patch of dogwood, self-seeded trees and scrub. This is another part of the gardens that has changed considerably over the last 100 years. Here Forest Service staff have discovered areas of old terrazzo flooring under a blanket of moss and leaves, the last remains of an impressive range of glass houses that used to stand in this area. These timber framed buildings collapsed long ago. Nothing remains of the formal flower beds, yew hedges and clipped bushes that used to enhance the ground in front of the glass houses. Old photographs of the site (numbers 4, 5, 6) show a charming ornament, an ivy basket planted with wallflowers, perhaps designed by the gardener to

please the lady of the house. Although this formal landscape is long gone, a few plants remain including two old tall pear trees hidden amongst self-seeded trees on the wooded slope. By the remains of a crumbling brick wall, an old ornamental vine with large heart-shaped leaves *(Vitus coignetiae)* still flourishes, twisting up and around the stems and branches of trees as it seeks out light.

Walking further along the path, you will see on the left a row of four impressive tall Monterey cypress. Behind these old trees are younger conifers, probably planted in the 1970s, with a group of young giant sequoia, Leyland cypress (including Castlewellan and Robinson Gold), golden Monterey cypress and incense cedar.

At a crossroads in the paths, stop and take in the views. In the foreground on the left is a low tree with an umbrella-shaped crown of long shoots. This is a Persian ironwood tree which is particularly attractive in autumn, when the leaves turn red and yellow. Behind it on the left is a magnificent tall giant sequoia *(Sequoiadendron giganteum)*, also known as Wellingtonia. The giant sequoia has a very distinctive tall, straight, tapering single trunk and thick, spongy bark. This tree species was first

discovered in California in 1852 and was soon introduced into Britain and Ireland where it grows remarkably quickly. On the stream bank by the bridge on the right are numerous short suckers of a wingnut growing in a patch of long grass. Not far in front, by the crossroads in the paths, is a deciduous tree, a sycamore that appears unremarkable in winter, but in spring produces yellow and green variegated leaves that are stunning on a sunny day.[7] The sloping ground ahead leads towards the old Breda graveyard and the golf course. Most of this area was formerly an orchard though there are some old arboretum trees, including a group of tall deodar cedars that form a conspicuous feature near the top of this slope.

Turn right and walk onto the humpback wooden bridge over the stream and pause awhile to take in the scenery. Nearby on the southern bank you can see the two huge atlas cedars that form a focal point to the gardens. The stream banks were also an important part of the garden design. The large blocks of stone that now lie on the banks are the remnants of old rockeries and stonework edging. Photographs of this area (numbers 7, 8) show that it used to be planted with shrubs and herbaceous material arranged around rocks and stepping-stones that led

Photograph 8: Waterfall and stepping stones. This view is upstream of photograph 7. A distinctive tree with an angled crown can be seen on the horizon in both pictures (early 20th century)

Photograph 7: Informal planting between blocks of stone along the stream in the garden (eatly 20th century)

to rustic bridges and little waterfalls. Most of the plants would have gone soon after the gardens became derelict in the mid 1920s, but some bamboos have flourished and a few other plants hung on. Forest Service staff recall seeing *Rodgersia* and *Peltiphyllum peltatum*, large-leaved plants suited to moist conditions, growing by the river bank.

Cross over to the southern side of the stream and turn left, following the path upstream. Pass an attractive multi-stemmed lime tree on your left and three young pines on your right. Notice a huge mass of roses on the far river bank, another rampant relic of the old gardens, and two lovely old Japanese red cedars on the right. This species of tree was first grown outside of Japan in 1842. On the bank behind the cedars is a group of three giant sequoias that were probably planted in the 1970s and, further up the bank, is an older tall, narrow, golden Monterey cypress, variety 'lutea'. Continuing along by the river, just before the junction with another path, on the left are two trees growing close together, a tall thuja[8] and a Lawson cypress. At this junction, turn right.

Thickets of bamboo, snowberry and the prickly branches and orange flowers of an old berberis (*Berberis darwinii*) hedge form the left-hand side of this path. On the slope on the right are young Monterey cypress and Lawson cypress. A short distance along this path there is an old spruce on the left. Turn right at the junction with yet another path and proceed up the small hill.

On the left-hand side is a large sycamore and, set back a bit from the path, another tall sycamore with variegated green and yellow leaves which are particularly impressive when the leaves first open[9] and, next to it, a tall maple with red/brown leaves.[10] On the right are several hazel bushes with numerous long straight branches growing from the base. These trees differ from the hazel trees that occur in the woods as they produce surprisingly large nuts in autumn. At the top of the hill it is worth taking a detour off the path and walking through the mown grass along the crest of the hill to the right through a grove of Lawson cypresses coloured dark bottle green, light green and golden yellow[11] to find a range of mainly deciduous trees. These include a group of roble beech (*Nothofagus obliqua*), hornbeam, lime, maple, London plane, beech, alder, two more old,

tall variegated sycamore, (one with a very yellow leaf[12] the other with a white and green leaf that has a purple tinge on the back[13]) and several different kinds of birch.[14] Young conifers to discover in this area include pines, spruce and a coast redwood (*Sequoia sempervirens*). Searching around the slopes of this hill one can find some old shrubs and small trees that were planted to add colour when this was a private estate. These include laburnum, rhododendron (one of which has a lovely light pink flower), mock orange (*Philadelphus*), azalea and eucryphia.

Return to the path and go down the far side of the hill, heading back towards the car park. This route passes between some oak and ash trees, including an attractive weeping ash. Further down the slope, on the left, there is another giant sequoia. On the right, close to the path, you pass some more young southern beech (*Nothofagus*) and an older deodar cedar. Continuing down to a little valley with a small stream, you come to a plantation of grey alder and larch that dates from the early 1960s.

When Belvoir was a private estate this part of the gardens used to be mown grass, shrub beds and hedges. This stream, which has only a trickle of

Photograph 9: One of the fish ponds (early 20th century)

Photograph 10: Eastern façade of the house from the gardens (early 20th century)

water, was dammed at regular intervals and the banks widened to create a series of rectangular ponds (photograph 9). These were labelled on Ordnance Survey maps as 'fish ponds'. It is now almost impossible to walk along the banks of this stream due to the dense undergrowth, trees and thickets of bamboo, though remains of some formal paths edged with cobblestones and the outline of the shallow ponds can still be traced. Photographs of the house from this area (number 10, 11) show that it must have dominated the top of the hill and looked very impressive from the gardens. Photograph 11 is of particular interest. The fish ponds cannot be seen in this view – they are obscured by trees and a hedge in the foreground. However, in the middle distance other features can be seen. Here there is a steeply sloping lawn, at the top of which is a path and a brick wall. There is another path above the wall, marked out by a row of yew trees. There is yet another steep bank above this, leading up to the flat platform on which stands the house. These features are probably the 'slopes and terraces' referred to by Harris in his 1744 description of Belvoir (see Chapter 2). Today this part of the old gardens is a larch plantation with dense undergrowth that

obscures the crumbling brick wall and terraces. However, the yew trees remain and now have quite large girths, giving them a timeless appearance.

Continue along the main path and cross the stream. Pass through the Japanese larch plantation and walk up the winding path. Here you come across one more old broadleaved tree, another Lucombe oak, before returning to the car park.

Before ending this tour, it is worth making a visit to a tall conical golden conifer which grows by the vehicle entrance to the courtyard, at the southern end of the buildings, in the garden to the right of the gate. This is a yellow form of Leyland cypress now known as Robinson Gold that was discovered growing in the forest by George Robinson, the first foreman and caretaker employed by the Forest Service, who transplanted it to its present location.[15] It has been propagated commercially through cuttings and an image of the tree appears in the Coat of Arms of Castlereagh Borough Council as well as in the centre of the medallion on the Mayor's chain.

Photograph 11: Eastern façade of the house. Terraces and yew trees embellish this part of the garden (early 20th century)

Acknowledgments

Thanks to Michael Lear, Forest Service, Reg Maxwell, Belfast City Council and Sabina Knees, Royal Botanic Garden, Edinburgh, for identifying many trees and Forest Service staff for providing information about the gardens.

Map of gardens based upon MapInfo image with the permission of the Controller of Her Majesty's Stationery Office © Crown Copyright 2005.

CHAPTER *Five-* WOODS, *meadows* and WETLANDS Dermot Hughes

Plant communities

THIS CHAPTER LOOKS AT the plantlife of Belvoir Park through a naturalist's eyes. Naturalists are forever categorising things into groups and associations, and in this case the plants tend to fall neatly into broad habitats, each with a fairly typical collection of plants. While Belvoir Park is clearly dominated by woodland of all sorts, there are other habitats to be found, such as open glades, grasslands, wetlands, streams and, of course, the River Lagan.

Although this survey did not look into every corner of Belvoir Park and not all plant groups were examined, the species found indicate that the best developed plant communities are associated with the more mature broadleaved woodlands. There are classic woodland habitats characterised by swathes of bluebell, wood anemone, lesser celandine and wild garlic with some interesting plants indicative of old woodlands such as wood sanicle. In younger woodland a few interesting plants can also be found, suggesting that Belvoir Park contains remnant populations of formerly more biodiverse habitats.

However, in other areas such as conifer plantations, areas where there are many young, tall, thin, self-seeded trees or where laurel dominates the woods, the ground flora is poor and in places almost non-existent. The least promising areas for studying plantlife in Belvoir Park are under the young conifer plantations and under the jungle of laurel on the southern side of Big Wood.

The grassland habitats around Belvoir tend generally to have an impoverished flora. This would be expected where the grass is regularly mown, where there has been reseeding, or where herbicides or fertiliser have been used. However, it is more surprising that Morelands Meadow does not have a particularly diverse flora. These kinds of riverside fields that occasionally benefit from organic-rich silt deposited during floods, are managed by low level grazing and are not improved, generally have many different wildflower species.

The margins of the small ponds and other wetlands at Belvoir are worth a visit by the botanist but, like the grasslands, can not be compared with the much more diverse wet grassland habitats across the river at Lagan Meadows.

Air photograph of Belvoir flown on 14 April 1962.

LAND PREPARED FOR FOREST PLANTING

GOLF COURSE

SEWAGE WORKS UNDER CONSTRUCTION

LAGAN MEADOWS

WOODLAND CLEARFELLED AND GROUND DISTURBED

RIVER LAGAN

FRAGMENTS OF MATURE WOODLAND

CANAL

MORELANDS MEADOW. THE SHADOWS CAST BY TALL TREES ARE VERY VISIBLE

OLD GARDENS AND ARBORETUM. THE TALL TREES CAST LONG SHADOWS

RUBBLE LEFT FROM DEMOLITION OF MANSION

CORBIE WOOD

BIG WOOD

TREES FELLED AND LAND PREPARED FOR FOREST PLANTING

COURTYARD BUILDINGS

© CROWN COPYRIGHT 2005 Permit 50161

Oaks in grazed grassland, Morelands Meadow

Woodland trees

The woodlands are surprisingly varied and, although large areas of conifers were planted in the 1960s, walking through Belvoir Park Forest you cannot fail to come across large broadleaved trees, mainly oaks, some of which have huge girths. Occasional massive oaks also occur in and around the Belvoir housing estate, in the golf course and in Morelands Meadow. These are places that originally formed the walled demesne that provided a setting to Belvoir House.

One of the most puzzling facts about Belvoir Park is that Victorian botanists seem to have made little or no reference to these huge trees. For example Ralph Tate, who in 1863 wrote a small book on the plants of the Belfast area with the wonderful title of *Flora Belfastiensis*,[1] made scant reference to Belvoir and only mentioned oaks in Colin Glen in the south west of the city (most of which were felled during the Second World War). Also Stewart and Corry's *Flora of north-east Ireland* (1888),[2] which included records collected by John Templeton, a naturalist who lived at Cranmore, across the river from

Belvoir, made few references to Belvoir and again ignored the oaks. Accounts of visits to Belvoir by the Belfast Naturalists' Field Club suggest that they walked past these monsters with hardly a glance. This is perhaps because there were so many big oaks that they did not attract the attention of botanists used to searching out rarities.

In Ireland we have two species of native oak, *Quercus robur* (called the common or pedunculate oak) and *Quercus petraea* (called the sessile oak). The differences between the two species are slight and the two species cross-breed easily, creating hybrids with characteristics intermediate between the species. A number of the Belvoir oaks were examined with the help of Paul Hackney of the Ulster Museum. Their physical characteristics suggest that many of the oaks

in Morelands Meadow and in the golf course are *Quercus robur*, but that in the area in between some are *robur*, some *petraea* and many seem to be hybrid trees. In this brief study the oaks in Big Wood were omitted as the dense woodland and high branches make many of them difficult to examine.

The area that has changed the least since the creation of the demesne is Morelands Meadow, where there are large, well-spaced oaks (and a few other species of trees such as horse chestnut, lime and beech) growing in grassland grazed by cattle. This type of habitat is called lowland wood pasture and parkland in Britain and is classified as a priority habitat in the Northern Ireland Biodiversity Strategy. In Morelands Meadow non-native shrubs are absent, the main understorey species being hawthorn, bramble and wild rose. The scattered trees have space to really spread out and the span of their branches can be quite enormous. If you view the area from the car park on the other side of the river when the sun is low, you can pick out regular lines of former cultivation ridges on part of the meadows, though there is no record of when or why this cultivation took place.

Left: Willows on the bank of the River Lagan with the Scots pine plantation at Bowling Green Hill

69

Lime tree, Morelands Meadow

The sloping ground between the River Lagan and the area of the main car park and courtyard is known as Corbie Wood (corbie is a Scottish word for a rook or crow). This used to be oak woodland, though most of these trees have gone and it is now mainly a conifer plantation. There is, however, some natural regeneration of oak (as well as beech and sycamore) in more open areas in the south of Corbie Wood. One glade has been planted with dogwood, which is particularly noticeable in winter, when it appears as a dense thicket of thin, whip-like red branches.

Big Wood, which comprises the slopes of a small river valley along the boundary with the golf course south of the old graveyard, contains many large oak trees. This area has not been planted with conifers and a wide range of self-seeded trees have grown tall and spindly, seeking out the light between the old oaks. Most of these young trees are birch and sycamore, the latter species dominating the eastern end of the wood. There is also quite a diverse range of other trees, including some horse chestnut, ash, beech and willow plus smaller growing trees such as hazel, hawthorn, holly and blackthorn. A number of hornbeam occur in this area, originally planted but

now seeding naturally. To the southeast of Big Wood, on land now managed by the Woodland Trust, there is a significant area of natural oak regeneration, with closely spaced trees over two metres high.

In southwest Belvoir Park Forest, towards the Red Bridge, large oak trees are absent. The main mature broadleaved trees in this area are lime (quite often multi-stemmed coppiced trees) and beech, the latter being particularly common on the steeply sloping banks above the River Lagan. Holly (occasionally forming large trees), elder, hawthorn and yew form the main understorey. Some sycamore and ash trees were also noted in this area.

In the grounds of Belvoir Park Golf Club there are quite a few magnificent old oak trees, some belts of broadleaved woodland with mainly sycamore and beech and some young conifer plantations. Some non-native specimen trees have also been planted by the fairways and greens in recent years. In some of the woodlands there is regeneration of beech and there are areas with an understorey of native species such as holly, hawthorn and elder. Where there has been recent disturbance there is a dense growth of nettle and bramble. Along the northern margin of the old demesne, near Galwally Lake and the sewage

works, there are occasional old lime trees and numerous tall, thin self-seeded trees. The ground here is wetter, and alder, birch, willow and sycamore dominate, with an understorey of laurel, holly and some elder. Areas of dense laurel growth, bramble, nettle, honeysuckle and thick carpets of ivy make it difficult to walk through these woods. A different type of woodland occurs to the south of Galwally Lake, where the ground is organic-rich and dry. In this area there are mainly birch trees (many of which are multi-stemmed) with some rowan and young oak with bracken, though laurel is starting to spread through the area.

Some common native tree species are perhaps less often seen at Belvoir than might be expected. For example, there are relatively few mature ash trees, rowan is common only by Galwally Lake, birch is only seen in a few areas and hazel is common only in Big Wood and parts of Corbie Wood. Cherry is also not frequently seen except in a small area of Big Wood and blackthorn, which forms areas of dense scrub in some Irish woods, is not particularly noticeable. Relatively few old hawthorn trees were noted, and these were mainly associated with former hedgerows. In Belvoir, like the rest of Ireland, big elm

Primrose (Primula vulgaris) under oak at Morelands Meadow

trees have all succumbed to Dutch elm disease and only one or two dead standing elm remain. A few young elm were noted, for example at the northern end of Corbie Wood not far from the courtyard, but elm is no longer a significant component of the Belvoir woods.

Throughout most of the deciduous woods in Belvoir Park Forest, and in some of the woods on the golf course, laurel has become literally a growing problem. Laurel, an exotic evergreen species, was often planted along with rhododendron in old estates to add winter colour and cover for game birds. If not controlled, in time laurel can create fairly sterile woodland because practically no light can reach through the foliage to the ground. Laurel has been cut back in some areas, for example in parts of Big Wood, but is shooting up again and on the southern side of Big Wood it is growing unchecked to such an extent that it has formed an almost impenetrable mass of branches. Although such areas can look superficially attractive, the reality is a loss of biodiversity. Rhododendron similarly blankets the ground but spreads much less rapidly and is not a significant problem in Belvoir. Another exotic plant that is common in most of the Belvoir woods is

snowberry, a wiry deciduous bush with small white spherical fruits. This seems to coexist with, rather than dominate, the native flora.

Conifers were first planted at Belvoir Park when it was a private estate, mainly in the Arboretum in the river valley between the car park and old graveyard. Two other long established conifer plantations remain at Belvoir, a belt of Scots pine and larch by the southern wall of the demesne in Belvoir housing estate and a plantation of Scots pine at the southern end of Corbie Wood towards the Belvoir footbridge. There are also some mature conifers that were planted around much of the demesne as specimen trees to enhance views. There are no old conifers in the area of the golf course, probably because this was originally farmland and not considered to be worth landscaping.

An interesting feature is the remains of an avenue of yew trees planted along the side of the wide path that parallels the boundary with the golf course. Yew trees are traditionally planted in churchyards and graveyards and these trees probably formed an avenue to the old Breda graveyard which lies on this route.

The main conifer plantations date from the early 1960s when the Forest Service took over the management of a large part of the former demesne. The plantations include Scots pine, Japanese larch, Lawson cypress and Norway spruce. These are generally unfavourable sites for understorey and groundcover plants, though holly, bramble and grasses do grow under the larch which has a less dense canopy and is deciduous.

Woodland plants

To really appreciate the wonderful display of woodland flowers one must visit Belvoir Park from March to May. This is when the flowers are at their peak, grabbing what sunlight they can before the trees burst into leaf overhead. In some of the younger deciduous woods in Belvoir groundcover is

Wild garlic (Allium ursinum) by the banks of the River Lagan

Early dog violet (Viola reichenbachiana) Lagan Meadows under alder/ash

Bluebell under beech at Belvoir

Toothwort (Lathraea squamaria) under yew at Breda graveyard

dominated by ivy, although in many areas plant communities are more diverse and typically include primrose, wood anemone, wood-sorrel, ground ivy, lords and ladies, bluebell and cow parsley. Lesser celandine is particularly common in the open woodland at Bowling Green Hill in the north of Belvoir. In the parts of Bowling Green Hill planted with Scots pine, there are thickets of bramble and snowberry, large ferns, mosses and other plants including bugle and red campion. Wood speedwell has been noted along paths and in hedgerows.

Regular visitors to the Belvoir woods have located some interesting species. For example, in Big Wood Roy Anderson has found early purple orchids scattered along the main path, and large bitter-cress

near the stream. This is a species with a very local northern distribution in Ireland (though as mentioned later in the text it has been noted at several other places in Belvoir). In the southern end of the Belvoir demesne, Doris Murphy has noticed large numbers of common twayblade growing under the poplar plantation alongside the path that follows the edge of the forest and leads to the playground at Belvoir Drive. In this area, toothwort is common under poplar and horse chestnut trees. At the side of this path, further towards the southern end of Corbie Wood, there is a large patch of bugle. On a grass bank by the edge of woodland near the footbridge to Morelands Meadow she has noticed goldilocks buttercup, best searched for in April.

Descriptions of visits to Belvoir by the Belfast Naturalists' Field Club give some hint of a time gone by.[3] In May 1921, 71 members were hosted by the Right Honourable Sir James Johnston J.P. A visit in May 1927 was attended by as many as 120 members. Reference in reports of the visits to 'a profusion' of adder's tongue ferns suggests areas of old pasture. Other old plant records include three-nerved sand wort (common in 1877 and recorded again in 1929), bird's nest orchid and thin-spiked wood-sedge, the latter re-found recently by Richard Weyl.

Ragged robin (Lychnis flos-cuculi)

A good area to see woodland plants is around the old Scots pine plantation in the southern part of Corbie Wood. Here conditions are more open and there is wood-sorrel, wood anemone, dog violet, wood sedge, red campion, hogweed, primrose and bluebell. Roy Anderson has also seen early dog violet (*Viola reichenbachiana*) in this part of Belvoir. Sanicle was noted on a bank at the side of the wide path through Corbie Wood and nearby, in a more open but damp area by the path, figwort, opposite-leaved golden-saxifrage, lords and ladies, red campion, hogweed, sedges and creeping buttercup carpet the ground. On the edge of the wood by the River Lagan plants include Saint John's-wort, bugle and wood speedwell. Broad-leaved helleborine, a striking woodland orchid, has also been recorded in Corbie Wood.

In spring the strong smell of wild garlic is particularly noticeable in areas of the Arboretum where it grows in patches of ground that are not regularly mown, for example by the stream and on sloping banks under brambles. Plants such as red campion and primrose are also common on the woodland fringe. An unexpected spring sighting has been a small group of cowslip growing under

Nothofagus in the southern end of the Arboretum. This may have been introduced by accident, perhaps in the soil of a potted tree. A less welcome plant which reappears each year is a patch of Japanese knot-weed by the stream in the Arboretum, an invasive non-native that is difficult to control.

The dappled shade under beech and lime trees on the steep, well-drained western side of the motte, and adjacent land alongside the riverside path just to the north, has a good flora. Here the plants include herb-robert, greater stichwort, bluebell, sanicle, pignut, angelica, cow parsley, hedge parsley, herb bennet, barren strawberry, dog violet, lords and ladies, red campion, wood sorrel, wood anemone, lesser celandine, wild garlic, tutsan, ground-ivy, toothwort (under lime) and tuberous comfrey. There are also woodland grasses, wood sedge and wood rush. Ferns include polypody, scaly male fern and hart's-tongue fern. Mosses are common. There are many tree seedlings (beech, sycamore, oak, conifers), honeysuckle and wild rose. Another interesting plant reported near the motte is bird's-nest orchid, though it has not been seen for many years.

Grassland

The most biodiverse grasslands in the region are the Lagan Meadows, which lie across the river from the Belvoir demesne. Here in the drier pastures you can find quite a range of scarcer grasses such as tall fescue and quaking grass along with classic meadow plants such as knapweed and sneezewort. Where the pastures are damper and flushed with springs, soft rush is abundant and here can be seen great drifts of ragged robin and common spotted orchid with scattered marsh ragwort, a beautiful sight in early summer. Between Lester's Dam and the Lagan is a patch of marshy ground dominated by greater tussock sedge forming shaggy humps over one metre high. Spring time in Lagan Meadows is a great time to see lady's smock, a delicate pink flower that persists to midsummer.

In the Belvoir demesne there are several different areas of grassland. The grassland in the more open ground between the trees in Morelands Meadow receives no fertilizer and has not been reseeded or tilled in living memory. The area is managed by grazing 18 cows and suckler calves, rotated between Morelands Meadow and the dry grasslands around Lagan Meadows from April to October. This low-level grazing is the best way to manage these riverside meadows and provides an attractive pastoral scene for visitors. The cattle keep the vegetation from growing rank, eating small tree seedlings and so preventing the area from turning into scrub woodland. They also dig up the ground a bit, providing space for new plants. However, although the flora is fairly diverse, it is not particularly noteworthy. Plants include meadow buttercup, creeping buttercup, lady's smock, ragwort, ribwort plantain, cat's ear, white and red clover, sorrel, meadowsweet, field wood-rush, spring sedge and soft rush. In the better drained eastern edge of the Meadow yellow rattle was seen at one location.

Big Meadow (also sometimes called the Sculpture Meadow from the timber sculpture that used to stand here) lies within Belvoir Park Forest, south of Morelands Meadow. In the 1970s this was regularly cut and used as playing fields, when it may have been reseeded, though now it is only cut once a year and the grass removed for silage. It is species-poor, with common grasses, rushes and grassland plants like creeping buttercup, meadowsweet, ribwort

plantain, dandelion, sorrel and chickweed. Around the periphery of the meadow tormentil and pignut have been seen.

Other grasslands at Belvoir including the grounds of the housing estate, the Boys' Brigade playing fields and the golf course greens and fairways, tend to be species-poor. These are areas that are regularly mown to create a short sward and only where the grass is not mown, for example around the margins of the golf course are species like lady's smock and common spotted orchid seen. The fields by the Lagan just north of the old demesne wall, at the bottom of Hampton Park, have a much finer sward complete with pignut, knapweed, common spotted orchid and meadow buttercup.

Common spotted orchid (Dactylorhiza fuchsii)

Wetlands

In the Lagan Meadows, grasslands merge into wetlands. Springs at the foot of the sloping ground towards Malone feed small streams and Lester's Dam which was an early water supply for Belfast. Lester's Dam contains some rarities such as whorl grass and large bitter-cress along with the more common bur-reed, reed-mace and water starwort.

Southwest of Big Meadow there is a small area of damp woodland and wetland around a small shallow pond close to the River Lagan. Here, plant species include an abundance of wild garlic, marsh marigold, bluebell, herb bennet, toothwort, lords and ladies, sedges, lesser celandine, cow parsley, goosegrass (cleavers), remote sedge, garlic mustard, wood anemone, ground elder, hogweed, hedge parsley, hedge woundwort, meadowsweet and creeping buttercup. In the wetter areas plants include creeping buttercup, marsh marigold, hemlock water-droplet, bittersweet and greater bitter-cress.

Towards the northern end of Morelands Meadow there is a pond which has been recently enlarged. Nearby there is an area of shallow water

Marsh marigold (Caltha palustris) in wet alder wood, Belvoir

under willow and alder scrub. Plants in this area include lesser spearwort, marsh marigold, meadowsweet, remote sedge, lady's smock, willowherb and bur-reed.

Galwally Lake lies to the north of the golf course, just within the demesne wall. It can be seen from Galwally Avenue, though much of the lake and adjoining wetland is surrounded by private gardens. Around the margin of the lake are stands of reedmace and flag iris with giant hogweed, branched bur-reed, water cress, water mint, greater willowherb, marsh marigold, creeping buttercup, marsh horsetail, brooklime, bittersweet, angelica, lady's smock,

hemlock water-droplet and floating sweet-grass. Tree species on the margin of the lake are alder, grey willow and birch.

The River Lagan near Belvoir has mainly steep banks with alder and willow trees and few wetland plant species. Near the river are patches of reed canary-grass, great water dock, butterbur and giant hogweed, the latter growing to a height of around two metres each year. Giant hogweed is a plant to avoid, for if the spines on the stem come in contact with skin they can cause very unpleasant blisters when exposed to sunlight. The most noticeable plant along the river banks is Himalayan balsam, an introduced species, which each spring grows rapidly to produce stands up to one metre high in summer. Although it is largely confined to the river edge, it has started to grow in damp areas by the roadway through Corbie Wood and it is hoped that it will not invade other wetlands. In the water of the River Lagan there are patches of yellow water-lily, broad-leaved pondweed and arrowhead.

In conclusion

One of the questions we need to ask is why there are huge oak trees hundreds of years old throughout much of Belvoir Park, but only locally are there the rarer kinds of plants that are associated with old long established woodland. In part, the reason may be the lack of appropriate management of the woods and meadows from the time when the house was last occupied in the 1920s until more recent years. Plants would have been affected by disturbance of the ground associated with the building of temporary structures in the woods during the Second World War, the large-scale tree planting that took place in the 1960s, works such as creating paths and running the large sewer pipes through the area to the sewage works. Plant diversity has also been reduced by competition from the extensive conifer plantations and from non-native plants like laurel and snowberry. Being largely surrounded by the urban conurbation does, unfortunately, mean that air and water pollution affect the area. In the grasslands, species diversity will have been affected by any application of fertilizers or reseeding on the golf course and playing fields.

Yellow water lilly (Nuphar lutea). River Lagan by Morelands Meadow

It is, however, very important to recognise that Belvoir Park does include pockets of good plant diversity and plant communities that can develop if the environment is suitable. Belvoir Park is also of great importance as an environmental resource. The patchwork of coniferous and deciduous woodlands, meadows and riverside walks attracts wildlife and thousands of visitors all year round. Belvoir Park

demesne was always a worked landscape with woodland, farmland and open space. Some of the woods were managed for game and large areas were allowed to grow naturally or were planted simply to please the eye. More recently, the land has been managed for forestry and amenity.

It is fascinating to walk round Belvoir Park to try to unpick the historical development of the landscape, to try to understand what natural processes have taken place and in what ways people have affected the landscape over time. These different influences have led to the development of the vegetation patterns we see today and hopefully can retain for the future. Only by understanding the story being told by the plantlife of Belvoir can we hope to secure its future by wise management.

Acknowledgments

Thanks to Roy Anderson and Doris Murphy for contributing plant records. Roy also very kindly provided photographs he had taken of plants in Belvoir Park.

Air photograph of Belvoir is reproduced with the permission of the Controller of Her Majesty's Stationery Office © Crown Copyright 2005.

CHAPTER *Six~* VETERAN TREES Ben Simon

ALL OF THE TREES with a trunk circumference of three metres or more were surveyed in the area formerly enclosed by the wall of Belvoir Park demesne, including the land between the River Lagan and the old canal. In addition to this study of the Belvoir demesne, a brief search was made for trees of particularly large girth throughout the northern Lagan Valley. This was to try to determine if the records for the Belvoir trees, in particular the oaks, are exceptional in a regional context. Finally, a deadwood survey was undertaken to locate the fallen trees in Belvoir demesne with a trunk circumference of over three metres. Details of the methodology used in the survey and results are given in Appendix 3, which also gives the grid reference for each tree.

The author measuring one of the larger oaks (tree 2362). This oak has a girth of 6.92m at a height of 1.5m.

Size and distribution of large-girthed trees

In the area of the former Belvoir Park demesne 270 trees that had a single trunk with a girth of 3m or greater were noted. An additional 16 large multi-stemmed trees were recorded. These were omitted from the analysis of the data as there is no generally agreed procedure for recording the girth of multi-stemmed trees.

Within the boundary of the old Belvoir Park demesne most of the trees with a girth of over three metres are located in Belvoir Park Forest, the grounds of Belvoir Park Golf Course, Morelands Meadow and the open space between the Belvoir housing estate and Belvoir Park Forest. Land at the northern and southeastern margins of the old demesne (Galwally, Belvoir housing estate) has few large trees.

The large-girthed native oaks are probably the most ecologically important trees at Belvoir and are of particular value as long established lowland oak woods are rare in Ireland. In the survey 130 native oaks with a single trunk of three metres or greater were noted, and these include 55 trees with girths of between four metres and six metres and three trees with girths of over six metres. These exceptional trees

Number of trees within the former Belvoir demesne with a girth of 3m or more

Belvoir Park Forest (Forest Service land)	128 trees	(47%)
Belvoir Park Golf Club	73 trees	(27%)
Open space between the forest & housing estate	29 trees	(11%)
Belvoir housing estate	5 trees	(2%)
Ardnavally (Scout Association land)	12 trees	(5%)
Morelands Meadow (Belfast City Council land)	20 trees	(7%)
Galwally (gardens, around lake)	3 trees	(1%)
TOTAL	270 trees	(100%)

Number of each species of tree within the former Belvoir Park demesne with a girth of 3m or more

Native oak	130 trees	(48%)
Beech	47 trees	(18%)
Non-native conifers	26 trees	(9%)
Horse chestnut	18 trees	(7%)
Sycamore	15 trees	(6%)
Lime	14 trees	(5%)
Yew	5 trees	(2%)
Ash	4 trees	(1%)
Turkey oak	4 trees	(1%)
Lucombe oak	3 trees	(1%)
Sweet chestnut	3 trees	(1%)
Holm oak	1 tree	(1%)
TOTAL	270 trees	(100%)

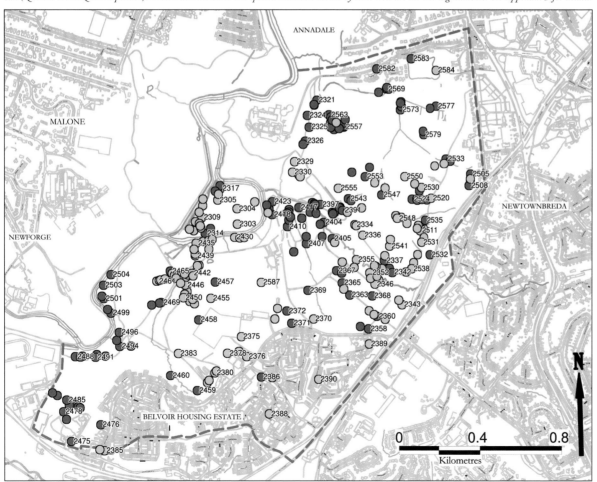

Location of the trees 3m or greater in girth in the area of the former Belvoir demesne. The line of the demesne wall is shown in red. Green dots are native oak (Quercus robur/Quercus petraea). Brown dots are other tree species. Numbers shown by some trees are the tree tag numbers. See Appendix 3 for details.

are tree 2509 (6.35m girth measured at 1.5m height), tree 2362 (6.92m girth at 1m height) and tree 2453 (8.8m girth at 0.1m height). The biggest girthed native oaks at Belvoir are some of the most impressive in Ireland. In 2005 the Tree Council of Ireland published *Champion Trees,* a book which lists a selection of the biggest trees in Ireland.[1] In this survey only a small number of oaks were found that had girths of over 8m and the largest oaks noted in Ireland were a sessile oak *(Quercus petraea)* at Baronscourt estate in County Tyrone with a girth of 8.35m and a pedunculate oak *(Quercus robur)* with a girth of 9.9m growing at Stradbally, County Laois.

The multi-stemmed oaks at Belvoir include some huge trees such as the oak between the car park and motte (tree 2424). This has several massive boughs that grow from just above ground level. Placing a tape measure around the base of the tree gives a girth of 8.64m.

The ash with the largest circumference is a magnificent, straight, tall tree (number 2556) on the edge of the seventh fairway of the golf course with a girth of 4.77m. There is a very impressive sycamore with large boughs near the Big Meadow (tree 2465, with a girth of 4.84m) and a sycamore at Bowling

Green Hill with a larger girth of 6.05m measured near the ground (tree 2328), though this is another example of a multi-stemmed tree. Only three sweet chestnut trees were noted in the area of the former Belvoir Park demesne, the largest girthed being a tree (number 2423) on the top of the motte with a circumference of 5.32m at a height of 0.5m. There are three Lucombe oaks with girths of between three metres and four metres and one large holm oak (4.5m girth measured at 1.75m) on the sloping ground between the car park and Arboretum. Four Turkey oaks with girths of between 3.78m and 4.23m were also noted at dispersed locations around Belvoir.

Within the boundary of the old Belvoir Park demesne many of the oaks with girths of over three metres are growing in rows or are growing close together in groups. A notable exception is Morelands Meadow where the oaks are well separated and form a more typical parkland landscape. The main areas where there are large oak trees growing very close together are the Big Wood and Corbie Wood. The most noticeable row of oak trees with large girths is at the southern end of the golf course.

Distribution of native oaks (*Quercus robur/petraea*) within the former Belvoir demesne with a girth of 3m or more

Belvoir Park Forest (Forest Service land)	61 oak
Belvoir Park Golf Club	31 oak
Open space between the forest & housing estate	18 oak
Belvoir housing estate	4 oak
Ardnavally (Scout Association land)	0 oak
Morelands Meadow (Belfast City Council land)	15 oak
Galwally	1 oak
TOTAL	130 oak

Number of native oaks (*Q. robur/petraea*) of different girths in the former Belvoir Park demesne

Number of oaks of 3-4 m girth	72
Number of oaks of 4-5m girth	44
Number of oaks of 5-6m girth	11
Number of oaks of 6-7m girth	2
Number of oaks of 7-8m girth	-
Number of oaks of 8-9m girth	1
TOTAL	130

Distribution of the native oaks (*Q. robur/petraea*) with largest girths

	5-6m girth	6-7m girth	7-8m girth
Belvoir Park Forest (Forest Service land)	5	-	1
Belvoir Park Golf Club	4	1	-
Open space between forest & housing estate	2	1	-
Belvoir housing estate	-	-	-
Ardnavally (Scout Association land)	-	-	-
Morelands Meadow (Belfast City Council land)	-	-	-
Galwally (around pond and gardens)	-	-	-
TOTALS	11	2	1

The beech trees with girths of over three metres are mainly located in the southwestern end of Belvoir Park Forest and in the golf course. The other broadleaved species with large girths are scattered throughout the area. Ash trees with a girth of over three metres are surprisingly rare, given the frequent occurrence of this species in many Irish woods.

The large girthed conifers (non-native species and yews) are mostly located in the Arboretum, though a few occur at other sites (Morelands Meadow, Housing Executive open space).

A survey of trees in the land surrounding the old demesne and a brief examination of large trees throughout the northern Lagan Valley indicates that the former Belvoir Park demesne contains an exceptional concentration of trees of three metres or greater girth.

Form and appearance of the native oaks

The Belvoir oaks are predominantly growing in parkland, woodland or woodland edge. Although there are some multi-stem large girthed trees, there is no evidence that pollarding or coppicing was a regular practice. The oaks are nearly all upright, have a single stem and still retain a full canopy and most of the crown. However, some degree of epicormic growth (twiggy growth from major limbs) is common and may indicate that many of the trees are under some degree of stress. A very small number of the oaks are retrenching, with a number of dead boughs throughout the crown. These are tree 2316 (Morelands Meadow), tree 2334 (Big Wood, on boundary with golf course) and tree 2453 (southern part of Corbie Wood). In the golf course two of the oak trees have shed many of their main boughs (trees 2513, 2516) and one tree appears to be dying (tree 2552).

Squat oak trees with a wide base, hollow decaying trunk and predominantly thin, short branches are generally considered to have reached a later stage of life. Only a few of the trees in the Belvoir area have these characteristics, the main examples being tree 2453 (east of Big Meadow), tree 2383 (between Belvoir Park Forest and the housing estate) and perhaps tree 2316 (Morelands Meadow).

Some trees have dead lower branches (e.g. trees 2444 and 2445 northeast of Big Meadow, tree 2330 in northeast Belvoir Park Forest, trees 2333 and 2335 in the Big Wood and tree 2464 close to the Big Meadow). This seems to occur generally where there is dense shade from surrounding trees, though this is not always the case – for example tree 2302 growing

Development too close to a large oak in Belvoir housing estate (tree 2388). Both a road and building have been constructed under the crown of this tree.

Above and above right: Retrenchment in an oak. Tree 2316, Morelands Meadow

in open conditions in Morelands Meadow has shed several of its lower limbs.

Few of the trees have had any significant recent management, though in the golf course and Belvoir housing estate many of the oaks show the signs of old tree surgery. Two oak trees in Corbie Wood are of interest as they were felled but subsequently put out new growth from the trunks. These trees (numbers 2585 and 2586) now have tall, thin (less than 50cm circumference) branches growing from massive old butts. The history of the felled trees is discussed in Chapter 7.

Development has taken place close to some of the oaks in the Housing Executive open space and within the crown spread of a number of the oaks in Belvoir housing estate (tree 2388, tree 2390). This is likely to have caused root damage and to have affected the health of these trees, many of which have since been pruned. In more recent years thankfully few of the veteran trees have been directly affected by building work or other kinds of development. However, there have been minor changes in soil level near some trees (for example tree 2380). Excessive shading of oaks is considered to be a more significant problem in Belvoir Park Forest and in parts of the Housing Executive open space where plantations of trees are causing heavy shade onto some of the oaks, and in a few instances this shade is from above as well as from several sides (tree 2453, tree 2383).

The future management of the veteran trees at Belvoir is an issue that requires careful consideration. In particular, where possible, development should not take place near the veteran trees (including the construction of buildings, paths and roads, trenching and the dumping of soil and other material). Where these kinds of activities are unavoidable, careful site management is required and the least damaging methods should be used.

The impact of shade from plantations and new woods on adjacent veteran trees needs to be considered by all of the main landowners in Belvoir Park. This is a particularly significant issue in Belvoir Park Forest. Here, factors that need to be considered include –

- The present impact of shade from conifer plantations on veteran trees.
- The future likely impact of shade from conifer plantations on veteran trees.
- The impact of localised felling or clear felling on veteran trees.
- The impact of felling on flora and fauna associated with the veteran trees.
- Scrub/grassland management if conifer plantations are felled.
- Providing opportunities for the natural regeneration of oaks.
- Possible vandalism of veteran trees (e.g. fires in hollow trees) if they become more visible as a result of the removal of other trees.

Given the historical, cultural and biodiversity value of the large girthed trees, it is of great importance that these issues are carefully considered and incorporated into management plans.

The most urgent issue that needs to be addressed is the shading of old oaks by surrounding fast-growing trees (in particular tree 2453, a low tree which has the largest girth of all the oaks and is now very heavily shaded). However, experience from

This is the largest girthed oak in Belvoir (tree 2453) with a circumference of 8.80m measured near the base. However, it is very heavily shaded by fast growing conifers. It is retrenching and has very little new growth.

England has highlighted the importance of not removing all of the trees that are shading a veteran at the one time. The adjacent trees need to be gradually removed over a period of years so that the environment around the veteran is slowly modified. It therefore follows that where veteran trees occur in conifer plantations clear felling is likely to be detrimental. A discussion of these issues is presented in the publication *Veteran Trees. A guide to good management* published by the Veteran Trees Initiative.[2]

Dead Wood

Dead wood is important for invertebrates and fungi and locating fallen trees can provide useful information about this habitat and also information concerning the former distribution of woodland and the rate of loss of large trees. A dead wood survey was undertaken of the woods and meadows in the former Belvoir Park demesne. Tree stumps with a girth of 3m or greater were identified and measured in the area of Belvoir Park Forest, Morelands Meadow, Ardnavally and the open ground between the forest and Belvoir housing estate. It was decided to exclude the golf course from the deadwood survey as in this area all traces of fallen trees are generally removed by the grounds staff.

The locations of the dead trees are given in Appendix 4. A total of 55 stumps over three metres in girth were noted. Of these, 37 (67% of the total) were oak and most of these were felled trees in Corbie Wood, which prior to felling must have been the most important oak woodland at Belvoir.

Only a small number of large-girthed trees have fallen in the last few years. Most had died at some time in the past and are now covered in a growth of ivy, moss and ferns. Some of the trees were too rotten

The Deramore Oak

to determine why they had fallen, but slightly more than half (56%) had been felled, about 10% had been uprooted and 16% had fallen because the trunk had fractured. Most of the uprooted trees are located on the edge of woodlands, where windthrow would be expected to be more of a problem. The trees that had fallen because the trunks had fractured are situated in a range of locations and appear to have collapsed because the trunks became too rotten.

A total of 27 stumps have a girth of four metres or greater and four stumps have girths of 5m or greater. These are the remains of a sweet chestnut tree at Bowling Green Hill (tree 0002, 7m girth), a hollow Turkey oak just outside of the entrance to Belvoir Park Forest that was felled in about 1995 because it was considered to be dangerous (tree 0012, 5m girth) and two oak stumps in Corbie Wood, tree 0036 (6.5m girth) and tree 0024 (girth estimate of 8.5m).

Stump number 0024 is about 27m (30 yards)

from the bank of the River Lagan, situated in low lying level ground. Only a short crescent shaped section of the outer part of the hollow trunk remains standing, 1.8m high, 2.5m long and 30cm thick. The former circumference of the tree was estimated at 8.5m by placing a tape around the remnant of standing trunk and along a line marked by small pieces of *in situ* timber and a roughly circular depression in the ground. This oak stump is of particular interest as it is the only tree noted that might be the last remains of a huge oak that was known as the Great Oak or Deramore Oak.

The Deramore Oak was described by Loudon in his book *Arboretum et Fruticetum Britannicum* (1844) as being the largest in Ireland, with a girth of 28 feet (8.5m) at 6 feet and located at Belvoir about 50 yards (45.7m) from the banks of the River Lagan in rather moist soil.[3] In 1899 The Belfast Naturalists' Field Club described it as having a girth

of over 30 feet (9m).[4] A photograph of the Great Oak was taken by Robert Welch at some time around the end of the 19th century or the early years of the 20th century and a reference was noted to the tree in an article about Belvoir in the Belfast Telegraph in 1919 which referred to it as '…still a commanding object of interest.'[5]

Acknowledgments

I would like to thank Forest Service staff for their help in providing grid references for the veteran trees and Richard McCrea of ISB Services at Belfast City Council for his help in using this data. I am also grateful to the landowners who have permitted detailed surveys to be undertaken over a number of years including the Northern Ireland Housing Executive, Belvoir Park Golf Course, The Boys' Brigade, Belfast City Council, Forest Service and Woodland Trust.

This oak at the northern end of Morelands Meadow (tree 0053) fell in a storm in living memory.

CHAPTER *Seven* –
how *old* is that OAK? David Brown and Mike Baillie

Background

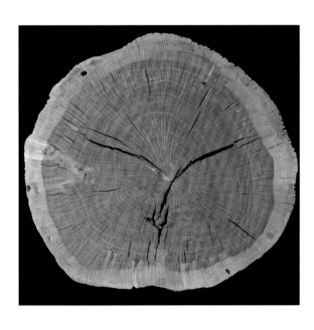

DENDROCHRONOLOGY – OR TREE-RING DATING – is a coverall term for studies of the growth rings of trees to establish their history and when they lived. It was first used by A. E. Douglass in North America who spent many years deriving long, year-by-year records of pine growth from the arid south-west regions.[1] The idea is to start with the patterns of living trees which are anchored at the present day at the time of sampling. The growth-ring patterns of these living trees can then be extended by overlapping the patterns from the living trees to those from older timbers from ancient buildings, archaeological sites or natural deposits. Once such a chronology is built it can be used to date new samples by comparing their ring patterns against the master chronology. Douglass perfected this work and by around 1930 had an American chronology back to AD 700 and could precisely date timbers from many Amerindian ruins.

The Belfast long oak chronology was constructed during the 1970s and 1980s. In this case, the anchor was provided by samples from modern estate trees from around the north of Ireland. The overlapping procedure was then used to extend an Irish oak chronology back for a total of 7400 years from the present.[2]

In that early Belfast work most of the modern oak samples were derived from slices from felled trees and from recently felled stumps. It is possible to sample trees non-destructively by extracting thin cores. Coring a tree involves screwing in a Swedish Increment Corer and extracting a long core, a few mm in diameter, from the centre to the outside of the tree. This provides a chronological anchor because, if we were to core a living oak in the winter of 2004-2005, while the tree is dormant, the last ring of the core will represent the complete growth ring for the year 2004. As oaks only put on one growth ring per year, the pattern of rings, anchored at 2004, will then extend back for as many years as the tree grew.

Dendrochronologists have perfected the methods necessary to study locally-grown oaks. Each ring pattern can be compared both with all of the other ring patterns from the site and with the existing regional master chronology. This allows each ring, in each sample, to be assigned to a specific calendar year. Once this chronological aspect has been completed the entire assemblage can be studied within the historical context of the site.

As this chapter is going to look at particular aspects of the Belvoir demesne, it is appropriate to briefly consider what the construction of the Belfast long chronology has indicated about oak growth in the north of Ireland. For example, in collecting modern oaks to anchor the chronology, it was discovered that the longest-lived examples extended back only to the mid-17th century. One old stump from Shane's Castle, County Antrim, gave a ring pattern that extended back to 1649. In the following three decades of sample collection no longer-lived oak was found anywhere in Ireland. Thus oak in Ireland is not the long-lived tree of legend. In fact, it has become obvious that the oaks that we see in the landscape today were mostly planted by landowners in the 18th and 19th centuries. No certain trace has been found of any 'primeval' oak forest anywhere on the island of Ireland. This planting activity also raised another issue, namely that many of the planted oaks may have been of imported stock. Thus when we stand under an oak tree today in Ireland we have no easy way of knowing whether it is an 'Irish' oak or an 'English' or even 'continental' oak. Another observation made during the construction of the Belfast chronology is that the modern oaks of the last few centuries tend to produce growth rings of around 2mm on average per year whereas more ancient Irish oaks, dating from 5,000 BC to AD 1,700 consistently averaged only 1 mm.[3] This could be due to one of two factors. The modern oaks could be of Irish stock and they simply grow more rapidly (wider rings) in parkland conditions, or they could be introduced trees specially chosen for their majestic or decorative configuration.

From collecting ancient timbers it soon became clear that oak was a preferred building timber across the 17th century and into the early 18th century. The last oak-timbered building identified turned out to be Gloverstown House (now in the Folk Museum at Cultra) whose timbers dated to 1716. All major buildings after this date were constructed using imported pine from either Scandinavia or the Americas.[1] This is likely to have been due, at least in part, to a lack of suitable local oak timber by about the second decade of the 18th century. As the chronology was extended back further in time it was also discovered that the longest-lived trees, used for building purposes in the period 1550 to 1720, had all started to grow after 1350. This surprising observation meant that most of the Irish oaks and certainly those from the east of the country were not primeval forest but were the product of a regeneration event after the Black Death.[4] This in turn implied that the woodlands in eastern Ireland had been under a management regime at the time of the Black Death. It could even be suggested that this management regime would have been introduced by the Normans in the 12th century as the same pattern is not observed in areas to the west which were not in Norman control.

Any study of an oak site in Ireland has to take account of this general background, namely that oak forests exploited in the 17th century were not primeval. Use of oak as a building timber seems to have ceased by about 1720 at the latest. There do not appear to be any really long-lived modern oaks and many modern oaks may derive from a different genetic stock to that of native Irish oaks.

The Belvoir Park trees

When checking through the tree-ring files relating to the Lagan Valley it was found that a few trees had been collected from Barnett Demesne and from Sir Thomas and Lady Dixon Park to help build the chronology, but none was taken from Belvoir. At the start of this study we therefore had no prior tree-ring information from the estate. Tree ring dating was undertaken at Belvoir merely because large oak stumps had been noted, particularly in north Corbie Wood near the River Lagan, and it was hoped that information could be obtained about the age of the woods and development of the demesne.

In December 2002 members of the Palaeoecology Centre (Queen's University, Belfast) collected slices from seven stumps in Belvoir Park Forest. The samples were collected from three locations. Four samples were collected from Bowling Green Hill, including one subsequently identified as sweet chestnut. Another sample was collected from beside the sewer pipe in south Corbie Wood (the area between the main path through Corbie Wood and the courtyard), and two were taken from stumps in north Corbie Wood (the area between the main path through Corbie Wood and the River Lagan).

The initial results were very surprising. Firstly, one of the tree stumps from north Corbie (Q10373) produced the earliest date recorded for a tree that had grown into the 20th century in Ireland – its innermost ring dated to AD 1642. The last growth ring for this weathered stump was 1940, and it could be estimated – by allowing 32 ± 9 rings for missing sapwood – that the tree had been felled somewhere in the range 1972 ± 9 years. Thus, after three decades of sampling, a modern oak tree had finally turned up that extended further back than the previous record at 1649. Given that oaks had been sampled all over Ireland, it was ironic that the oldest modern tree so far discovered was in Belvoir within a few miles of the

Left and below: A few large girthed oaks show clear evidence of felling and subsequent growth from the stumps. These trees (2585 and 2586) are in Corbie Wood.

Palaeoecology Centre. A second stump from north Corbie Wood (Q10374) had an innermost surviving ring that dated to 1662 but with some rings missing at the centre. It is likely therefore that it would have had a similar germination date to Q10373. The tree close to the sewer pipe in south Corbie Wood, Q10372, had a start date of 1722 and was felled in late 1968 or early in 1969 (its last growth ring had been produced in 1968 and there was no sign of growth relating to 1969, thus it must have been felled between about September 1968 and May 1969).

Table 1 lists the initial series of dates obtained from the tree stumps in the park. It should be noted that Q10368 was sweet chestnut (*Castanea sativa*) and was of no interest from a dendrochronological point of view as a chronology for this species has never been compiled. However, its start date of 1801 was broadly consistent with the start dates of three of the oaks at 1794, 1798 and 1815, implying a possible planting (or regeneration) episode around the time of the Napoleonic Wars, indeed bracketing the 1798 Rebellion.

From Table 1 it seems that Corbie Wood contained ancient, indeed very ancient, trees. The trees at Bowling Green Hill were somewhat younger. There was at least one episode of felling at Belvoir close to 1970 and most probably in the winter of 1968/1969 based on the actual felling date for Q10372. One curiosity was sample Q10374 that has an outer ring dating to 1897, which would normally suggest a felling date around 1930. However, the complete absence of sapwood and the good condition of the heartwood suggest (in the absence of evidence to the contrary) that it was probably also felled in the 1968/1969 episode. Overall, these observations of phases of growth in the 17th and 18th centuries, involving some of the oldest trees in the north of Ireland, encouraged the collection of a second set of samples in July 2004. In this case nine samples were taken and Table 2 provides details about the trees.

These samples provided additional evidence that Corbie Wood contained particularly old trees. One of the felled trees that was sampled, Q10640, started to grow in the 17th century and re-sprouted after having been felled and is still living. Today it is therefore the oldest living tree dated in Belvoir. The

QUB number	Tree tag number	Location	Number of years	Start date	End date	Estimated felling date range
Q10368	0002	Bowling Green Hill	141	AD1801	AD1941	AD1973 ± 9 years
Q10369	0004	Bowling Green Hill	121	AD1815	AD1935	AD1964 ± 9 years
Q10370	0005	Bowling Green Hill	118	AD1794	AD1911	AD1943± 9 years or later
Q10371	Dead branch	Bowling Green Hill	137	AD1798	AD1934	AD1966 ± 9 years
Q10372	0015	South Corbie Wood	247	AD1722	AD1968	AD1968/AD1969
Q10373	0028	North Corbie Wood	299	AD1642	AD1940	AD1972 ± 9 years
Q10374	0031	North Corbie Wood	236	AD1662	AD1897	AD1929 ± 9 years or later

Table 1: The samples were of stumps or fallen trunks beside stumps except sample Q10371 which was a branch lying on the forest floor. As this branch was not obviously associated with any particular tree it was not given a tag number. Sample Q10368 was sweet chestnut and the others were oak. See Appendix 3 and 4 for further details about the location of trees.

early end date for this tree in Table 2 is because the outer growth rings of the trunk were unmeasurable. Big Wood was also identified as very old woodland with one tree dating to 1700.

A final group of samples was taken in February 2005. This consisted of four trees cored with the kind permission of Belvoir Park Golf Club. These large-girthed trees were targeted as they form part of a long line of big girthed oaks which are thought to have been hedgerow trees. It should be said that the use of increment corers with hardwoods is not ideal. It can be very difficult to get the corer (originally designed for use with conifers) into the centre of the

Row of large girthed oaks in the southwest of Belvoir Park Golf Course.

QUB number	Tree tag number	Location	Number of years	Start date	End date	End date or estimated felling date range
Q10631	2361	Between forest & housing estate	136	1869	2004	2004 core
Q10632	2362	Between forest & housing estate	16	-	-	Failed core
Q10633	0009	Big Wood	271	1700	1970	1970/1971
Q10634	2354	Big Wood	143	1862	2004	2004 core
Q10635	No number	Big Wood	133	1872	2004	2004 core
Q10636	Dead branch	Big Wood	245	1753	1997	1997/1998
Q10637	0037	North Corbie Wood	152	1782	1933	1965 ± 9 years
Q10638	0035	North Corbie Wood	114	1714	1827	1859 ± 9 years or later
Q10639	0028	North Corbie Wood	ca. 140	-	-	Undatable
Q10640	2586	North Corbie Wood	99	1686	1784	1816 ± 9 years or later

Table 2: Trees with tag numbers 0009, 0028, 0035 and 0037 are dead stumps. Trees with tag numbers over 2361, 2362, 2354, 2586 are living trees. See Appendix 3 and 4 for further details and grid references. Tree Q10635 was just less than 3m in girth and therefore had not been given a tag number. The dead branch (Q10636) lying on the forest floor was not obviously associated with any particular tree and therefore had no tag number. All samples were oak.

tree. There are other difficulties, for example we tried twice without success to obtain a core (sample Q10632) from tree 2362, which is the second largest girthed tree in Belvoir demesne; in this case the heartwood was rotten and the tree was too soft to core. Also, the smallest tree sampled had a girth of 2.56m at 1.5m height while the largest that was cored was 6.92m at 1m height. Even with a 600mm Swedish increment corer it would be impossible to obtain a complete radial core from these trees.

Estimating felling and start dates for incomplete samples

Obviously in an exercise of this kind the primary information required is the exact start and felling date for each tree. Unfortunately, dendrochronologists are at the mercy of the available samples which are often incomplete due to rot. The centres of trees are often hollow, while sapwood is normally missing on stumps or trunks that have lain around for decades. As noted, we can make allowance for missing sapwood by applying the 32±9 ring allowance for Irish oaks. For missing rings at the centre of the tree there are two possible routes to estimating the likely planting or regeneration date. With a core the procedure is to measure the length of the core and separately estimate the actual radius. Then by measuring the mean ring width of the rings in the core an estimate can be made for the missing portion of the radius. An alternative is to use published Forestry Commission estimates of the ring widths that are to be expected in large and veteran trees. Although the figures were worked out in

Britain and are therefore not ideal in an Irish context, they do provide a rough and ready way of estimating for missing core. We estimated the start dates for any incomplete Belvoir samples using both methods and the results based on these calculations are presented in Table 3.

The start and felling date ranges for all the tree stumps and cores are shown in Figure 1 where the horizontal shaded sections represent sapwood. Bars indicate estimates of start dates and the vertical shading indicates suggested phases of planting or regeneration. Samples marked with black squares are those with definite centre rings present.* It should also be noted that all inner ring estimates need to carry a 'health warning'. It was observed that individual trees could put on either very narrow bands of juvenile rings, or sometimes enormously wide rings. It needs to be stressed therefore that the estimates (indicated by horizontal bars) are inferior in terms of information quality from measurements on trees which have a datable centre ring.

QUB number	Tree tag number	Location	Girth	Start date	End date	Maximum estimated start date	Calculated estimated start date
Q10712	2536	Golf Course	4.29m	1826	2004	ca. 1738	ca. 1766
Q10713	-	Golf Course	2.56m	1780	2004	ca. 1777	ca. 1776
Q10714	2538	Golf Course	4.86m	1834	2004	ca. 1725	ca. 1731
Q10715	2539	Golf Course	5.10m	1818	2004	ca. 1673	ca. 1713
Q10716	2362	Between forest and housing estate	6.92m	-	-	-	ca. 1700
Q10631	2361	Between forest and housing estate	5.52m	1869	2004	ca. 1694	ca. 1713
Q10634	2354	Big Wood	3.85m	1862	2004	ca. 1800	ca. 1802
Q10635	-	Big Wood	2.98m	1872	2004	ca. 1848	ca. 1831

Table 3: Trees Q10635 and Q10713 were less than 3m in girth and had no tags. Q10713 is located between trees 2536 and 2537. All are living oak trees. See Appendix 3 and 4 for further details about the location of trees.

*Note: It has to be understood that when a slice is taken from the stump or trunk of a mature oak, the date of the centre ring is not the date when the parent acorn was planted. Since most samples are taken some distance above the ground there will be an interval of several years between the date of planting and the date of the innermost growth ring. However, as estate oaks were probably often brought on in nurseries and only planted out when they were some years old, it follows that the date of the innermost ring may well be very close to the date of planting out (see below).

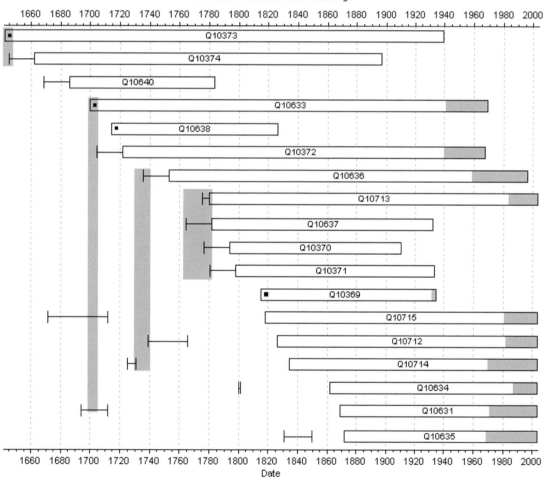

Belvoir Park Forest, Belfast

Start date or estimated start date range

Figure 1. The time spans of the various ring patterns from Belvoir. Shaded horizontal bars represent sapwood; thin bars represent estimated start years; vertical shading indicates likely planting phases; black squares represent start years present.

Planting or regeneration phases

With all the tree-ring patterns constrained in time and with estimates for both start and felling years, it is possible to review the information from Belvoir Park. Referring to Figure 1, there is clear evidence for oaks starting to grow just around the time of the 1641 Rebellion. Sample Q10373 has a definite start date at 1642 and Q10374 has an estimated start date just at this time. Sample Q10640 could well belong to the same phase.

The *second* start phase is just around 1700, constrained by the definite start date of Q10633 and backed up by estimated start dates for Q10372, Q10715 and Q10631, with the *third* phase at 1714 constrained by the start date for Q10638. There is a hint of a *fourth* phase in the 1730s represented by the estimated start dates for samples Q10636, Q10712 and Q10714. A *fifth* phase in the 1770s is hinted at by samples Q10713, Q10637, Q10370 and Q10371. There is a *sixth* phase defined by the 1801 start date for the Spanish chestnut Q10368 which is backed up by the strangely tight estimated start date 1800-1802 for Q10634. The *seventh* phase is represented by Q10369 with its 1815 start date; it cannot be ruled out that the estimated start date of Q10635 might belong to this same episode. A critic could argue that we are over-interpreting the data and that we can only stand over phases one, two, three, six and seven with their definite start dates, and that there may have been a random scattering of plantings and/or regenerations across the century from 1715 to 1815. For example, tree Q10372 could as easily fit with a planting phase in 1700 as one in 1714, or neither. We would argue that the evidence is perfectly reasonable for the seven planting phases *as a basis for discussion*, and would point to the tight clustering of the estimated start dates of phase five in our defence. It would seem churlish to dismiss this apparent phase of activity and replace it with a 'blur' of late-18th century planting. We think the evidence is better than that.

In summary, the trees in Belvoir Park would support the notion of planting/natural regeneration episodes in or around the following dates: 1642, 1700, 1714, the 1730s, the 1770s, 1801 and 1815. Of these dates, 1642 falls so close to the date of the start of the 1641 Rebellion that it is hard to imagine there is not some causal connection. It is known that there were a number of forges (iron smelting works) in the Lagan Valley in the early 17th century, including one at Newforge, across the river from Belvoir.[5,6] Interestingly, this was destroyed in the 1641 Rebellion.[7,8] It would have used large quantities of local timber and it is probably not a coincidence that the end of this industry is also the time when oaks that were to remain untouched for hundreds of years started to grow at Corbie Wood, next to the River Lagan. The tree-ring pattern of the two oldest trees at Corbie Wood also gives some indication of the local environment at the time. From 1642 to 1684 tree Q10373 was what could best be described as a runt. It was growing at only a fraction of a millimetre each year. From 1684 it rapidly escalated to over 1mm and by the 1690s it was producing rings up to 5mm in width. This could well have been a tree struggling to develop under the canopy of

other trees until it was 'released', most likely by the felling of trees around it. Interestingly, or confusingly, tree Q10374 suggests a different landscape. It was growing healthily from its earliest surviving ring at 1662. Unfortunately, there are not enough of these early trees at Belvoir to create a coherent picture.

The planting/natural regeneration episodes near the beginning of the 18th century cannot be easily linked to any particular events in the area, but do perhaps suggest that there was woodland management of some kind during this period. The earliest reference to the development of Belvoir Park demesne was in 1722 when Arthur Hill acquired the townland of Ballylenaghan and, by the 1730s, his address is given as Belvoir, suggesting that he was resident (see Chapter 2). Trees sampled in this study with a start date of around 1730 could

The largest girthed oak at Belvoir. Tree 2453.

well indicate planting and woodland management associated with the formation of the demesne. The trees growing in a straight line in the golf course that are thought to have been hedgerow trees (Q10712, Q10713, Q10714, Q10715) have start dates estimated from short core samples. It is interesting to note that two are estimated to date from the early 18th century while one was older and one younger. Accounts of Belvoir Park from the 18th century refer to 'enclosures' (Chapter 2) and the start dates may indicate that this hedgerow was planted around 1730, when the estate was founded, and that it may have included an existing old tree and later planting.

Indications of planting/natural regeneration episodes around the 1770s and 1801 are intriguing when considered in relation to the history of the estate (Chapter 2). Arthur Hill died in 1771 and the estate was inherited by his grandson, who was only a child at the time. We know from newspaper articles that during the 1770s there were many instances of vandalism at Belvoir and it seems likely that the grounds were neglected. There are also records of some large trees being felled at Belvoir at this time. During the period 1796 to 1809 the Dungannon family were not resident and the grounds were

Perhaps the best known tree at Belvoir, the multi-stemmed oak near the motte. Tree 2424.

described as being in poor condition. The only record found to large-scale felling in the estate took place during this period. Between 1809 and 1813 the demesne was acquired by three businessmen who probably acquired it as a short-term investment and were more likely to have sold trees than to have planted.

The most likely explanation would seem to be that during these periods tree felling and perhaps changes in woodland management and grazing provided opportunities for self-seeded trees to survive and grow. Support for this suggestion is provided by an observation that many of the samples examined exhibit much wider ring widths across the period

1800 to 1815. This faster growth may have been due to other trees being felled, thereby reducing competition.

In 1811 Robert Bateson, who is known to have been an improving landlord with an interest in agriculture, acquired Belvoir demesne. We also know that large numbers of trees were planted in the Belvoir area in the early nineteenth century (Chapter 2 and Appendix 2) and it seems likely that the trees with a start date of around 1815 are an indication of tree planting and regeneration of the woods undertaken by Robert Bateson.

This analysis, based on limited tree ring data, must be treated with a degree of caution and it has to be stated that we have failed to find evidence of planting/natural regeneration following the Great Wind of 1839 which devastated Ireland,[9] and is known to have affected the Belvoir woods (Chapter 2). There would have been significant natural regeneration in open spaces where large woodland trees had fallen and it is likely that planting would also have taken place. The absence of any trees with start dates around 1839 in the samples taken is probably an indication that our sample size was too small.

One other aspect of the Belvoir trees is worth mentioning. It was observed on the basis of the original tree-ring work in Belfast that from 5400 BC to AD 1700 the mean ring width of Irish oak is close to 1.0 mm per year. It was also observed that parkland oaks of 1700 to the present tend to have average growth rings closer to 2.0mm. This led to suggestions that such trees represented imported stock from Britain or Continental Europe (presumably large impressive oaks would be desired by landowners improving their estates). The Belvoir oaks, taken overall, have a mean ring width of 2.4mm, consistent with the earlier observations on Irish trees and this could suggest that they are of non-native stock. However, a different conclusion has been reached from the genetic study of the living oaks at Belvoir (Chapter 8) which suggests that they are of Irish origin.

Other events recorded in the Belvoir trees

Tree-ring data can be used to reconstruct some aspects of past climatic regimes, date archaeological and environmental events and can be used as a record of social and economic activities from a regional context. Much work has been carried out to try to reconstruct past climatic conditions from tree rings (for example by Briffa and Matthews[10]). In some cases, especially in areas where tree growth responds to one single aspect of climate (such as moisture availability or summer temperature) this has been very successful. In Ireland, because of the temperate climate, only about 25% of the variation in annual tree growth represents the effect of climate; the rest is a complex combination of factors including soil and forest conditions, human interference and other unknowns. However, even if we cannot reconstruct climate directly from Irish tree-rings, many trees in Ireland do reflect specific regional and in some cases global events.[4] Some such examples are described below.

1816 is recalled as 'the year without a summer'. In the previous year there had been the large volcanic eruption of Tambora which had had a dramatic effect on climate. The cold, dark summer of 1816 resulted in narrower than normal tree-rings for 1816 and 1817 in the vast majority of the Irish oak trees. The Belvoir Park oaks are no exception. All the trees produced narrower tree-rings in these two years (see Figure 2). While they are not dramatically narrow, it has to be remembered that these trees were probably growing in near ideal parkland conditions.

The Great Wind of 1839 referred to earlier in this chapter might have been expected to cause a major reduction in ring width for oaks throughout Ireland due to factors such as salt dumping and physical damage. However, in the original Belfast work there was little sign of such effects though it was noted that almost all Irish oaks show notably reduced growth in 1840-1844. The trees at Belvoir also register the early-1840s reduction though it is clearly not catastrophic in nature.

What was particularly interesting about Belvoir was the remarkable similarity of the site master chronology (the mean of all the Belvoir trees) and the original Belfast Long Chronology.

Figure 2 shows a section of the two chronologies from 1780 to 1850. The degree of similarity is much higher than even dendrochronologists might have expected.

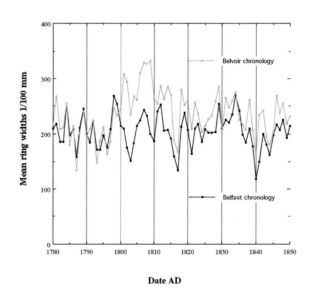

Figure 2: Section of the original Belfast long oak chronology and the Belvoir Park site chronology from 1780 to 1850. Both chronologies are straightforward yearly means of the available trees.

Oak logs from the Lagan at Shaw's Bridge

In *Tree-Ring Dating and Archaeology*[1] there is a description of the problems encountered with the dating of a series of heavy oak timbers from the bed of the River Lagan near Shaw's Bridge, a short distance southwest of Belvoir. A difficulty arose because the timbers were dated by dendrochronology to felling years 1617 and 1631, whereas there were references that Shaw's Bridge had first been constructed around 1655 by 'Captain Shaw of the Train' (Cromwell's Train). The issue was resolved by the construction of a Scottish oak chronology. This confirmed the accuracy of the Belfast tree-ring series and it is now known with certainty that a substantial timber structure was constructed with timbers felled in 1617, while a sluice on the Antrim bank dated to 1631. Interestingly, Moses Hill, who owned large amounts of land on either side of the Lagan in the early part of the 17th century, was created Earl Marshal of all Ulster in 1617. It is possible that the timbers of 1617 represented improvements in line with his new status and as he died in 1630 the timbers dating to 1631 might be explained by a successor undertaking further work.

The close proximity of Shaw's Bridge to Belvoir provided an opportunity to compare the samples taken from the two sites. The Shaw's Bridge oak timbers were over 8m long with cross-sections up to 45cm square and we assume they were local simply because it would be difficult to transport massive beams any great distance. The oak beams at Shaw's Bridge provide ring patterns from 1360 to 1617/1631. Given that we know that oak trees have been growing at Belvoir since the mid 17th century, we can now state with a reasonable degree of certainty that there has been an uninterrupted growth of oak in the northern Lagan Valley from the 14th century to the present.

We can also compare the growth rates for the oak timbers from near Shaw's Bridge with those from Belvoir. We have noted above that the overall mean ring width for the Belvoir trees was 2.4mm. However to compare the groups objectively we chose two time intervals where consistent groups of trees were represented (this irons out end effects to some extent). Ten trees from Belvoir covered the period 1873 to 1969; for this 97-year period the mean annual ring width was 1.82mm. From Shaw's Bridge eight trees covered the period 1444 to 1566. For this 123 year period the mean annual ring width was 0.85mm. This suggests that the Belvoir and Shaw's Bridge trees either grew in very different environments (e.g. forest as compared with parkland) or differed in some other way. As 'imported stock' seems to have been ruled out by genetic studies (Chapter 8), currently it looks as though 'different environmental regime' is the most likely solution.

Interestingly the Shaw's Bridge timbers were from long straight trees growing to at least 10m without branching. While such trees do exist at Belvoir, many others exhibit quite large branches at a few metres. This would seem to reinforce our prejudice that the Belvoir samples were growing in ideal parkland type conditions while the Shaw's Bridge trees probably came from a more forested context.

Above: Construction of the new Shaw's Bridge

Above: Oak timbers recovered during excavation

Conclusions

An oak at Belvoir that was growing until recent years has provided a record of growth from 1642. This was the oldest Irish oak tree ever recorded by the Palaeoecology Centre at Queen's University. Although the age of a tree cannot be accurately estimated from girth, it is worth noting that some of the fallen trees dated at Belvoir undoubtedly had girths of around 4m. Since a number of the oaks still growing in the woods at Belvoir have girths of over 5m, and even a few over 6m, it seems highly likely that some of these trees are well over 300 years old.

North and south Corbie Woods, which lie between the courtyard buildings at Belvoir and the River Lagan, contained most of the oldest oaks sampled. However, some very old trees also occur in Big Wood and in the golf course grounds. The four samples from Bowling Green Hill are of slightly younger trees. Large-girthed oaks in the golf course near Big Wood that are growing in a very straight line appear to be remnants of a hedgerow most likely planted in the early 18th century and incorporating an earlier tree.

The most important insight that the data give is that the woods at Belvoir Park predate the formation of the estate in the 1720s-1730s. On reflection, this is not an unexpected conclusion. A new estate would be more likely to be developed in an attractive verdant landscape than in open farmland. However, this conclusion is contrary to the normally held view that trees in Irish estates post-date the building of the houses.

At Belvoir there is also some evidence for a series of planting/natural regeneration episodes from 1700 to 1815. Some of these seem to correlate with periods of likely tree planting and development of the demesne. Others, however, seem to correlate with periods when the demesne was known to have been neglected and might indicate natural regeneration. Evidence from Belvoir and older oak timbers from the River Lagan at Shaw's Bridge suggest that oak trees have, without interruption, been part of the landscape of the northern Lagan valley since at least the 14th century.

This study has been the first dendrochronology investigation of the history and development of a living Irish wood. Even though the number of samples has been relatively small, it has provided new insights into the history of the area and helped corroborate information from other sources. These techniques should prove of use in examining other Irish wooded estates.

Acknowledgments

We would like to thank Prof. Jonathan Pilcher and Mr Phil Barrett for assistance with sampling. This work was carried out partly under the auspices of, and using equipment provided by, 14CHRONO.

CHAPTER *Eight–* OAK *fingerprints –*

where did that oak come from? **Colin Fleming and Stephen Clarke**

Native woodlands

A MUCH STATED, yet nevertheless significant fact, is that Ireland is one of the least wooded regions within Europe. Most put the area of woodland in Northern Ireland at 6%, compared to 10% in the United Kingdom and 24% in the rest of the European Union. Approximately 75% of Northern Ireland woodland consists of non-native conifer plantations, which highlights the particular importance of our existing broadleaved woodland.[1,2] In 1996 Northern Ireland Environment Link in its Environmental Strategy for Northern Ireland proposed a planting programme to increase the amount of tree cover in Northern Ireland and recommended that trees grown from local genetic stock should be used where possible. Further to this, in 2000 the Northern Ireland Biodiversity Group called for a review of the past and current effects of introduced genetic material in Ireland.[3]

Initiatives for planting native broadleaves have come from both public and voluntary sectors. For example, the Woodland Grant Scheme run by the DARD Forest Service was introduced in 1988 and offered grants for planting trees, with financial help considerably greater for planting broadleaved species and preference given to 'species which are, or might have been, native to the site'.

Conservation Volunteers Northern Ireland, in its 1996 publication *Our Trees, a guide to growing Northern Ireland's native trees from seed,* recommended avoiding not only planting non-native provenances, but also translocations between, for example, Co. Antrim and Co. Fermanagh.[4]

It is generally accepted that the effective use of local forest resources in this way can enhance and help maintain biological diversity in a region, as well as improving the quality of forestry products. These regional objectives must also be seen in an international context. For example, the UK has signed up to international commitments such as those specified within the Rio Principles Article 4, Biodiversity Convention Articles 8 & 9 and the Helsinki Guidelines Resolution 1, which require protection, characterisation and use of native genotypes.[5] The UK response to fulfilling the Convention on Biodiversity was the Biodiversity Action Plan[6] which included a number of recommendations for enhancing woodland biodiversity:

- Creating new woodlands, especially in areas of low wildlife value.
- Encouraging the use of native species of local provenance.

- Promoting the use of good quality, local genetic hardwood stock where native broadleaved tree species are being planted.
- Careful selection of seed sources in order to help ensure that local genotypes are preserved and that trees being planted are well suited to local environments.

Genetic diversity in native tree species

In the past, the forestry industry has successfully exploited population differences within species by paying attention to the provenance and origin of reproductive material. The term 'provenance' is used to describe the location of the woodland from which seed, plants and parts of plants were collected. In practice, the actual origin of the material is more important, since this term is used to describe that part of the natural species range from which the material was originally derived. However, since the origins of planted stands are often unknown, local provenance is normally considered sufficient on the assumption that collections are made from stands of trees that appear well adapted.

Woodlands, especially ancient (before 1600) and semi-natural woodlands, are widely accepted as being of high biodiversity value and the genetic diversity of the constituent tree species is seen as a key component of that biodiversity. Genetic variation falls into two classes, adaptive variation and selectively neutral variation, though the distinction between them is not always clear. Adaptive genetic variation is important as it ensures a high fitness across a wide range of environmental conditions and allows a species to respond to environmental change (e.g. climatic change). For many plant species, often genes in a particular region will have co-evolved to interact well together. Crossing with individuals from other regions can break these relationships, resulting in progeny with lower fitness and having a knock-on effect on other species in the ecosystem, for example those dependent on timing of leaf flush.[7]

Numerous experiments have been conducted to examine how plant species are adapted to local conditions. In Europe, studies have focused mainly on commercially important species, for example oak, hawthorn, Scots pine and birch.

Worrell[8] demonstrated that in the oak *Quercus petraea* British provenances showed marginally faster growth rates than those of continental origin and they also showed marginally higher survival rates, though the differences between provenances was not as marked for oak compared to other species. Ducousso *et al*[9] studied the timing of bud burst in *Q. petraea* populations at fifty sites in France, concluding that northern provenances and those nearest the sea were latest and that early flushing trees were more likely to suffer from frost damage. They recommended avoiding moving acorns from region to region and that foresters should use oak of local origin. This view has been supported by Jensen[10] who, in a trial of *Q. petraea* and *Quercus robur* provenances from across Europe in Denmark, found that flushing is under strong genetic control, as are growth and stem form. A strong influence of coastal climate was also detected. Deans and Harvey,[11] in an examination of frost hardiness of sixteen European provenances of *Q. petraea* from five countries, found significant differences between them. French provenances were less hardy than those from Britain, with a tendency to flush early and grow late in autumn whereas German, Polish and Danish provenances were hardier than local material.

In the case of most native tree species the lack of scientific information requires that the designation of local provenances is usually based on subjective data and a 'best guess assessment' of population differences. For example, in Britain where the importance of local seed supplies is recognised, the island is divided into four regions of provenance. These are defined areas within which similar ecological and climatic characteristics are found and they provide a framework for specifying sources of Forest Reproductive Material (FRM). For native species these Regions of Provenance have been split into a total of 24 native seed zones (http://www.forestry.gov.uk/pdf/Provmap.pdf/$FILE/P rovmap.pdf). Seed zones are in turn divided where appropriate into two altitude zones, below 300m and above 300m. Key to the maintenance of local genetic diversity in native woodland species is the restriction of movement of FRM between zones. A notable exception to this is the Scots pine (*Pinus sylvestris*) where genetic analysis has identified distinct genotypes amongst the remnant Scottish woodlands. Consequently, seed zones for Scots pine reflect these actual and characterised biological differences rather than the ecologically based seed zones used for most other species.

As is the case in Britain, hard data on genetic differences among populations of Irish woodland tree species are generally lacking and recent studies (notably on oak and ash) have attempted to provide information on the patterns of genetic diversity within Ireland.[12,13] While attempting to characterise Irish woodland tree species, we can ask a number of important questions including:

- Are Irish trees genetically different from those in the rest of Europe?
- Where are the remaining native Irish woodlands located?
- Can we identify introduced non-native trees?
- Are there genetic differences among trees within Ireland?
- Are native Irish woodlands genetically healthy?
- Why bother with native seed if non-native seed is less expensive?
- Will the use of non-native seed damage our woodlands?

In this chapter we will report on the results of a genetic study of oak trees within the area of the former walled Belvoir Park demesne and evaluate the significance of these oaks as a genetic resource within Ireland.

Origins of native trees in Ireland

The events of the last 13,000 years in Ireland have been pieced together from pollen studies, Carbon-14 dating, dendrochronology, molecular markers and written records. Around 13,000 BP (Before Present) climate improved rapidly, and Ireland moved from arctic to temperate conditions in a relatively short time.[14-17] Temperate plant and animal species that had been confined to refugia in southern Europe began to move north to occupy the now favourable northerly regions. Data based on Carbon-14 and pollen analysis have given an idea of the development of vegetation in this post-glacial period. Following a period of grass-dominated tundra, willow and juniper increased, then a steep rise in birch at about 10,000 BP preceded the spread of Scots pine and hazel around 9000 BP. Oak and elm appeared around 8,000 to 7,000 BP, alder slightly later (7,000-6,500 BP) and ash arrived later still, perhaps around 4,500 BP.

From around 8,000 BP, mixed deciduous forest covered 80% of Ireland with the midlands dominated by hazel and elm, the south and northeast containing mainly oak woods and Scots pines along the west coast. The first evidence of humans dates to around 9,000 BP,[15] although these hunter-gatherers appear not to have had a major effect on Irish woodland. Agriculture appeared in Ireland around 5,000 BC.[15] This was shortly after the 'elm decline' which was apparently brought about by a disease, possibly via human vectors.[16] In common with most of Europe, the agricultural period saw a decline in woodland cover[18] but this was by no means a steady process.

Evidence for temporal variations in tree cover comes from a number of sources. Pilcher[16] interpreted a pollen diagram from Fallahogy, Co. Londonderry, as indicating woodland clearance and farming *ca.* 5,400-5,300 BP followed by about 400 years of regeneration. In a pollen study on Slieve Gallion[19] there is an indication that while oak decreased from *ca.* 1,500-500 BC, alder, ash and hazel were increasing. Cruickshank and Cruickshank[20] studied the pollen deposition in soil at Breen Wood, Co. Londonderry and found two periods of clearance, one at 2,000-1,700 BP and another at 1,400-1,100 BP, yet in both cases the wood was allowed to regenerate without an intervening period of cultivation. The historical period in Ireland has been an eventful one for woodlands. Written

records for Irish woodlands are poorer than for those from England[18,21] but indicate that in 1600 over 12% of the Irish land area was wooded, dwindling to about 2% in 1800.[21]

Clearly, major woodland clearance has occurred between 1600 and today. This may not have been at a higher rate than preceding clearances and regeneration this time may have been minimal.[22] During this period Ireland went from being a net exporter to a net importer of timber.[23] Tree species which had failed to reach Ireland in the post-glacial period were now imported, for example beech, chestnut, sycamore and conifers[24] and non-local provenances of native species were imported from a range of localities including Scotland, England and Holland.[23,25] Interestingly, of the woodlands recorded in the Civil Survey of 1654-1656, only 10% had survived up to the Ordnance Survey of 1834-1844, with woods appearing on the later map that had not existed in the 17th century.[18] The influx of alien provenances of native trees (especially to estate plantings) has made the identification of ancient woodlands and truly native trees a difficult process. This is particularly true in the case of estates such as Belvoir where past plantings of non-native provenances is likely.

Oaks in Belvoir

Two species of oak are generally considered to be native to Ireland, *Quercus petraea*, the sessile oak and *Quercus robur*, the pedunculate oak. As the two species can hybridise (levels of 10% are not uncommon) and produce viable offspring, their taxonomic status has been questioned. However, *Q. petraea* and *Q. robur* display clear morphological differences and habitat preferences. *Q. robur* has a shorter leaf stalk (petiole) than *Q. petraea* and there are obvious auricles at the leaf base (absent in sessile oak). The acorns of *Q. robur* are produced in groups on a long peduncle, whereas the acorns of sessile oak exhibit either no peduncle or a very short one. Hybrids generally exhibit characters intermediate between the two parent species. Ecologically, *Q. robur* prefers to grow on wetter and more alkaline habitats while *Q. petraea* is more generally found on well drained substrata. In Ireland *Q. petraea* is much more common than *Q. robur* and tends to dominate most of the wooded areas.[26]

The Belvoir Park demesne used to comprise the land which is now the Belvoir Park Golf Course, Belvoir Park Forest, most of the Belvoir housing

estate and Morelands Meadow. Within the
boundaries of the former demesne there are 260 trees
with a girth of 3m or more, which includes 130
native oaks (i.e. *Q. robur* and *Q. petraea*). As in most
genetic analyses of oaks, larger-girthed trees were
selected for study because they are more likely to
represent the original native stock. In addition to the
native oaks, in the area of Belvoir Park demesne there
are a small number of other species of oaks with
girths of over 3m. Most are Turkey oaks, though in
the Arboretum near the site of the old mansion
house there are one large holm oak and three oaks
that are generally referred to as Lucombe oaks (see
Chapter 4).

Quercus robur

Quercus petraea

Genetic analysis of oaks

In order to grow, survive in a complex
environment and reproduce, living organisms require
thousands of proteins to build and maintain their
cells and to regulate their biochemical processes.
DNA contains genetic information in the form of a
sequence of four bases A-adenine, T-thymine, C-
cytosine and G-guanine. These sequences code for
the proteins and DNA analysis can provide the
information required to distinguish and genetically
characterise populations of animals and plants.
Within plants two sources of DNA are particularly
useful.

1. Most DNA and the majority of plant genes are
   found in chromosomes located in the nucleus of
   each cell. Chromosomal DNA in species such as
   oak is derived from the male and female parents
   with both contributing equally to the genetic
   make-up of their offspring. Different types of gene
   (e.g. microsatellite genes, structural genes,
   ribosomal genes) in the chromosomal DNA can

be examined, allowing a range of levels of genetic variation to be assessed (e.g. the relatively small amounts of variation found between individuals up to the larger differences present between species).

2. A smaller but equally informative type of DNA found in plants is located in the chloroplasts. These cellular components are the plant's machinery for converting light energy into sugars and they contain their own set of genes within a circular molecule of DNA. The chloroplast DNA generally displays uniparental inheritance.[27] In most species including oak, chloroplasts are inherited from the maternal line[28] so their DNA can disperse via seed but not in pollen. Thus it is possible to compare chloroplast DNA variation with that of the nuclear (chromosomal) genome to obtain data on the relative influences of seed and pollen on genetic diversity. In general, chloroplast DNA is less variable than nuclear DNA[29] and its usefulness tends to be confined to examining 'higher level' genetic variation such as that between subspecies, species or genera,[30] though this is dependent on the region of the chloroplast genome studied.

Present-day genetic variation in oaks has been greatly influenced by events during and since the last glaciation. During the period when most of Europe was covered by ice a number of southern glacial refugia maintained much of the present-day northern European flora and fauna.[17] In the case of oak the main glacial refugia are considered to have been in the Iberian Peninsula, Italy and the Balkans. Genetic variants (known as haplotypes) identified from European oak have been used to support the existence of these glacial refugia and to trace the subsequent routes of postglacial migration through a number of lineages.[31,32] Kelleher et al.[13] and Muir et al.[12] have shown that native Irish oak exhibit chloroplast DNA haplotypes characteristic of a lineage which originated in the Iberian peninsula and today is present in Britain, France, Portugal and western Spain. Oak originating from five other genetically and geographically distinct lineages throughout Europe exhibit different haplotypes. Consequently, in Ireland chloroplast haplotypes can be used to identify non-native oaks which have originated from outside the western European zone.

Three types of genetic marker were employed to assess both genetic diversity and genetic structure (the spatial pattern of genetic diversity) of oak in Belvoir.

1. DNA sequence analysis of chloroplast genes.
2. Microsatellites.
3. Inter Simple Sequence Repeats (ISSR).

Microsatellites and ISSRs were chosen because of their proven ability to detect genetic variation in populations, whilst the chloroplast DNA regions were included to provide an indication of the provenance of the Belvoir site. All three marker types were generated using the polymerase chain reaction, a process which amplifies millions of copies of specific target DNA sequences from complex mixtures of genomic and other DNA. Detailed descriptions of these markers and the methods used to detect them are presented in Appendix 5.

Collection of oak samples in Belvoir

Leaf samples were collected from 45 oaks including many of the larger-girthed trees at Belvoir (most of the trees sampled had a circumference of 4-6m). Outside of the boundary of the former Belvoir Park demesne, there are a smaller number of native oaks with a girth of over 3m. Samples were collected from two large native oaks at Annadale (just north of the boundary of the former Belvoir Park demesne) and four samples were taken from large oaks in the Lagan Valley (Sir Thomas and Lady Dixon Park, Barnett Demesne and a field near Edenderry footbridge). The reason for collecting these samples was to assess if Belvoir oaks were genetically distinct from those in the surrounding region, though the small sample size for the trees outside of Belvoir was likely to make any conclusions tentative. These 54 leaf samples were frozen at -40°C until use. Technical information concerning the analysis of the samples is given in Appendix 5.

To provide a more comprehensive comparison of the variation detected in Belvoir, data from a previous analysis of supposedly native Irish and introduced oaks were included in the data analysis. The native Irish tree sample included leaves from ten trees from Breen wood, Co. Antrim, eight trees from Correl Glen, Co. Fermanagh, five trees from Tomies, Co. Kerry and ten trees from Derrycunihy, Co. Kerry. Tomies and Derrycunihy belong to a collection of woods in the Killarney valley thought to represent the largest collection of semi-natural remnants in Ireland. Although historical records indicate that Tomies wood was felled and replanted at the beginning of the 19th century, it is highly likely that regeneration of the wood was natural at this time rather than artificial. On the other hand, pollen profiles from Derrycunihy indicate a continuous *Quercus* pollen record for at least the last 5,000 years and, most probably, direct continuity with post-glacial primary forest. Material from additional woodlands within the British isles were also examined as were samples of non-native *Q. robur* and *Q. petraea* from France, Spain and Serbia and a sample of *Quercus cerris*.

Chloroplast variation in Belvoir oaks

With no significant differences in chloroplast variation in trees from different parts of the forest, all the Belvoir oaks displayed either haplotype 10 or 12 (Figure 1). Previously these have been shown to be the commonest of the four chloroplast haplotypes (7, 10, 11, 12) recorded in Ireland to date and are indicative of a native Irish gene pool. Interestingly, haplotype 7 found in a single specimen by Kelleher *et al.*[13] is characteristic of Balkan oaks and its presence in Ireland may reflect a historical alien introduction. Haplotype 10 has been found mainly in the south and centre of Ireland, while haplotype 12 predominates in the north and coastal woodlands. The much higher frequency of haplotype 12 at Belvoir supports this apparent geographical difference and also suggests a higher *Q. petraea* contribution to oaks at Belvoir. Kelleher *et al.*[13] reported haplotype 12 to be present at a significantly higher frequency than haplotype 10 in Irish sessile oaks. The absence of chloroplast haplotypes other than 10 and 12 at Belvoir also provides strong evidence that the woodland comprises oaks originating from the same post-glacial lineage as native Irish oaks (i.e. the western European lineage). On the basis of these chloroplast data, it is not possible to determine if the Belvoir oaks are solely of Irish origin or if they contain individuals originating from other parts of the western European lineage (i.e. Britain, France, Portugal, western Spain).

ISSR analysis of Belvoir oaks

The generation of DNA fingerprints using ISSR PCR primers allowed the broad genetic relationships between Belvoir oaks and other oak populations within the British Isles and Europe to be assessed. DNA fingerprint data were converted to binary codes and a phylogenetic tree showing the genetic relationships to be constructed (Figure 2). A number of key points were apparent from the ISSR analysis:

1. Mainland European populations were distinct from oak populations in the British Isles.

2. Oak populations from southern and south-eastern Ireland were genetically distinct from those in Northern Ireland.
3. Belvoir oaks showed a close genetic affinity with oak from the Northern Irish semi-natural woodlands at Breen, Correl Glen and Rostrevor.
4. The Fermanagh oak woods at Reilly and Annagariff were distinct from other Northern Irish woodlands.
5. Ervey wood (Co. Londonderry) showed most affinity with the Scottish oaks from Killicrankie.

The observation of a genetic similarity between Belvoir oaks and native north-eastern Irish genotypes provides support for the view that most Belvoir oaks are native in origin.

Microsatellite analysis of Belvoir oaks

Having examined the broad genetic relationships between Belvoir oaks and other European populations, microsatellite analysis was used to individually genotype the Belvoir trees. The

microsatellite data were then used to assign the trees into genetically distinct groupings, each comprising individuals separated by only minor genetic differences. Genetic groupings and individual tree codes are shown in Appendix 5, Table 1. From this it is clear that none of the groupings for the oaks shows a clear association with location within the different parts of the Belvoir Park demesne or with the sites outside of Belvoir.

Genetic distances among the groupings were estimated and used in the phylogenetic analysis. The resulting phylogenetic tree is presented in Figure 3.

The major dichotomy within the phylogenetic tree was the separation of the Lucombe oaks and *Q. cerris* from the other material. This was not unexpected as Lucombe oaks are thought to be a cross between *Q. cerris* and *Q. suber*. The result may be of local interest in helping to support the identification of these three trees.

Within the remaining oak material, three clear groupings were apparent. Groups 5, 6 and 12 clustered with the native Irish oak populations indicating that trees within these three groups showed most affinity with native Irish material. Assuming future seed collections were to target native

Irish trees, the individual trees within these groups are probably the best source of 'native' seed within the Belvoir area.

Groups 5 and 6 also included seven of the twelve trees sampled with girths of over 5m, including the two largest trees at Belvoir (girths of 8.8m and 6.92m), though excluding the third largest tree (girth of 6.34m). As Groups 5 and 6 comprised just under 30% of the Belvoir oaks sampled, this may indicate a link between native origins and size of tree.

Groups 8 and 9 included few large-girthed trees while group 3 (comprising just two trees!) had no large-girthed trees. Groups 3 and 10 clustered with the mainland European germplasm and together with Groups 4, 7, 8, 9 and 11 (which clustered separately from this material) comprise trees which are more likely to have non-native origins. All of the trees in Group 7 were over 4m, with 6 of these over 4.5m in girth. This may be a group of older trees that are genetically distinct to groups 5 and 6 and which may have a non-native origin.

An important aspect of genetic diversity is the actual level of genetic variation present in populations. Low genetic diversity indicates that populations may have suffered influences such as population crashes or inbreeding and can point to potential problems for populations in coping with environmental change.

Two assessments of the genetic variability present at microsatellite loci were made:
1. Variance in repeat number.
2. Heterozygosity.

The data presented in Figures 4 and 5 show that Irish oak populations, including Belvoir, contain similar levels of genetic variation to those found in the larger European oakwoods. Apparently, despite the contraction in size of oakwoods in Ireland there has been no significant decrease in genetic variability. This suggests that many Irish oakwoods, including Belvoir, are genetically healthy and a potential source of genetically viable native seed.

Microsatellite analysis can also provide an indication of the species status of oaks. *Q. robur, Q. petraea* and their hybrids are found throughout Ireland and an assessment of the species status of the Belvoir oaks was undertaken using an assignment test based on allele frequencies.[33] Confirming the results of the chloroplast haplotype analysis, the microsatellite data indicated that *Quercus petraea* dominated the oakwoods at Belvoir.

Area where trees were sampled	Species assignment
Morelands Meadow	*Petraea*
Belvoir Park Golf Course	*Robur/Petraea*/hybrids
Belvoir Park Forest	*Robur/Petraea*/hybrids
SE Belvoir Park Forest	*Petraea*
NE Belvoir Park Forest	*Petraea*
Land between Forest and Housing Estate	*Robur/Petraea*/hybrids
Annadale	*Petraea*
Upper Malone	*Petraea*/hybrids

Table 1: Species assignments to a sample of oak trees from different areas of Belvoir

Conclusions of the genetic study

- Within Belvoir the presence of genetically distinct oak, showing an affinity with what we believe to be native Irish germplasm, suggests that the Forest contains a genetic resource which merits protection.

- The Belvoir trees have apparently originated from the western European chloroplast lineage and haplotypes indicative of other European lineages were absent.

- Relatively high levels of genetic diversity show the oakwood to be in good genetic health and also give a scientific basis for resourcing the conservation of oakwood around Belfast.

- Worries that high levels of planting of non-native provenances have occurred during the history of the Belvoir estate seem unfounded.

- The woodland appears to be an acceptable and valuable source of seed for use in new plantings and woodland improvement in the Belfast area.

- Confirmatory data for these conclusions comes from the three different genetic marker types.

Acknowledgments

Thanks to Maggie McDowell for help with the DNA extraction, to Brendan Moreland and Ronald Hunter for assistance with the DNA sequencing and microsatellite analysis and thanks to Ben Simon for collecting the leaf samples.

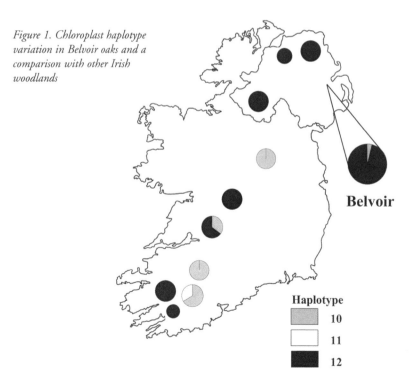

Figure 1. Chloroplast haplotype variation in Belvoir oaks and a comparison with other Irish woodlands

Belvoir

Haplotype

- 10
- 11
- 12

Figure 2. Genetic relationships between the Belvoir population and oak provenances from the British Isles and Europe. Numbers on branching points (bootstrap values) indicate significant genetic differences between groups of oak populations. Shorter branch lengths between populations indicate closer genetic relatedness. Data based on ISSR fingerprints. Populations names: Killiecrankie (Scotland), Breen (Co. Antrim), Reilly, Correl Glen, Annagariff (Co. Fermanagh), Ervey (Co. Londonderry), Rostrevor (Co. Down), Derrycunnihy, Tomies (Co. Kerry), Garranon, Pollnaknockaun (Co. Clare), Glengariff (Co. Cork).

Figure 3. Phylogenetic tree showing genetic relationships among DNA groups of Belvoir oak and their similarity to native Irish oaks, introduced oaks and Q. cerris.
'Native' = cluster for native Irish oaks. 'Introduced' = cluster for mainland European oaks. Group 1 and Group 2 are two Belvoir oaks generally considered to be Lucombe oaks. Trees that comprise Groups 2 to 12 are described in Appendix 5, Table 1.
Tree constructed using microsatellite data and UPGMA cluster analysis.

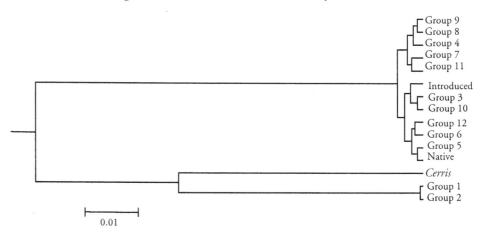

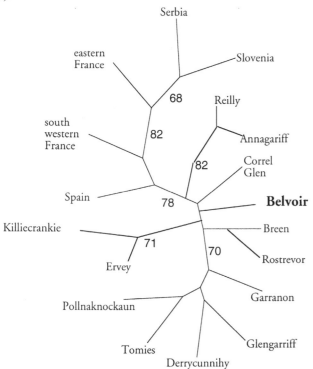

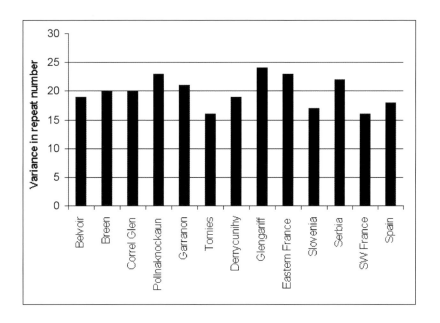

Figure 4. Levels of genetic variation (variance in repeat number) at microsatellite loci from Belvoir oak and other Irish and European oakwoods.

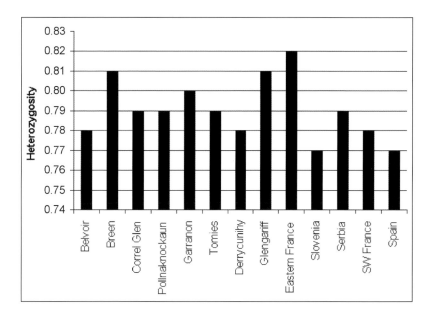

Figure 5. Levels of genetic variation (heterozygosity) at microsatellite loci from Belvoir oak and other Irish and European oakwoods.

CHAPTER *Nine*
PENNY BUNS to *milk caps* and *stinkhorns* to BIRDS' NESTS
a great diversity of fungi   **Roy Anderson**

Fly agaric (Amanita muscaria) under birch

Snakeskin agaric (Amanita inaurata) under oak

THE APPEARANCE OF MUSHROOMS and toadstools in autumn heralds the year's end and the end of plant growth in the forest. For many it is an opportunity to collect edible mushrooms and other fungi for the pot. For others it is a seasonal prelude to Hallowe'en and a reminder of witches' brews, fireworks and autumnal decay. Few realise the pivotal role of these strange, often brightly-coloured objects in maintaining the health of the forest. For fungi are not only agents of decay but recycle vital nutrients to enable the continued healthy growth of trees.

We only see the 'fungus' when it is ready to reproduce and forms a fruiting body, the familiar mushroom or toadstool. Most of the fungus is actually underground, existing as tiny threads called mycelia in the soil. This is a reason why the fruiting bodies of most large fungi appear in the autumn. As well as decomposing wood and leaves on the forest floor, many fungi grow in association with the roots of large trees and are known technically as mycorrhizae. When the tree sheds its leaves in autumn, the nutrients from the dying leaves travel down the tree to the roots for storage and here the almost invisible mycelia of fungi benefit and are

helped to produce their fruiting bodies. The result is, quite literally, flushes of fungi appearing near the roots of their host trees from late summer onwards. The relationship between trees and fungi is a complex one, but the tree benefits by receiving micro-nutrients collected by the fungus in exchange for energy foods (carbohydrates) delivered to the fungus from the tree's root system.

Belvoir has a wide variety of fungi. The larger ones collected for the pot or famous in folklore have interesting names such as ceps, penny buns, waxcaps and milkcaps. Many are edible, but great caution is advisable with wild fungi as serious poisonings are not unknown and it is advisable to have at least one good reference guide and to stick to a few of the more easily identified edible fungi.[1]

One of the most poisonous fungi known, the aptly-named destroying angel (*Amanita virosa*), was recorded in Belvoir by visiting experts from the British Mycological Society in 1948[2] and there are a number of other poisonous species in the Forest which are less rare. The genus *Amanita*, to which the destroying angel belongs, is notorious for poisonous species. The familiar bright scarlet, white-spotted, fly agaric (*Amanita muscaria*), for instance, grows in association with birch and is common in good years on Belvoir Park Golf Course. This secretes a hallucinogen called muscarin and was famously used to promote psychedelic trances by the Siberian indians. However, don't try this one at home as the most likely outcome will be a severe cramping diarrhoea! The Siberian shamans wisely used lesser mortals to 'clean up' the raw extract and consumed a filtered urinal decoction to achieve their trance state! Other Amanitas found in Belvoir include the delicate snakeskin agaric *(Amanita inaurata)*, the panther cap *(Amanita pantherina)* and the blusher *(Amanita rubescens)*, so called because it reddens when bruised. All have been found growing under oak or beech in the Arboretum. None of them is safe to eat. The edible mushrooms *(Agaricus)* are, alas, quite rare in Belvoir and only the woodland mushroom *(Agaricus sylvaticus)* has been seen recently under Monterey cypress in the Arboretum. All mushrooms have reddish to brown gills whereas the Amanitas are white-gilled, a point to remember if you are ever tempted to try wild fungi for the pot.

In and around the conifer plantations at Belvoir in late summer one may encounter the small yellow boletes of the genus Suillus. Slippery jack *(Suillus luteus)* occurs rarely under Scots pine, the larch bolete *(Suillus grevillei)* under larch, and several others under larch and spruce. These are highly prized for food in other cultures such as the Chinese, but not in Ireland. Another yellow fungus which grows in Belvoir and is more routinely eaten is the chanterelle *(Cantharellus cibarius)*. It is solid, waxy and bright yellow all the way through, but delicious grilled with a little lemon or on toast. In recent years it appears to have declined and is only rarely encountered under its host tree, beech. The large brown ceps or penny bun *(Boletus edulis)* is used commercially to flavour soups and sauces. Once again, it is fairly rare in Belvoir but may be found growing under conifers. Most of the other large fungi are of marginal or no culinary value. These include the brittlegills *(Russula)* and milkcaps *(Lactarius)* species which abound in parkland at the Arboretum, in the grassland of Belvoir Estate, or in the golf course. The brittlegills are a colourful lot with white stems and gills but bright caps of various shades. Examples of colours you can find are: yellow, in the common brittlegill *(Russula ochroleuca)* which is found widely under conifers; red, in the beechwood sickener *(Russula mairei)* found commonly under

Larch bolete (Suillus grevillei) under larch

Penny bun (Boletus edulis) under beech

111

Coral brittlegill (Russula velenovskyi) under lime

Common puffball (Lycoperdon perlatum) under oak

Striate earthstar (Geastrum striatum) under Monterey cypress

Common stinkhorn (Phallus impudicus) emerging from its 'egg'. In mixed woodland

Witches' butter (Exidia glandulosa) on an oak branch

Beefsteak fungus (Fistulina hepatica) on an old oak log near the River Lagan

Resin bracket (Ganoderma resinaceum) on a parkland oak

Chicken of the woods (Laetiporus sulphureus) on willow by the River Lagan

Yellow fan (Spathularia flava) in litter under spruce

Scarlet elfcap (Sarcoscypha austriaca) on alder twigs

Green elfcup (Chlorociboria aeruginascens) on willow - note the green stain

Eyelash fungus (Scutellinia crinita) on twigs buried in mud

beech; pink- or purple-grey, in the charcoal burner (*Russula cyanoxantha*) which is also found under beech; pale green, in the green brittlegill (*Russula aeruginosa*) found under birch; reddish-orange, in the coral brittlegill (*Russula velenovskyi*) under lime; brown-black, in the blackening brittlegill (*Russula nigricans*) under oak and beech – this turns red, then black on bruising. The milkcaps (*Lactarius*) 'bleed' a milky sap when cut and, although most are inedible, one or two are highly prized for the pot. The saffron milkcap (*Lactarius deliciosus*) is the most desirable and grows under Scots pine, but although known from about 20 locations in Northern Ireland, has not been recorded from Belvoir.

Aside from the familiar 'mushroom' design, fungi come in all shapes and sizes. There are the puffball fungi, familiar white or brownish spheres with or without short stalks, or the earthstars, like a puffball seated on a fleshy star. The earthstars are scarce, but one species, the striate earth star (*Geastrum striatum*), occurs commonly on litter under a large Monterey cypress in the Arboretum. It fruits in October to November but the fruiting bodies are very durable and can be seen at most times of year. The 'ball' part of puffball species contains the spores which 'puff' out of the fruiting body when this is pressed or flicked. Although puffballs mostly occur in great numbers in dry places such as well-drained pastures and sand dunes, several species are commoner in woods where they can be seen in grass under large trees or at the sides of paths. Two very unusual members of the group conform to the puffball shape only when young. These are the stinkhorns. Stinkhorns are named for the ferocious scent of decay (ammoniacal or amine-like) which emanates from mature fruiting bodies and can be detected 30 or 40 metres away in still conditions. The 'egg' or ball of the stinkhorn develops just below the soil surface in mixed woods. At this stage it is quite heavy and gelatinous inside. Fluid pressure builds in the egg until the top ruptures and a rapidly expanding phallus-like 'horn' emerges. The overall shape of this is reflected in its scientific name *Phallus impudicus*. The cap of the horn is covered in a greyish-green slime which contains the spores and most of the vile smell. This attracts flies, mainly bluebottles, which gorge on the spore material and defaecate undigested spores far from the original fruiting body. In this way the spores are dispersed. A smaller species, the dog stinkhorn (*Mutinus caninus*), occurs sporadically in Belvoir. It differs in the more slender and reddish-coloured horn.

The jelly fungi are so-named for their irregular shape, sometimes bright colours and tendency to absorb water and inflate to a jelly-like consistency in wet weather. The commonest is the yellow brain (*Tremella mesenterica*) which grows out of dead gorse stems or tree branches in wet weather and is a gaudy orange in colour. Witches butter (*Exidia glandulosa*) by contrast is black and glistening, with irregular clumps growing on dead oak branches (including those still attached to the tree) in autumn and winter.

The brackets are an important group of forest fungi. These occur, stiff and bracket-like, on tree trunks and branches and may either feed off dead tissue (saprophytic) or the living phloem of the tree (parasitic). The latter group are known to be forest pathogens and may eventually kill trees. The former are much more common and do not affect tree growth but cause only the decomposition of dead heartwood. In breaking down and hollowing out the heartwood, the fungus probably extends the lifespan of the tree as hollowed trees are lighter and more flexible, so avoiding damage in gales. Interesting brackets on oak include: the beefsteak fungus

Acorn goblet (Ciboria batschiana) on a blackened acorn from the previous season

(Fistulina hepatica) which sprouts from the base of trunks or long dead heartwood of logs from July onwards; the resinous bracket *(Ganoderma resinaceum)*; and the brilliant yellow and orange chicken of the woods or sulphur polypore *(Laetiporus sulphureus)*. Beefsteak and sulphur polypore are good edible fungi but must be harvested young to be palatable and sliced thin for grilling or frying. The best season for beefsteak is July when it sprouts from old oak logs near the Lagan, and for sulphur polypore as early as June when it erupts from oak or willow. Resinous bracket is relatively common on oak in Northern Ireland but rare in Britain. It is mildly parasitic but rarely kills trees and is a very efficient hollowing agent.

The final group I am going to mention are the cup fungi or Ascomycetes. These are generally tiny and require a practised eye to see and record. As the name suggests, most are cup-shaped and many are delicate and beautifully coloured. A very unusual and rather rare species is the yellow fan *(Spathularia flava)* which has been found growing on the ground under larch in Belvoir. More familiar and typical are the elfcups. Typically these can be relatively large in size (2-5cm) and various dull yellow, brown or blackish colours. An exception is the beautiful scarlet elfcup *(Sarcoscypha austriaca)* which grows commonly on alder branches on wet ground near the River Lagan from January to March.

There are literally thousands of species of cup fungi, mostly growing on dead wood or leaf litter in forests where they do an essential job of breaking down dead plant remains to release the nutrients back into the forest nutrient cycle. Tunbridge Ware, essentially kitchenware made from oak wood, gets its characteristic green colour from the tiny green elfcup *(Chlorociboria aeruginascens)* which stains dead oak wood a bluish-green. The equally tiny eyelash fungus *(Scutellinia crinita)* also grows on rotten wood, but this is bright red and the cup is surrounded by fine dark hairs, hence the name. Some cup fungi are not cup-shaped at all but form variously coloured spots, pustules and spheres on leaves, twigs and branches. The coral spot fungi are a case in point. Most, like the common coral spot *(Nectria cinnabarina)*, are red in colour but some are orange, including the rare Ralfs' coral spot *(Nectria ralfsii)* which grows typically on dead sycamore bark in the Big Wood. It has only been recorded from the extreme west of Britain and from Ireland. Some of these are important plant pathogens and the apple coral spot *(Nectria galligena)* will perhaps be more familiar as apple canker.

Practically every tree and shrub species has one or even a number of cup fungi which grow only on it. The alder-seed goblet *(Ciboria lentiformis)* parasitises alder seeds and appears in spring. The very similar alder goblet *(Ciboria caucus)* grows only on dead alder flowers and appears only in autumn. Oak has its own form which grows on acorns, the acorn goblet and, although not recorded for Belvoir, it is highly likely to occur there. The alder-seed goblet was first reported in the British Isles from alder woods on the north bank of the Lagan opposite the Big Meadow (in biological records this site is known as the Sculpture Meadow).[3] New species of cup fungi are still being described from the British Isles and some interesting species grow even on exotic plants naturalised in Belvoir, such as the cultivated bamboos. A grove of arrow bamboo (*Pseudosalsa japonica*) on the stream entering the Arboretum has several cup fungi not previously seen in Europe, but obscure enough to have been overlooked until now (see Appendix 6).

Grassland fungi are not well represented in Belvoir, even on the golf course and the lawns of the housing estate. The reason for this can be summed up in a word; fertilizer. The most important grassland in the Lagan Valley lies in Barnett Demesne between Malone House and the River Lagan. This has a rich flora of waxcap fungi, so-called for their brilliantly coloured fruiting bodies, and glossy caps – the whole fungus is shades of red, pink, orange, yellow or green. The grass here has been unfertilised for decades, hence its high biodiversity value. Fertiliser application often results in over-enrichment and the growth of weed grasses to the exclusion of more interesting and varied wild flowers and fungi. Enriched habitats can be rehabilitated. For example, the Big Meadow at Belvoir is cut annually and the grass removed so that, provided no fertiliser is applied, it will eventually produce a more varied and interesting flora. It is also worth noting that the common tree associates (mycorrhizae) appear much less sensitive to fertiliser and often fruit under trees on high fertility soils.

Despite the enrichment of the grasslands at Belvoir, some rare species of fungi do occur under mature trees on the golf course, including the duck brittlegill *Russula anatina* (under oak) and the swamp brittlegill *Russula claroflava* (under birch). The duck brittlegill has also been reported from oak in Barnett Demesne.[4] Doubtless there are other as yet undiscovered rarities like these in the parkland around Belvoir.

However, although overall the fungi at Belvoir are interesting (see Appendix 6), the area is perhaps less impressive than might be expected given that this is now known to be a very long-established woodland.

Most of the fungi at Belvoir are in the broadleaved woods and unimproved grasslands.

Although some notable fungi do exist under conifers, such as the earth star, which is found under Monterey cypress in the Arboretum, the worst areas for fungi are the extensive conifer plantings. These plantations of exotic trees are also poor for other flora and for fauna. In some areas of former broadleaved woodland that were cleared and planted with conifers, fungi associated with the original native woodland still linger on. For example, in a Norway spruce planting at Corbie Wood near the River Lagan, there are residual colonies of the rare mazegill *Daedalea quercina* on large oak logs. These huge logs also still yield good quantities of beefsteak fungus and colonies of the tiny cup fungus *Cudoniella acicularis*, whose fruiting bodies mimic tiny capped mushrooms. Retention and enhancement of this biodiversity is difficult if not impossible while the spruce remain, but may be possible if these are replaced by oak plantings after they have been felled.

In addition to increasing the area of broadleaved woodland at Belvoir, creating habitat for fungi should be considered in management plans for the woodland and grassland. For example, dead wood habitats could be created by retaining some or all of the fallen branches and logs of deciduous trees such as oak and beech. Standing deadwood should also be retained where possible. These provide living space not only for fungi but also for the multitude of tiny invertebrates which feed on fungoid wood, and for the birds which in turn depend upon the invertebrates to feed their young. Over-tidied woodlands are in general less interesting and biodiverse than woods with habitat piles and rotting logs. Retaining wet areas also benefits fungi, as does restricting the use of fertilisers and pesticides. Biodiversity in general also tends to decline where non-native plants are allowed to dominate the woodland floor. Mention has been made of the influence of exotic conifers. At Belvoir, the highly invasive laurel *(Prunus laurocerasus)* is a considerable problem as it sterilises the soil over large areas due to the deep shade it casts and to a phytotoxic fungus which grows in association with its root system. However, the impact of all management work in woodlands has to be carefully considered, including the control of exotic species. For example, the arrow bamboo which grows along streambanks in the Arboretum has quite interesting fungi growing on dead woody stems. Managing woodland for biodiversity is therefore not straightforward and can be expensive, especially where problems have built up over long periods.

Finally, a word to the would-be gastronome collecting fungi for the pot. It is very important to get expert instruction and on no account to collect or eat wild fungi without guidance. The best way to achieve this is to join a special interest group. The Northern Ireland Fungus Group has a very large and entertaining website (http://www.nifg.org.uk) where regular forays are advertised to observe and collect wild fungi. These trips are aimed at stimulating interest in native fungi and provide guidance on identification, with resident experts on hand to emphasise the dos and don'ts of collecting for the pot.

CHAPTER *Ten~*
SLUGS and *snails* and PUPPY DOGS' TAILS

the invertebrates of Belvoir   **Roy Anderson**

Author wielding a sweep net under oak trees in Belvoir

THE WORD 'INVERTEBRATE' probably conjures up very little to the average visitor to Belvoir. The name means 'lacking a backbone' and encompasses a wide range of creepy-crawlies including worms, slugs and snails, slaters, millipedes, centipedes, beetles, flies, wasps and bees, grasshoppers and dragonflies. Despite being small and apparently insignificant, they are important to the life of the forest and exceed just about everything else except fungi for sheer numbers of species and numbers of individuals.

I have had a life-long fascination with these animals. I remember frogspawn-collecting trips to a marshy area behind the towpath on the River Lagan at Stranmillis when the houses at Sharman Drive were being built. Frogs and newts were mixed in with lots of other things and my interests quickly expanded into a more general interest in pond life. Freshwater snails abounded in those days in ditches along the towpath and it wasn't long before molluscs in general were in the driving seat. Next came beetles, then a variety of other invertebrates and finally, in my middle age, the fungi (mushrooms). Today I retain an interest in all of these and, living in Newtownbreda, greatly value the proximity of

Belvoir where I collect regularly. This chapter summarises some of the more interesting fauna encountered over the years and hopefully will stimulate others to take an interest in what is literally 'under foot'.

Worms, slugs and snails

Life in the forest, even tiny life, moves very much with the seasons. Cold and water-saturated winter soils are more congenial to slugs, snails and flatworms than the heat and drought of summer. Forests of course provide cool shade and are an important habitat for sensitive species. The human destruction of forests has led to a widespread decline of many animals including a number of snails which evolved in wet, cool climatic conditions. These are unable to survive exposure to drying winds and the sun's heat for very long and tend to be restricted to old and undisturbed woodlands on the western fringes of Europe.

The tiny plaited snail *(Spermodea lamellata)* for example, though widespread in the British Isles, occurs on mainland Europe only at one site on the

Plaited snail (Spermodea lamellata), an old-forest (Urwald) relic species

Pyrenean glass snail (Semilimax pyrenaicus) on bracket fungus (Phlebia)

Irish yellow slug (Limax maculatus) a forest and garden scavenger from south-east Europe

north German plain and in a small area of southern Scandinavia. Even in Britain it doesn't occur everywhere and has largely disappeared from England and Wales.[1] The Irish climate suits it and it is commoner and more widespread here with about 80 sites in Northern Ireland. The English chrysalis snail, a tiny little fellow shaped like a chrysalis and with teeth in the mouth aperture, has a similar distribution and is, again, more common in Ireland than Britain.[1] Both occur in Belvoir where conditions are suitable. Trees such as oak and beech which produce durable litter are favoured and are probably essential for their survival in many areas.

The English chrysalis snail also occurs in one or two pockets of alder carr along the River Lagan. These wet woodlands are also home to a strange little mollusc, the Pyrenean glass snail (*Semilimax pyrenaicus*) which, as its name suggests, has a very fragile glassy shell and is native to the Pyrenees in western France. Its presence in Ireland is puzzling as it does not occur in Britain and opinion is divided upon whether it is a native species. It certainly does well here and has been increasing in recent years, apparently spread around by forestry operations.[2] Unlike the majority of shelled snails, it is relatively indifferent to the presence of alien conifers which tend to produce acidic ground conditions which most snails avoid. The shell is too small for its voluminous mantle so it cannot withdraw inside like most snails and at rest looks like a tiny slug. This makes it vulnerable to drying and it seems to do best in permanently wet places.

Again, because of climatic factors, Ireland is a pretty good place for slugs, something gardeners don't need to be reminded of. In Belvoir about 11 species of slug are officially recorded but a good few more (up to 19 species!) occur in nearby gardens. Most slugs adapt well to human disturbance and thrive in the mix of cultivation and hedge bottoms where there is a richer food supply than in semi-natural woods. Nevertheless, a few slugs are more fussy and need undisturbed forest conditions, rarely venturing into gardens.

The hedgehog slug (*Arion intermedius*), so-named for the tiny pointed warts or tubercles along its back, is a good example and, though common in leaf litter throughout Belvoir, is never found in gardens. The similar but larger Inishowen slug (*Arion owenii*) occurs sporadically in litter and under logs in the Arboretum. It appears to be endemic to the British Isles (found nowhere else) and was described new to science from Buncrana, Co. Donegal, as recently as 1977.[1] The Arion slugs are often called roundback slugs because they lack a keel on the back. One of the biggest is the large black slug (*Arion ater*) which is common throughout the Forest. Very recently, a few specimens of the closely similar Lusitanian slug (*Arion vulgaris = lusitanicus*) have appeared in the Arboretum. This is a notorious pest which has devastated arable crops in Europe. It is turning up all over the British Isles and is likely to do considerable damage to garden plants, unlike the large black slug, which prefers dead organic matter to fresh green plants.

Among the keeled slugs the largest native species is the ash-black slug (*Limax cinereoniger*) which favours old native woodland and minimally-disturbed environments. This has not been recorded from Belvoir. A close relative, the great grey or tiger slug (*Limax maximus*) is, however, common throughout the forest under logs and dead branches where it feeds on fungi. Unlike these strongly keeled species, the Irish yellow slug (*Limax maculatus*) has only a very short keel near the tail. This is common throughout Ireland but is local and rare in Britain.

SLUGS and *snails* and PUPPY DOGS' TAILS
the invertebrates of Belvoir

This flatworm (Kontikia andersoni), origin unknown, feeds on invertebrates in forest litter

New Zealand flatworm (Arthurdendyus triangulatus) a serious predator of earthworms

Rather appropriately, it is coloured green with large yellowish blotches. The name is deceptive, however, as it is now considered to have been introduced to Ireland from eastern Europe in the nineteenth century. Like the other keeled slugs it is predominantly a fungus or lichen feeder but in gardens and outhouses its appetite extends to the stripping of old wallpaper from damp walls and devouring odd scraps including pet food and bread or grain left for birds. The keeled slugs in general avoid consuming green vegetable matter.

Flatworms exist in much the same sorts of places as slugs but are much more primitive and lack the highly structured eyes and internal organs of the latter. Flatworm eyes are visible as tiny black dots, usually near the head end or arranged in lines around the margins of the long, flat body. Most are predatory and feed on a range of animals in forest litter from springtails to earthworms. We have only three native land-living forms, all small and retiring. Several alien species also occur. These are generally larger and more colourful and come from exotic places like the Antipodes and the South Pacific islands. Just about every garden in Belfast has the large (up to 10cm) earthworm-eating New Zealand flatworm *(Arthurdendyus triangulatus)* but a second species, *Kontikia andersoni,* is also present in Belvoir, though it is smaller, rarer and restricted to undisturbed wet places. It was described new to science from Rea's Wood near Antrim in 1981 but probably comes from the South Pacific.[3] Little is known about its feeding habits but it has been seen consuming springtails in forest litter. A similar-looking but quite different animal is the Australian land nemertine *(Argonemertes dendyi)*.[4] This conceals a sticky and barbed lassoo in its fore-parts which it shoots out by increasing the fluid pressure in its body to pinion and stick to prey. The hapless victim is then 'roped in' and swallowed. Flatworms approach their prey more slowly and attach themselves by a sticky pad near the front end. The procedure is to hang on until the victim tires, at which point the flatworm's stomach is pushed out to pour strong digestive juices directly onto the captive. The resulting pre-digested 'soup' is then lapped up at leisure. Charming creatures! All three are widespread in Belvoir.

But why are there so many alien animals you might say? Ireland has an impoverished native fauna through the destruction of its ancient fauna by a long series of glaciations. It remained attached to the European land mass for only a very brief period after the last glaciation, and the migration of fauna from Europe to recolonise the island was accordingly limited. Alien animals introduced by accident through horticulture, the garden plant trade and holidaymakers therefore find few competitors for the available food supply and have plenty of 'space' to establish themselves. Successive waves of 'colonists' from around the world, but particularly from New Zealand with its similar oceanic climate, have been reported in recent years. Some argue that these are making our impoverished fauna more varied and interesting, but there may be a hidden cost to both the environment and agriculture. There can be little doubt that the New Zealand flatworm, for instance, has damaged soils by removing vast numbers of earthworms and probably has had a knock-on effect upon native earthworm feeders.

Beetles

Moving on now from the wet and the sticky to something altogether drier and harder, not to say crunchy. Belvoir has much to offer the amateur coleopterist or beetle collector. Beetles present an almost infinite series of variations on a theme, with their great range in size and widely varying but intricately decorated protective shells, which are in fact hardened wing cases. They make nice subjects for a collection and are the most varied (biodiverse) group of animals, not just in our little island, but everywhere, with an estimated 2-3 million species worldwide. They have entered and found food sources in a bewildering range of environments including dead wood, dung, animal carcases, straw, hay, stored grain, horn, stuffed animals, textiles, carpets and even the dried dead remains of other beetles stored in museum collections. One species of spider beetle, *Gibbium aequinoctiale*, has managed to complete its life-cycle and survive for long periods on the dung of people working in mines deep underground.[5]

Beetles are prime elements in the overall biodiversity of any forest ecosystem. A group of beetles known as the dead wood fauna, or saproxiles, are intimately associated with dead wood, fungi and the whole cycle of decay and re-birth in the forest ecosystem. These are becoming endangered across Europe because modern forestry leaves little if any room for old-growth forests. Before the organised harvesting of wood by man, trees would have grown to immense size and would have been hollowed out by the activities of forest bracket fungi and associated saproxylic beetles. Such old scarred giants are no longer part of the vision of a modern forest and have been extensively culled across Europe. The demise of these plant Methuselahs has resulted in the decline of many associated animals, but particularly beetles. This has had a profound impact on the ecology of woods, to the extent that we can now measure the 'conservation value' or quality of a woodland entirely by the number and range of saproxylic or dead wood beetles present.[6]

Forest history in Ireland seems to preclude there being a lot to offer in terms of woodland biodiversity compared to other parts of Europe. Around 1800 over-population was at such an advanced state that only about three-quarters of one percent of the land area was under woodland cover – and it is likely that most of that was degraded scrub. In some areas diarists complained that even the hedgerows were cut for fuel. Evidence of the great animal and plant extinctions which accompanied this over-burden of humanity are everywhere. The native Scots pine together with many forest insects, plants and fungi have long disappeared. Even the red squirrel, so valued as an inhabitant of our woods, is a foreigner, derived from a late re-introduction from Britain. Our beetle fauna has fared no better.

The good news is that Belvoir still retains some of its primaeval fauna, though probably only a small percentage. Evidence presented in other chapters indicates that there has been a continuity of native oak on the site during the most damaging period of woodland destruction (the century preceding the Great Famine). This has probably enabled the survival of animals such as the hairy spider beetle (*Ptinus subpilosus*) which has its only known Irish site in Belvoir.[7] It occurs very sparingly under the bark of an old sycamore east of the Big Meadow, but is probably also present on oak.

Other rarities include the following which, being very small and obscure, have no individual English names, only family names:

SLUGS and *snails* and PUPPY DOGS' TAILS
the invertebrates of Belvoir

False ladybird (Endomychus coccineus), a ladybird mimic, on bracket fungus

Name	Family	Status
Adalia bipunctata	Coccinellidae – ladybirds; 2-spot ladybird	Common in and around willows in the Lagan Valley.
Scymnus auritus	Coccinellidae - ladybirds	On one large oak at the entrance to Belvoir – 2nd Irish record – first record, Charleville Co. Offaly, May 2003.
Agathidium nigripenne	Leiodidae – round fungus beetles	Rare but widespread in old woods
Coryphium angusticolle	Staphylinidae – rove beetles	Rare generally; under bark
Gyrophaena pulchella	”	Red Data Book species in Britain (pRDBK); 1 other Irish record
Homalota plana	”	3 other Irish sites; under bark
Datomicra zosterae	”	2 other Irish records; in rotting fungi
Bessobia occulta	”	1 other (old) Irish record; in rotting fungi
Cryptophagus ruficornis	Cryptophagidae – silken fungus beetles	1 other Irish site (also Lagan Valley); in fungi
Dacne bipustulata	Erotylidae – shiny fungus beetles	3 other Irish sites; in old bracket fungi
Cis bilamellatus	Ciidae – small fungus beetles	2nd Irish record; introduction from New Zealand – on dead brackets
Endomychus coccineus	Endomychidae – false ladybird	Recent colonist of Ireland from Britain
Xyloterus domesticus	Scolytidae – bark or ambrosia beetles	Scarce wood-boring beetle.

It may be seen how many of the rarer and more important species are found in and around forest fungi (mushrooms, brackets etc.). Two of these are recent arrivals in Ireland, examples, if you like, of an ancient fauna re-asserting itself. The false ladybird *(Endomychus coccineus)* is widespread in Britain and is like a rather large, but oval, ladybird. However, it has only four large black spots on a brilliant red ground, fewer and larger than in any native ladybird except the 2-spot. It probably derives protection from the ground colouration as red is a warning colour, used to train potential predators who associate it with the rather disgusting and bitter taste of true ladybirds. False ladybirds came into this country sometime prior to 1976 when the first was found at Rea's Wood near Antrim.[8] Unlike ladybirds, which feed on greenfly, these develop in fungi growing on logs or on dead branches on the ground. They now occur along the Lagan Valley and around Lough Neagh up to Castlerock on the north coast and are fairly common in Belvoir.

The 2-spot ladybird is another common species in Britain that was of very restricted distribution in Ireland and confined to the south coast. In the mid 1980s a few were found on willows at Greenmount

Orange ladybird (Halyzia sedecimguttata), a mildew feeder and quite common on trees such as sycamore

Holly weevil (Mesites tardyi) on driftwood, which is probably how it originally got to Ireland

College near Antrim and in Lagan Meadows across the River Lagan from Belvoir. Since then it has spread rapidly along the Lagan Valley and around Lough Neagh.[10] It probably came in via a mass eruption from Scotland. More mysterious is the case of the tiny ladybird *Scymnus auritus*. This has no common name but feeds on the oak aphid *(Phylloxera glabra)*. It was first discovered in Ireland when one was swept from a large oak in native woods at Charleville outside Tullamore Co. Offaly in May 2003. By an extraordinary coincidence a large colony came to light in May 2004 during a routine survey of the Woodland Trust site at the entrance to Belvoir. It was found to be common on one of the large oaks (number 2359, see Chapter 6) by the old (now abandoned) entrance to Belvoir estate.[9] It is quite possible that being small and dark (black with some red on the head and pronotum) it has simply been overlooked in Ireland. Alternatively, like the others, it could have arrived comparatively recently, and be in the process of expanding its range. There are a number of other ladybirds in Belvoir, including the pretty orange ladybird *(Halyzia sedecimguttata)* which is common on sycamore where it feeds on mildew. Most ladybirds are carnivorous, feeding on

greenfly, but the orange ladybird is an exception.

But it is not only European natives which are coming in across the Irish Sea. The small fungus beetle *Cis bilamellatus* is a New Zealand species accidentally introduced to Britain some decades ago but now turning up in Ireland. It was seen for the first time in May 2003 at Glengarriff, Co. Cork, but was found at the entrance to Belvoir Forest in April 2004 on small bracket fungi growing on a red squirrel wood sculpture! Finds like this are turning up with increasing frequency and suggest both that the spread of insects, including aliens, is increasing and that global warming may be assisting this trend. It is largely conjectural by which route alien insects enter this country. However, climatic conditions in Ireland are fast becoming tolerable to a wide range of 'international travellers'. Forest pests such as the Asian longhorn beetle *(Anoplophora glabripennis)* and the great spruce bark beetle *(Dendroctonus micans)*, which can devastate plantation forestry, are probably out there just waiting for a suitable untreated log or plant destined for a local garden centre on which to hitch a ride. In this context, the author notes with some alarm an increasing tendency to ship large wild shrubs and trees with their attached root balls from

exotic places to satisfy the garden trade. This practice has the potential for environmental devastation, as alien insects and plant diseases hitching a ride in this way can destroy native plants and animals not adapted to deal with them. The impact of the New Zealand flatworm on our earthworms furnishes a cautionary example.

The various leaf beetles and weevils recorded in Belvoir *(Chrysomelidae, Brentidae, Curculionidae*, Appendix 7) feed directly on living plants. Exceptions are the holly weevil *(Rhopalomesites tardyi)* and the New Zealand weevil *(Euophryum confine)*. The larvae of both bore into dead wood creating, in the case of the holly weevil, extensive galleries and large exit holes (about 3-5mm) through which the adults emerge. As its name suggests the holly weevil is frequently found in old holly branches but other broadleaf trees are also colonised. The smaller but similar New Zealand weevil is yet another introduction but now very common in dead conifer wood, reducing the heartwood of infested logs to a fine powder over time.

Ireland has few insects which specialise and feed entirely on living oak leaves. Entomological visitors often remark on the general scarcity of insects and

Small copper butterfly (Lycaena phlaeas), still common in fields with short vegetation

Adult cockchafer or May bug (Melolontha melolontha) on oak; the larvae feed on plant roots

the clean and undamaged leaves on oak here. However, as already seen, some interesting oak fauna still survives in Belvoir, and it may be getting more common. The tiny oak flea weevil *(Orchestes quercus)* occurs on large parkland oaks at the entrance to the Forest, and perhaps elsewhere. Though common in Britain it is scarce in Ireland with recent records in our area only for Correl Glen in Fermanagh and for Belvoir. A similar species *(Orchestes rusci)* occurs on birch in the Belvoir area while the beech flea weevil *(O. fagi)* is widespread in the Lagan Valley. The only

other beetle exclusive to oak at Belvoir is the tiny but fairly widespread oak gall weevil *(Archarias pyrrhoceras)*. A similar species *(Archarias salicivorus)* lives on willow in the forest. The ladybird *Scymnus auritus* should also be included, although it feeds on aphids rather than directly on oak leaves.

Many other types of beetle occur on oak but are not dependent upon it. In spring each year the cockchafer or May bug *(Melolontha melolontha)* makes its annual pilgrimage in search of egg-laying sites and often turns up on paths and in gardens. It has an unsteady and bumbling flight and a propensity for blundering into buildings at night to be found dazed on the ground in the morning. Its size (3-4cm) and shiny brown, whitish-hairy body set it apart. The adult feeds in and around oak trees, but females burrow in the soil to lay their eggs and this is where development takes place. The larvae or grubs feed on plant roots for about three years before pupating and emerging at the beginning of May. Hence its name, the May bug.

Showy insects – butterflies, bugs and hoverflies

The butterflies found in Belvoir are small in number but not without intrinsic interest and are obviously important from an amenity point of view.

The small copper butterfly *(Lycaena phlaeas)* breeds in the Big (Sculpture) Meadow and in Morelands Meadow and requires open conditions and short vegetation. The grazing at Morelands and the hay crop taken from Big Meadow are therefore important in maintaining the correct vegetation height to meet its requirements, or rather that of its food plant. The common blue *(Polyommatus icarus)* lives in the same area and has similar needs, but the caterpillars feed on birdsfoot trefoil.

Réal's wood white *(Leptidea reali)* occurs intermittently at the Big Meadow and is a woodland edge butterfly preferring sunny glades and pasture near woodland. It is a weak flier and avoids really exposed places, so the habitats in Belvoir probably suit it pretty well. This insect has spread throughout Ireland (from the south-west) in the not-too-distant

Réal's wood white (Leptidea reali), an Irish butterfly not found in Britain

Shield bug (Troilus luridus) feeding on a geometrid moth caterpillar

Bee mimic hoverfly (Criorhina berberina) removing pollen from its legs

past, using the railway system as a linear habitat to connect up with suitable woodlands. It is distinct from the common wood white *(Leptidea sinapis)* of Britain, a species which occurs in Ireland only in the Burren area of County Clare. The distinctiveness of Réal's wood white has only recently been recognized.[11] It does not appear to occur in Britain but is widespread, if local, near western coasts in Europe. It therefore has the distinction of being the only Irish butterfly which does not also occur in Britain. Other butterflies found at Belvoir are listed in Appendix 7.

The true bugs are a group of insects with hypodermic-needle-like mouth parts. Some species are carnivorous and the tube is used to suck out the juices of prey species. The shield bugs, so named because of their shield shape, are the largest kind of bug we have here. Most are herbivorous and live mainly in the foliage of trees and shrubs, though adults are not averse to the odd caterpillar. In Belvoir, *Troilus luridus* together with the closely related forest bug *(Pentatoma rufipes)* are not uncommon on oak. The bright green hawthorn shield bug *(Acanthosoma haemorrhoidale)* is a species more often noticed by the casual observer as it occurs commonly near

hawthorn and gives off a harsh, offensive smell if handled. Shield bugs are also known as stink bugs.

Another group of showy insects is the hoverflies. The great majority of species are bee or wasp mimics. This confers some protection against predators but the common wasp is rarely fooled by the subterfuge and may sometimes be seen on autumn flowerheads mutilating captured hoverflies. Several very local species occur in Belvoir.[12,13] The rarer forest hoverflies tend to use rot holes or the water-filled crevices at branching points in old trees for development. The larvae are aquatic and feed on decaying organic matter. So here is yet another group of animals which needs large, mature trees! A list of species is provided in Appendix 7 with the forest forms indicated. The attractive but rare bee-mimic, *Criorhina berberina,* and a peculiar green form of the uncommon wasp mimic, *Didea fasciata*, have both been seen recently in Belvoir Park Forest.

Wasp mimic hoverfly (Didea fasciata) on an umbel

Gall wasps

Everyone will be familiar with the oak apple which is seen on twigs and branches of oak in autumn. This and several other strange outgrowths on twigs and buds are the result of the activities of tiny gall wasps. Galls are common in Belvoir. Gall wasps lay their eggs on or in leaves and twigs and the larvae burrow into the living green material forcing the tree to form a knot of tissue, called a gall, around them. The inside of the gall is soft, green and

Cottonwool gall (Andricus quercusramuli) on male flowers of oak in spring

Current galls (Neuroterus quercusbaccarum) on oak leaves in spring

nutritious and provides the gall wasp larvae with food while they mature. When the time is right, the larva forms a pupa and this eventually hatches to produce an adult wasp. The wasp eats its way out of the gall to mate with others of its kind and to lay the new season's eggs.

Last year (2003) saw a bumper crop of common spangle galls *(Neuroterus quercusbaccarum)* with their tiny flat discs on the underside of oak leaves. Spangle galls have an asexual generation in spring called the currant gall. Also found was a species not previously seen in the area, the knopper gall *(Andricus quercuscalicis)*. This forms a strange

helmet- or hat-shaped outgrowth on the sides or base of infected acorns. It was first noted in the Belfast area about 1990 by Reg Maxwell, Area Manager for Parks in Belfast City Council, on oaks in the City Cemetery. It is apparently restricted to *Quercus robur*, the pedunculate oak, and does not occur on the sessile oak *(Q. petraea)* which is the commoner of the two in Ireland. It appears to have been introduced from southern Europe and colonises new areas via the Turkey oak *Quercus cerris*, which is scattered thinly across Belvoir. The infestation of acorns in 2003 was so severe that unaffected acorns were scarce and oak germination virtually ceased. Jays, which depend heavily upon acorns for food in the autumn, were forced to scavenge outside the Forest boundaries to survive. In spring 2004, there appeared to be a major crop of the spring generation of the spangle gall *(N. quercusbaccarum)* which is very different from the autumn generation and, as noted previously, is called the currant gall. This forms on the leaves and male flowers of oak. With it on male flowers in 2004 was the much rarer cottonwool gall *(Andricus quercusramuli)*. The cottonwool gall wasp was first recorded in Ireland as recently as 1993 from Co. Meath.[14] It is local in Britain and probably more

so in Ireland. The Belvoir record is a first for Northern Ireland.

This finishes our brief tour of invertebrate life in Belvoir. An impression may have been given that we know everything of importance about the fauna, but this is certainly not the case. New finds continue to be made several decades on from my own first visit to the forest and doubtless will continue for some time to come.

Belvoir is an important site for woodland invertebrates and includes some species indicative of ancient woodland. It is difficult to assess objectively its value compared to woodlands elsewhere in the Lagan Valley and further afield, mainly because it has been more intensively studied than anywhere else. However, present evidence suggests that it is very important.

CHAPTER *Eleven-* Birds of *Belvoir* PARK Chris Murphy

Feeding time on the Lagan towpath near Stranmillis

IN 1984 I CAME FROM SAFFRON WALDEN to work for the Royal Society for the Protection of Birds at their office in Belvoir Park Forest. After a few years we bought a house in Belvoir on the edge on the forest and I had a 15 minute walk through the trees to the office without seeing even a road, which I thought was a great way to start the day. Even though I have changed jobs and we have outgrown the house we are having difficulty in moving away from Belvoir because we love the forest so much.

A day does not go past without our seeing something of interest. Today, my wife Doris saw at least 250 frogs in the old canal by the lock-keeper's house. At this time of year, early March, they gather in ditches and ponds to mate. A highlight for me today was finding a mealy redpoll, probably the only one in Ireland; it breeds in Scandinavia. At the moment near our house we have about 300 lesser redpolls, 50 goldfinches, siskins, a cock brambling and a cock blackcap. Two buzzards were overhead a few minutes ago and birds like ravens and sparrowhawks are here almost daily. It is fantastic. Lots of rare birds have been clocked up here at our little kitchen window. In winter the forest regularly

features on Flightline, the bird news service for the latest sightings in Northern Ireland. A feature of this winter (2004-2005) has been the big flock of waxwings. We have had up to 200 at the front or back of the house and yesterday they were in the larches nipping off new needles. The larch plantation is a very good habitat for birds.

We have many blackbirds in the back garden; I saw 24 together last winter. Also last winter one day there were 14 robins together on the lawn. They are normally aggressive and territorial and they were getting worked up about seeing each other. However, finally they worked out that all the other birds were feeding and they stopped being so aggressive and got on with business of survival, eating.

Here on the edge of the forest, birdlife is much richer than in the centre of the housing estate. However, this winter most of the waxwings have been along Belvoir Drive, feeding on cotoneaster berries or fly-catching from treetops. I have seen crossbills coming down to drink at the pond near the entrance to the forest. In summer, swifts, swallows and house martins are constantly overhead. There is a noisy house sparrow roost in a cordyline, a non-native tree also known as a cabbage palm, on Belvoir

Waxwings at Belvoir, on trees at the motte and feeding on rose hips

Drive. Nearby, at Belvoir Park Primary School, the children put out food for birds. They attract blackbirds, robins, blue tits, great tits, coal tits, long-tailed tits, greenfinches and chaffinches. These birds are all great to watch. They are mainly attracted by the proximity of the larch plantation and beyond the larches the mixed deciduous woodland, the very old oak trees, big sycamores and beeches. There are also playing fields, meadows, the River Lagan, the old canal and little streams. Across the river is the Lagan Meadows Nature Reserve. We have a fantastic range of habitats within a few kilometres. Belvoir Park Forest is part of the Lagan Valley Regional Park which acts as a natural corridor for migration in spring and autumn.

Although I am writing about birds, I have to say something about the red squirrels. My family has always looked out for them in the garden. We are very upset at the loss of the reds since the greys appeared. I absolutely loathe and detest grey squirrels. I first saw red squirrels here in the summer of 1986 and they have been constantly on view from our kitchen window right up to June of last year, 2004. We had six different red squirrels coming to our feeders every single day. We could recognise each

of them by their different shades and shapes, perhaps a tatty tail, a dark tail or fluffy blond tail, long pointy ears, bitten off or chewed ears. We had names for them – fluffy, scruffy, blondie and the like. They are such attractive animals. However, since last July I have not seen any of these six individuals. All we see now are grey squirrels with just an occasional timid red putting in brief appearances. In this part of the forest I think there are just two reds left. We try to discourage the greys but they are very persistent.

Most winters the larches in Belvoir Park Forest attract large numbers of finches, especially siskins and redpolls, and every four years or so these delightful birds arrive in exceptional numbers. Ten years ago we had 500 redpolls, possibly the largest flock in the British Isles at the time. Crossbills can also come in numbers, sometimes as many as 200; one year we had such a flock every day from June until November. There is also a phenomenal population of coal tits in the forest. About 15 years ago I saw two coal tits with yellow cheeks and yellow napes. They are an extremely rare Irish race. One was stunningly yellow, the other a little less striking.

Buzzards may well breed here sometime in the future. They are now the most common bird of prey

in Britain and are doing very well in Ireland. In the early 1990s a pair of goshawks spent a month in the area. These big birds are very sensitive and did not stay to breed. The smaller birds of prey are more tolerant of humans and sparrowhawks are breeding just at the back of our house. The male, which has a beautiful blue-grey back and orange cheeks, was calling to his mate from a treetop three days ago. There are several pairs breeding in Belvoir Park. They have short, broad wings and a long tail. They dash through our garden or along the edge of the forest causing panic among small birds. Invariably you first hear the long-tailed tits and coal tits, they warn other birds with a high-pitched alarm call. A few seconds later you glimpse the hawk weaving through the trees. Sometimes right in front of you it pounces on a blackbird or starling, then stares at you with its bright yellow eyes before carrying it off to a favourite plucking post. Kestrels pass by occasionally but don't breed in the forest. The other breeding bird of prey is the long-eared owl. Again there are several pairs and you can hear them in the middle of the night in late winter and early spring. They make a single drawn out hoot, not the too-wit too-woo of the tawny owl. The female makes a long, low note similar to a

Great tit

Blue tit

collared dove when it lands. They also make a distinctive clap with their wings as part of their display flight. However, they are very secretive, strictly nocturnal and you have a much better chance of seeing one in June when the young are calling for food. They sound like a rusty gate creaking in the wind and often you can see these birds before dark. They feed on wood mice, rats and birds plus the occasional bat or frog. I know of five pairs of long-eared owls within three kilometres of this house.

Barn owls were last seen in Belvoir around 1990 and within the last 10 years nested in nearby Edenderry. They may return to Belvoir one day.

A feature of winter is the gathering of rooks and jackdaws on the playing fields by the Activity Centre on Belvoir Drive. It is a great spectacle and such a clamour. During the day these fields can appear white with gulls then at dusk turn black with crows. They roost in several parts of the forest and across the river in the trees around the Lagan Meadows, but they first gather for their evening chat on the playing fields of Belvoir. The jackdaws and rooks roost together, about 5,000 in total. This is possibly the biggest roost in Belfast. They don't breed here. There is also a roost of magpies in the larches by the Big Meadow. My son, Tim, counted 50 last winter, which is a high count for magpies.

When I started birding here 20 years ago the blackcap was a scarce summer visitor. Today it is the most abundant warbler in the forest. Its beautiful song is one of the dominant sounds of summer; it is the nightingale of the north. Increasingly, it is also becoming a winter visitor as the blackcaps of Denmark, Germany and other parts of northern Europe do not all migrate south to the

Mediterranean. A lot now come to Northern Ireland especially where there are gardens with bird tables. Here they can find food to survive the cold months then get back to their breeding sites sooner, which gives them an advantage. There was a male blackcap in our garden yesterday, it will soon be leaving; our breeding birds do not arrive until early April.

Another success story concerns the jay, a colourful member of the crow family that is now widespread and numerous. Crows just seem to love Ireland! The largest member of the crow family is the raven, they sometimes croak from the electricity pylon near Belvoir Close and may be prospecting for a future nest site, perhaps in one of the big conifers at Ardnavally. At present their nearest nest sites are at Cavehill and in a quarry a few kilometres from Belvoir. The only crow that is not doing well in Northern Ireland is the chough, which is reduced to just one pair at the Giant's Causeway.

Along the Lagan there are kingfishers which nest in holes they excavate in the river bank. The hole is about one metre long and at the end six or seven eggs are laid in an enlarged cavity. Many people look out for the kingfisher but never see it. In some parts of the world kingfishers can be very tame but

Jay

here they are shy, secretive birds. They hear you coming and as you get within about 50 metres they are away, fast out of sight. You know they are around because they nearly always make a high-pitched whistle. All the birds that live by rivers, including the wagtails and dippers, have penetrating calls, probably so they can be heard above the sound of rushing water. To get a good look at a kingfisher you need binoculars. Scan the bank-side vegetation, look ahead, think ahead, do not make yourself obvious when you approach a bend in the river. They do most of their fishing early in the morning, long before the first joggers, and then retire somewhere quiet for the rest of the day.

Herons fish all along the Lagan and regularly fly over Belvoir. They are generally hunting eels, though they will take anything, a rat or a frog, even a moorhen or little grebe. There are records of a heronry in Belvoir[1] and they may nest here again one day. The nearest heronry I know of is at Campbell College, where a few pairs remain. You can also often see them on the islands in Victoria Park. Herons are less tolerant of people than cormorants which will often sit still as you walk by. I sometimes see cormorants at the mouth of the Minnowburn, just

upstream from Shaw's Bridge. They are big, black birds typically sitting on a bit of exposed mud or swimming low in the water.

Another bird to look out for between Stranmillis and Shaw's Bridge is the grey wagtail which nests in old walls and bridges. Dippers nest along the Minnowburn. They like fast-flowing streams where they walk along the riverbed turning over little stones in their search for food.

Some of the commoner waterbirds you will see along the river between Stranmillis and Belvoir are mallard, little grebe and moorhen. In autumn you may see tufted duck, pochard, coot and great crested grebe. I have seen scaup here and on one memorable day in September 12 years ago a drake ferruginous duck, a rare visitor from south-eastern Europe.

Occasionally you will see mute swans on the river but they do not nest at Belvoir. They do regularly fly over the forest maybe commuting between the Waterworks or Victoria Park and Ballydrain Lake in Malone Golf Club or Willis's Lake in Upper Malone. We once found a whooper swan on the Lagan that was injured, tangled up with fishing line. Sometimes greylag geese graze on the fields by Belvoir Drive. They are feral birds rather

than truly wild and most likely come from Victoria Park or Kiltonga.

Galwally Lake is a good site for ducks. In harsh weather it can be full of pochard, tufted duck, mallard and teal as well as coot, moorhen and little grebe. Around the edges of the lake you can sometimes see water rail, heron and kingfisher. This tiny pond is very rich in birdlife. There has been a problem with sewage pollution in the stream entering Galwally Lake and indeed all of the waterways in Belvoir at times suffer from pollution. This obviously

Cormorant on the River Lagan at Belvoir

Jackdaws and rooks gathering at Lagan Meadows as dusk

impacts on invertebrates and fish which in turn makes these areas less attractive to birdlife.

Although some species of birds are increasing, others are not. Many species are having to change their habits. Some are moving into cities where there might still be natural habitats like the Lagan Meadows, which is full of snipe. However, those species that cannot adapt, the specialists, will disappear. Within the last 20 years the corncrake, partridge and corn bunting have become extinct in Northern Ireland. The problem is rapid change in farming practices. Farmland can no longer support the range of species that it used to. Lapwings, partridges, snipe, yellowhammer, cuckoo, linnet and tree sparrows, very common birds that my father grew up with in the fields around Newry, have now disappeared from much of the Irish countryside. Fields are so heavily fertilized that they are just bright green grass that can support little more than cows and crows. Much of our countryside is now dreadfully boring, just a grass factory. We need to leave aside ponds for mallard and moorhen, old grassland where barn owls can hunt mice and species-rich meadows for cuckoo and skylark.

The best way to see birds close-up is to put out food and water. Anywhere in Belvoir you could attract up to 20 species with the right mix of food. Apples for thrushes; ground peanuts for robins, dunnocks and long-tailed tits; whole peanuts in a feeder for greenfinches, goldfinches, siskins and coal tits. Keep the cats away and don't put out so much food that some is lying overnight. Hang up the feeder and most of the other food should be on a bird table, though blackbirds, robins and dunnocks prefer to feed on the ground. If you want to learn more all you need is an identification book and some binoculars. Speak to RSPB at their office in Belvoir Park Forest or ask a birdwatcher for advice. Pick up a good quality pair of binoculars second-hand; they will last for years. Try to learn the different bird calls. Belvoir is a great place for birding with one of the richest varieties of forest birdlife in Ireland. When you visit remember that you will hear much more than you see. Stop frequently and listen carefully. Enjoy.

Galwally Lake

CHAPTER *Twelve-*
The mammals of *Belvoir* PARK Peter Cush

IF YOU LIVE IN SOUTH BELFAST, the Lagan Valley Regional Park is on your doorstep. The Lagan Towpath stretches from Stranmillis all the way to Lisburn and beyond. A short distance along the towpath from Stranmillis, it passes along the edge of Belvoir Park Forest with the river between the walker and the woodland. This woodland edge is a good place to view the wildlife which inhabits the forest and the adjoining river and wetland areas. Less than 2km will take you to a wooden footbridge, the Belvoir Bridge, which links the towpath to Belvoir Park Forest.

Having lived in South Belfast now for close on 25 years I have regularly taken this walk. Since the Belvoir footbridge was opened in the mid 1990s, several circular walks are now possible through Belvoir returning to the towpath either at this footbridge or upstream at the Red Bridge by the old lock-keeper's cottage. As the seasons change these walks throw up new things to see and, depending on the time of the year and the time of day, there are opportunities to observe all kinds of plants, birds and – if you are lucky enough – mammals.

Wildlife is close to most people who live in Belfast. From the moment you go outside anywhere in the city you are likely to encounter nature. It may be a sparrow chirping in your backyard, the ferns growing from a wall where a drainpipe has leaked or the numerous birds and plants in parks and gardens. Belvoir, however, has a remarkable range of wildlife considering that it is so close to Belfast city centre. I am going to describe some of the mammals I have come across. It is by no means an exhaustive account, but I hope it may encourage you to watch out for mammals when you are out and about in the area. If you are already interested in mammals my sightings may encourage you to look more closely and maybe to send in your records to CEDaR (http://www.habitas.org) at the Ulster Museum.

Of Ireland's 29 species of land mammals around 18 regularly occur in Belvoir Park Forest. Unlike birds, which are generally conspicuous as they fly in and above the trees of the forest, mammals are much more secretive. In fact most of the species frequenting Belvoir and its surrounds are nocturnal. Even those mammals which are regularly in the forest by day are generally very shy and tend to stay under cover. To see a mammal as you walk through the forest is therefore a fairly rare event but any sighting can be very exciting and memorable.

Feeding badgers in a back garden at Malone

If you keep your eyes open, sooner or later you will almost certainly see some species of mammal. You can also look out for their tracks, the remains of what they eat, their burrows and other signs made by them as they move around, find their food and make their homes. As with birds, you are especially likely to see mammals if you are walking late in the evening or very early in the morning. Around Belvoir Park Forest you are likely to come across a fox, red or grey squirrels, an occasional rat and the odd rabbit. You will almost certainly see bats during the summertime if you are out in the evening and, believe it or not, you also stand a good chance of seeing the very shy and elusive otter.

The range of mammal species found in Belvoir forest now is somewhat different to that found in the days when the estate was private land managed for farming and shooting. Thus you are unlikely nowadays to see what one young lad reported around the 1850s. He put his hand into a magpie nest and was bitten by a pine marten! The late C. Douglas Deane, who knew the estate, its history and wildlife, recalled this story in an article in the Belfast Telegraph.[1] In this article he also mentions another early reference to mammals in Belvoir – in 1858 a gamekeeper shot a Leisler's bat. This had been only the second Irish record for this species. Birds and bats are now protected by law and the cause of death, which I will later describe, of a Leisler's bat in 2003 was as prey of a sparrowhawk and not as a result of being shot by a gamekeeper.

One mammal which is still fairly common in Belvoir but is very rarely seen is the badger. If you look carefully you can find the pathways they make in the forest. Sometimes you might come across bundles of dry or fresh grass lying on paths or at the entrances to setts. Some people whose gardens are close to or adjoin Belvoir Park Forest see badgers almost nightly because they feed them. Leaving out food such as peanuts or general food scraps is virtually certain to attract badgers if your garden is close to their regular foraging routes. They forage widely and their staple diet consists of earthworms, which they find in fields and other areas of grassland. It is a depressing fact that badgers are sometimes illegally hunted; the badgers are dug out of setts and then killed by powerful fighting dogs. If you find evidence of badgers in Belvoir, keep the knowledge of the location to yourself and keep an eye out for signs of anybody disturbing them. If you do see something

illegal or suspicious report it to your local police station.

For anyone leaving out food for badgers at night in gardens near or adjoining Belvoir the chances of also attracting a fox are excellent. In Belvoir Park Golf Club golfers catch sight of foxes around the greens where they are probably hunting rabbits. Foxes are expert at making use of cover and therefore you have a better chance of seeing them in more open country rather than in woodland. In spring and summer when they have cubs, the adults are often searching for food and can be active for periods throughout the day. In the late winter months, and especially during early January, foxes

Red squirrel at the feeder at Belvoir car park

can become very vocal. This is the time that they mate and their screams and shrieks can be heard at night as they call to attract mates and warn off rivals. This is a species which is probably more common now than it was in the days when the Belvoir estate had gamekeepers. In those days, every gun would have been turned against the fox.

Of all the mammals found in Belvoir, bats, despite being nocturnal, are the most noticeable and obvious provided one is out late in the evening or very early in the morning in spring and summer. It is their flight in open spaces which makes them obvious, as is the squeak they emit which can be heard by a lot of people but not by everybody. The younger you are the more likely it is that you will be able to hear them. In and around the forest and along the towpath at Belvoir, bats can be seen at dusk, dawn and throughout the night hunting for insects above and through the trees. Bats hunt at night not only to avail of the bountiful supply of insects, particularly moths, but also to avoid predators, mainly day-flying birds of prey. This fact was well illustrated one night in early April 2003 when I saw a sparrowhawk in rapid pursuit of a Leisler's bat hunting over the Lagan at the edge of

Belvoir Park Forest just before dusk. The hawk followed every twist and turn of the bat's flight and eventually succeeded in seizing it in its talons. The bat emitted a very loud squeak as the bird's talons gripped it. The sparrowhawk then flew into some hawthorn bushes where it proceeded to eat the bat. I watched it for a few minutes before it flew off into the trees of Belvoir Park Forest, still carrying the remains of the bat in its talons.

The sparrowhawk, a true hawk species, and the kestrel, which is a species of falcon, are both prone to hunting late in the evening. Any bat which ventures out too early in the evening over the river to avail of the insect prey massing above the water is in great danger from an agile hunter such as a hawk or falcon. Thus, the unfortunate bat caught by the hawk that evening on the River Lagan will not be passing its genes on to the next generation. Perhaps an evolutionary trend among some bats of being up in the early evening is constantly being suppressed by birds of prey who like to stay up late at night!

If you stand on the Belvoir bridge just as it gets dark, you may be lucky enough to see a number of bats hunting low and silent over the water. If they are flying in all directions and criss-crossing each other's

path as if performing in a bat ballet, then it is most likely that they are Daubenton's bats, sometimes called water bats. This species specialises in this low, silent, criss-crossing flight pattern. I have often observed these bats feeding late in summer evenings below both the Belvoir and Red Bridges and in sections of the river between the bridges. Sometimes up to 20 bats can be seen in a group feeding a few inches above the water. Their aerial ballet is a beautiful sight to behold and one can only marvel at their agility and supreme mastery of the air as they flit past each other, occasionally disturbing the water as they pick insects off the surface.

A large bat flying high and strong in a fairly defined flight pattern above the trees or along the edge of a row of trees is most likely to be a Leisler's bat. However, bats are difficult if not impossible to identify in flight unless the observer is an expert or is using a bat detector. With this instrument it is possible to detect the high-pitched sounds which the bats make as they echo-locate. The sound emitted by the bat and the signal frequency are characteristic of the particular species. Bat species likely to be observed in and around Belvoir Park Forest are pipistrelles, Leisler's, long-eared and Daubenton's.

The long-eared is the easiest bat to identify since its ears are nearly the same size as both its head and body.

Even if you don't know the species of bat you are observing, they are always interesting to watch. If you walk through Belvoir and along the towpath regularly, you will start to notice that bats will often follow the same flight paths each evening, especially if weather conditions are similar. When the weather changes the bats modify their hunting behaviour, for example by using lower flight paths or flying in more sheltered air at the leeward side of tree clumps where insect prey has gathered.

The otter is a shy and elusive mammal and is mostly nocturnal. Most people imagine that you have to go to wild lonely places on the coast or on upland rivers to see them, but if you are lucky enough you may encounter one in the River Lagan at Belvoir. In fact, if you want to see one it is just as likely you will see it in Belfast as anywhere else provided you keep your eyes open for the unexpected. A good place to look for signs of otters is the stretch of the River Lagan between the Belvoir Park Forest office in the courtyard and Morelands Meadow. Otter tracks are frequently seen in mud banks of the little stream which runs into the River Lagan from Belvoir near the motte.

I have seen an otter on more than one occasion crossing the towpath from the Ulster Wildlife Trust Nature Reserve in the Lagan Meadows and sliding down the bank into the River Lagan. A sighting is most likely at dusk when it is starting to get fairly dark. I saw glimpses of two otters last summer (2004) late in the evening moving through the stretch of canal between Lagan Meadows and Morelands Meadow towards Belvoir Bridge. They were splashing about in ponds and moving through wet vegetation in the bed of the disused canal. Forest Service staff working in Belvoir have regularly reported sightings of otters near the Red Bridge, including one sighting of four otters.

On a spring evening in late April 2003 I had my best-ever view of an otter when I was out for a walk with my wife. We were walking down the towpath towards Stranmillis at about 8pm when, at the side entrance to Lagan Meadows opposite the sewage works, we spotted an otter swimming close to the near bank of the river. At first glance we thought it was a dog, but we quickly identified it as an otter by its graceful and sinuous movement in the water.

It was a very bright evening and we were absolutely delighted to see the animal in such good light and for such a long time. We walked slowly along the towpath as the otter moved in a graceful and leisurely manner downstream. As it swam, dived and came up for air, it left trails of bubbles rising to the surface. It appeared quite relaxed despite people passing with dogs and it left the river a number of times to move through riverside vegetation on the far bank. In all, we watched the animal for about five minutes. It entered the river for the final time just at the old Belvoir demesne boundary wall and swam, submerging a number of times, as far as the small stream which joins the Lagan from the direction of Galwally wood and lake. Here it left the river and moved up the stream towards the houses at the bottom end of Hampton Park and Galwally Avenue before disappearing from sight. We were left stunned and

Otter

Red Squirrel

astonished that we had been able to watch such a wild and beautiful animal for so long so close to the city of Belfast. Don't rule out the unexpected. It is amazing what is about.

The red squirrel is another mammal which you have a good chance of seeing in broad daylight in Belvoir. The best place to look is probably around the carpark at the Forest Service buildings or in the Arboretum. The squirrels sometimes take food out for the birds and at times they are fed by Forest Service and Lagan Valley Regional Park staff. The person I most associate with the red squirrels at Belvoir is Norman Taylor who, until he left Northern Ireland a few years ago, used to photograph the squirrels from a hide he made in the forest.

Residents do not remember seeing squirrels at Belvoir in the 1960s and 1970s. They came in the mid-1980s when the conifer plantations had developed. However, red squirrels are now under threat from greys, a North American species introduced into Ireland in County Longford in 1911. In the past few years greys were occasionally reported around Belvoir Park Forest and in 2004 they were spotted in the southern end of the forest and sometimes in the housing estate. On one occasion a grey was noted running along the wall between the estate and the Belvoir dual carriageway, and on two occasions a grey was observed near the motte. However, by the summer of 2005, greys had become common around the car park and Arboretum, in the centre of the forest. The future of the red squirrel population in Belvoir is now a matter of concern to the many people who want to see this population remain and thrive.

The story of the interaction of the red and grey squirrels is not as simple as the grey driving the red out, but in general when the greys appear the reds disappear and find it impossible to retain a foothold. This is the situation that has developed in England and Wales, with the reds absent from most of their former range. The main tactic for trying to conserve the red squirrels in Northern Ireland is to safeguard their main strongholds, which are mainly in conifer plantations. In fact, the non-native conifer plantations which exist in Belvoir actually give the reds a better chance of surviving as they can utilise the limited food supplies in this type of woodland better than the greys. What a sad loss for Belvoir Park Forest and the people of Belfast if the red squirrel population were to disappear.

The rat is one mammal which you are very likely to see if you keep your eyes on the water's edge anywhere along the River Lagan in Belvoir. They are often seen moving along the riverbank with great agility, seldom getting their feet wet. They are, however, expert swimmers and I have regularly seen them crossing the width of the Lagan. Rats also dive and swim well underwater, to keep out of sight of predators and to seek food. They occur throughout Belvoir Park Forest but are seen most frequently near the river or near to any place where there is edible waste. Most people do not like rats, but fortunately for humans their numbers are kept in check not only by the amount of food available, but also by the hunting activities of the resident long-eared owls, day-flying birds of prey and mammal predators such as the fox and stoat.

Stoat

The mammal which is probably the easiest to identify is the hedgehog, although it is not that common in the Belvoir woodlands. You are more likely to come across a hedgehog in your garden if you live in Belvoir housing estate. Hedgehogs find food and shelter in gardens, and compost heaps are a favourite feeding and hibernating area.

Stoats live in Belvoir but are rarely seen. The most common way of encountering one is by chance as it sprints across open ground to cross a path. They are small brown animals about nine inches to a foot (20-30cm) long with a black tip to the tail. The body is about the same diameter as the shaft of a garden spade and the way they move will also give them away. Stoats take leaps as they cover open ground and progress along in a series of bounds. A rat, on the other hand, runs with its body close to the ground and its movement is very flat compared with the stoat whose sinuous movements and suppleness is very distinctive. The Irish stoat is a subspecies found only in Ireland and the Isle of Man. A family of stoats has recently been reported feeding at Shaw's Bridge car park and around the Minnowburn.

Long-tailed field mouse

Another mammal species which is sometimes reported along the Lagan at Belvoir is the mink, although I have never seen one in 25 years of walking the Lagan at this location. Although not direct competitors, the presence of otter on this stretch of the river may keep the mink in check or ensure that they do not linger for long. American mink were first 'farmed' in Ireland in the 1950s and unfortunately were soon escaping into the wild. They are predators of the young of water birds such as the moorhen, coot and mallard and will sometimes kill adult birds as well as small mammals, frogs and fish.

The long-tailed field mouse is almost certainly the most common mammal in Belvoir Park Forest. Conversely it is also the one that most people are least likely to see! It is because this animal, although very common, is almost exclusively nocturnal. The long-eared owl is its main nocturnal avian predator but this tiny little animal is also pursued by a host of other predators both furred and feathered, so it is no wonder that it is very reluctant to appear in daylight! Even those who don't like mice often think it a very pretty animal when seen up close. The only sure way of ever seeing one is to use a trap

Pigmy shrew

like a Longworth trap which is commonly used by mammalogists. It will capture but not harm small animals.

The pigmy shrew, the only shrew species found in Ireland, is widespread in Belvoir but very seldom seen. It hunts both by day and night and is a ferocious predator, mostly of insects. Your best chance of encountering a pigmy shrew is to listen for its high-pitched squeaking and twittering as it hunts or encounters another shrew. If you hear this high-pitched sound in grass as you walk woodland paths, stop, look, keep listening and you might be lucky. Even close up you may not see the animal since it is so small and tends to stay under cover. However, come the autumn you are very likely to come across dead pigmy shrews on woodland paths. They are unmistakable, being absolutely tiny, weighing on average only about five grams and measuring only about two inches (50mm) in length with a tail about three quarters of that length again and a long thin snout. Incidentally, cat owners generally have a very good idea of the local small mammal fauna since their pets regularly bring home trophies such as pigmy shrews and mice of various species and present them triumphantly to their owners.

137

The house mouse is a mammal which lives up to its name. It is rarely found far from human habitation and in fact some populations on islands die out if the island becomes uninhabited, such is the dependence of the species on man. However, house mice are regularly found in fields and hedgerows especially in spring and summer.

Rabbits are not that common in the Belvoir area, possibly never really recovering from the myxomatosis epidemic of the 1950s. When the Belvoir estate was in its heyday and actively managed for game birds such as pheasant, the control of predators would have helped rabbits to survive in much greater numbers than they do now. The mixed agriculture practised in former days would also have provided more food and suitable habitat for their survival. Rabbits are not a woodland species, preferring to live in clearings and grassland and bramble areas adjoining woodland. The best chance of seeing rabbits in Belvoir is along the golf course. Douglas Deane, in his book *The Ulster Countryside*, referred to an advertisement of 1792 concerning the removal of a rabbit warren at Belvoir.[2] Here rabbits had probably been protected and bred for their pelts and for food.

Hares would also have been common at one time in the estate when the countryside was more open, predators were controlled and there was less disturbance. Hares disappeared from Belvoir a long time ago and they were last seen at the Lagan Meadows in the 1960s. The Irish hare is now a priority species for conservation in Northern Ireland. It is not a woodland species but prefers to live in the open, preferably in meadows or arable fields. The large numbers of domestic dogs which are taken for walks in the Belvoir area are a deterrent to any reintroduction of the hare into the grassland areas.

The most unusual mammal I ever saw in the Belvoir area was, believe it or not, a seal! Not for the first time a common seal made its way up the River Lagan from Belfast Lough in 2004 and climbed up the Stranmillis Weir, which separates the tidal salty water of the estuary from the freshwater river. At least one of these crossings was captured on video by the Department of Agriculture and Rural Development Science Service camera used to record the movement of salmon and sea

trout up the river. I saw this particular seal as far upstream that year as Morelands Meadow! Two days later I saw the same individual making short work of a fairly large salmon in the stretch of river near Annadale a few hundred metres above Stranmillis weir!

What about the future for Belvoir mammals in the 21st century? The range of mammal species found will depend on the use to which the land is put by man, the kind of woodland, the extent of woodland cover and the amount and type of grassland and wetland. The mammal fauna of Belvoir has changed over the years and will probably continue to change. The quality of the natural environment will be critical. If there is clean water, clean air and a range of natural or semi-natural habitats, then the mammal fauna will reflect this. The growth of the urban area will have an impact, though many mammals have the ability to live close to man in gardens, parks and farmland.

It is almost certain that the bank vole, first found in Ireland in 1964 and Ireland's only vole species, will eventually reach Belvoir and add to the mammal fauna found there. Perhaps with a rapidly

Irish hare

expanding deer population in Northern Ireland, some species of deer will reach and inhabit the forest. Global warming will have an effect so far unknown and the impact of the accidental introduction of other alien species to Ireland will also be hard to predict. The natural world is continually evolving and changing and that is why studying and observing mammals is so fascinating. If your interest has been aroused by what you have read here and you want to learn more about mammals found locally or in the Belfast area and beyond, the internet now provides easy access to information via such sources as the Ulster Museum Website. There are some excellent books on the mammals of Ireland by James Fairley, who is one of Ireland's foremost mammalogists, and another good source of local information is Robert Scott's recent excellent book *Wild Belfast: on safari in the city*.[3] However, there is nothing quite like the buzz of excitement and joy you will get when you see a wild creature in its natural state. Good luck with your mammal watching in Belvoir and remember to keep your eyes open. You will be surprised at what you see.

Author and family on mammal watch in Belvoir Park Forest.

The largest girthed oak at Belvoir. Tree 2453.

References and Notes

Appendices

Picture Credits

Chapter One

1. Reeves-Smyth, T. (1997) Demesnes. In: Aalen, F. H. A., Whelan, K., Stout, M. (Eds). *Atlas of the Irish rural landscape.* Cork University Press, Ireland.

2. Dooley, T. (2001) The decline of the Big House in Ireland. Woolfhound Press, Dublin.

3. Packenham, V. (2000) *The big house in Ireland.* Cassell paperbacks, London.

4. Anon (2000) *Biodiversity in Northern Ireland.* Recommendations to Government for a Biodiversity Strategy. HMSO, Belfast.

5. Planning Service (1999) *Planning Policy Statement 6 (PPS6). Planning, Archaeology and the Built Heritage.* Department of the Environment Northern Ireland.

6. Planning Service (2004) *Draft Belfast Metropolitan Area Plan 2015.* Department of the Environment Northern Ireland.

7. Reeves-Smyth, T. (1997) The natural history of demesnes. In: Foster, J. W. and Chesney, H. C. G. (Eds) *Nature in Ireland.* The Lilliput Press, Dublin, Ireland

8. Terrence Reeves-Smyth *Pers. Comm.* 2005

9. Kelly, D. L. and Kirby, E. N. (1982) Irish woodlands over limestone. In: White, J. (Ed). *Studies on Irish vegetation.* Royal Dublin Society.

Chapter Two

1. Anon (1966) *An Archaeological Survey of County Down.* HMSO, Belfast

2. MacAnally, D. (1982) *Belvoir Park. A Background History.* Forest Service, Department of Agriculture.

3. Reeves, W. (1847) *Ecclesiastical antiquities of Down, Connor and Dromore.* Hodges and Smith, Dublin. p. 15.

4. O'Laverty, J. (1880) *An historical account of the diocese of Down and Connor.* M. H. Gill, Dublin. Volume 2 pp. 222-223.

5. Green, E. R. R. (1949) *The Lagan Valley.* Faber and Faber, London.

6. Greeves, J. R. H. (1960) North Down at the end of the 16th century. *Belfast natural history and philosophical society* **5**: 5-15.

7. Tomlinson, R. (1997) Trees and woodlands of County Down. In: Proudfoot, L. and Nolan, W. *Down history and society.* Geography publications.

8. Owen, D. J. (1921) *History of Belfast.* W & G Baird Ltd, Belfast pp. 55-56.

9. Chart, D. A. (1942) The break-up of the estate of Con O'Neill, Castlereagh, County Down. *Proceedings of the Royal Irish Academy* **48**: 119-151.

10. Carleton, T. (1976) Aspects of local history in Malone, Belfast. *Ulster Journal of Archaeology* **39**: 62-69.

11. Barry, J. (1982) *Hillsborough. A parish in the Ulster Plantation.* William Mullan and son, Belfast.

12. Anon (1993) *Hillsborough Castle.* Ulster Architectural Heritage Society. W&G Baird, Antrim

13. Anon (1939) *Burke's genealogical and heraldic history of the Peerage.* Burke's Peerage Ltd, London. p. 2437.

14. Rev. Charles Ward of Mountpanther, Co. Down, and Michael Ward of Castleward, Down, esq., to Arthur Hill of Dublin esq. 7 May 1722. Lease for a year, with intent that a release follow, of the lands of the town and lands of Ballylenaghan. Public Records Office Northern Ireland D/778/58. Michael Ward had acquired the townland from the Hamilton family on his marriage to Anne Catherine Hamilton. See Public Records Office Northern Ireland D/778/49 and D/778/54.

15. Final Concord. Arthur Hill of Dublin, Charles Wardde of Mountpanther, Co Down, Clerk, Michael Wardde of Castleward, Co Down and Catherine his wife. June 1722. Clwyd Record Office, Ruthin, Denbighshire. DD/BK/I/111.

16. William Johnston of Belfast esq to Arthur Hill of Bellvoir, Co Down. Bargain and sale of lands in Co. Down 9 November 1731. Public Records Office Northern Ireland D/778/68a.

17. Samuel Hill of Strangford Co Down, Gent, to Arthur Hill of Belvoir, Co Down. Release of lands and rent-charges by way of mortgage for £1,890 28 June 1773. Public Records Office Northern Ireland D/778/79A.

18. Michael Merrifield of Dublin, gent. to Arthur Hill of Bellboy, County Down esq. 12 May 1732. Public Records Office Northern Ireland D/778/71.

19. Dobbs, R. (1683) Description of the County of Antrim. In: Hill, G. (1873) *An historical account of the Macdonnells of Antrim.* Archer and Sons, Belfast.

20. Bigger, F. J. (1925) Old Knock-Breda. Belfast News-Letter April 18 p.10.

21. Deane, C. D. (1976) Demesne spelt death to a village. News Letter February 7 p. 5.

22. Wood, R. E. (1987) *Set on a Hill. The story of Knockbreda Parish Church.* University Press, Belfast.

23. Reported in - Robb, C. J. (1955) Site for Ulster Folk Museum? Belvoir Park. Belfast News-Letter November 14 p.4. and Robb, C. J. (1959) Belfast's first greenhouse. The Irish News and Belfast Morning News, July 30 p.4. The original source of this information is not known.

24. Map of County Down by Oliver Sloane, 1739. Copy in Public Record Office, Northern Ireland. T/1763/2.

25. Harris, W. (1744) *Ancient and present state of County Down* A. Reilly, Dublin.

26. Copy will of Ann Lady Viscountess Dowager Midleton. 10 July 1746. Clwyd Record Office, Ruthin, Denbigshire Record Office. Reference DD/BK/I/336.

27. Deane, C. D (1983) *The Ulster Countryside*. Century Books, University Press, Belfast. p. 73.

28. Advertisement in the Belfast News-Letter 4 September 1753 p. 2.

29. Delany, M. G. P. (1861) *The autobiography and correspondence of Mary Granville*. R. Bentley, London.

30. Willes, E. (1990) *The letters of Lord Chief Baron Edward Willes to the Earl of Warwick, 1757-1762*. Edited by James Kelly. Boethius Press, Aberystwyth.

31. To the rear of Knockbreda Church is a gravestone inscribed - HEARE LYES THE BODY OF IEAN SUTHERLAND & CHIELD WIFE TO KENNETH SUTHERLAND GARDNER AT BELVOIR WHO DEPAIRTED THIS LIFE JUNE THE 17 1776 AGED 25. The wording is given (slightly incorrectly) in *Journal of the Irish Memorials Association* 11: 1921-1925 p.150.

32. Death notice for John Lomas in Belfast News-Letter 29 January 1771 p. 2.

33. See note in Belfast News-Letter 1759 February 20 p. 2.

34. Johnston-Liik, E. M. (2002) *History of the Irish parliament 1692-1800*. Ulster Historical Foundation, Belfast.

35. Death notice of Viscount Dungannon. Belfast News-Letter February 8 1771 p. 2. The text of the Dungannon plaque in Knockbreda Church reads as follows – SACRED TO THE MEMORY OF ARTHUR 1ST VISCOUNT DUNGANNON OBT JANY 31ST 1771

HE WAS THE 2ND SON OF MICHAEL HILL ESQR OF HILLSBOROUGH IN THE COUNTY OF DOWN AND BROTHER OF TREVOR VISCT HILLSBOROUGH IN 1727 HE WAS ELECTED ONE OF THE REPRESENTATIVES IN PARLIAMENT FOR THE COUNTY OF DOWN ON THE 6TH OF APRIL 1754 HE WAS APPOINTED CHANCELLOR OF THE EXCHEQUER IN IRELAND IN 1759 HAVING SUCCEEDED TO THE ESTATES OF HIS MATERNAL GRANDFATHER SIR JOHN TREVOR OF BRYNKINALT IN THE COUNTY OF DENBIGH NORTH WALES AND KNIGHTSBRIDGE IN THE COUNTY OF MIDDLESEX SOMETIME SPEAKER OF THE HOUSE OF COMMONS AND MASTER OF THE ROLLS IN THE REIGNS OF KING WILLIAM III AND QUEEN ANNE HE ASSUMED THE NAME AND ARMS OF TREVOR AND IN 1765 WAS RAISED TO THE PEERAGE

HE MARRIED IN 1737 ANNE DAUGHTER OF EDWARD FRANCIS STAFFORD ESQR OF BROWNSTOWN COUNTY OF MEATH AND BY HER WHO DIED AT HAMPTON COURT JANY 12TH 1799 HAD ISSUE AN ONLY SON AND TWO DAUGHTERS ANNE WHO MARRIED GARRETT EARL OF MORNINGTON BY WHOM SHE HAD ISSUE RICHARD MARQUIS WELLESLEY AND ARTHUR DUKE OF WELLINGTON AND PENOLOPE PRUDENCE MARRIED TO CHARLES POWELL LESLIE ESQR OF GLASSLOUGH IN THE COUNTY OF MONAGHAN

IN MEMORY ALSO OF HIS ONLY SON THE HONBLE ARTHUR TREVOR BORN DECR 24TH 1738 DIED JUNE 10TH 1770 HAVING MARRIED FEBRUARY 27TH 1762 LETTITIA ELDEST DAUGHTER OF HARVEY VISCOUNT MOUNT MORRIS WHO ON THE 3RD OF JULY 1774 REMARRIED WITH RANDAL WILLIAM 6TH EARL OF ANTRIM AND HAD ISSUE ARTHUR 2ND AND LATE VISCOUNT BORN OCTOBER 2ND 1763 AND HARVEY JOHN BORN IN 1767 AND DIED THE FOLLOWING YEAR

THIS TABLET IS ERECTED BY THEIR ONLY SURVIVING REPRESENTATIVE AND LINEAL DESCENDANT ARTHUR PRESENT AND 3RD VISCT DUNGANNON IN THE PEERAGE OF IRELAND AND ONE OF THE REPRESENTATIVES IN PARLIAMENT FOR THE CITY OF DURHAM WHO SUCCEEDED TO THE TITLE AND ESTATES OF HIS ANCESTORS DECR 14TH 1837

36. Anon (1852) Birthplace and infancy of the Duke of Wellington. Belfast News-Letter September 24 p. 2.

37. Cansdale, P. (1949) The victor of Waterloo spent happy boyhood days at Belvoir Park House. Belfast Telegraph January 6 p. 4.

38. Kernohan, J. W. (1920) Iron Duke and Belfast. Belfast News-Letter January 31. Annadale is briefly described in an advertisement for the sale of the house in the Belfast News-Letter March 2 1819 p. 1.

39. Death of Arthur Trevor. Belfast News-Letter June 26 1770 p. 2.

40. Advertisement. Belfast News-Letter December 4 1772 p. 3.

41. Advertisement Belfast News Letter December 30 1783-January 1784 2 p. 3.

42. Bigger, F. J. (1926) Belvoir Park. Belfast's finest and most historic mansion. Belfast News-Letter October 1 p. 7

43. Agnew, J. (1998) *The Drennan-McTier Letters*. 1776-1793. Irish Manuscripts Commission Dublin. Volume 1. pp. 273, 313.

44. Anon (1796). The ball at Belvoir. The News Letter January 4-January 8 p. 3.

45. Anon (1796) The ball at Belvoir. The News Letter January 8-January 11 p. 3

46. Lloyd, J. E. and Jenkins, R. T. (1959) *The dictionary of Welsh biography down to 1940*. B. H. Blackwell, Oxford.

47. Hurdsman, C. N. (1996) *A history of the parish of Chirk*. Bridge Books, Wrexham.

48. Advertisement in The News Letter September 5 to September 9 1796 p. 3. His previous agent in Belfast, Edward Kingsmill, had died earlier in the year (see note in the Northern Star 1796 July 4-9 p. 2)

49. 1 September 1796. Lord Dungannon, Belvoir (Belfast) to Lord Downshire asking for a commission as a magistrate of County Down for (Cortland) Skinner, his agent. Public Records Office Northern Ireland D/607/D/145.

50. Kernohan, J. W. (1919) Belfast and suburbs. Creation of Belvoir Park. Belfast Telegraph October 10 p. 6.

51. Agnew, J. (1999) *The Drennan-McTier Letters* Irish Manuscripts Commission, Dublin. Volume 2 p. 300.

52. Wood, R. E. (1987) *Set on a Hill. The story of Knockbreda Parish Church.* University Press, Belfast. p. 115.

53. Hoare, R. C. (1807) *Journal of a tour in Ireland.* W. Miller London. p. 226.

54. Agnew, J. (1999) *The Drennan-McTier Letters* Irish Manuscripts Commission Dublin. Volume 2 p 696 and Volume 3 p.18.

55. Letter from Davin Ker, Belfast to David Ker, Junior, London dated 20 August 1808. Public Records Office Northern Ireland. D/2651/2/178. Transcription seen, original missing.

56. Advertisement in Belfast News Letter on January 10 1800 p. 3.

57. Advertisement in Belfast Commercial Chronicle 1808 for February 17 p. 2.

58. Advertisement in Belfast Commercial Chronicle 1808 July 30 p. 3.

59. Advertisement in Belfast Commercial Chronicle 1808 September 19 p. 1.

60. Advertisement in Belfast Commercial Chronicle 1808 October 5 p. 3.

61. Arthur Trevor, Viscount Dungannon of the first part John Gilles, Robert Davis and William Blacker of Belfast, Merchants of the second part. Cortland Skinner of Belvoir, Esq. of the third part (1808). Lease for a 1,000 years by Viscount Dungannon to Cortland Skinner. Public Record Office Northern Ireland D/778/576.

62. Arthur Trevor, Viscount Dungannon of the first part John Gilles, Robert Davis and William Blacker of Belfast, Merchants of the second part. Cortland Skinner of Belvoir, Esq. (1809) Renewal of lease for 1,000 years. Public Record Office Northern Ireland D/778/582.

63. Arthur, Viscount Dungannon; Charlotte, Viscountess Dungannon; George, Lord Southampton; and Major General Charles Fitzroy to John Gilles, Robert Davis and William Blacker of Belfast, merchants. (1809) Conveyance of the mansion house of Belvoir and of parts of Ballylenaghan, Bredah and Galwally. Public Record Office Northern Ireland D/778/583.

64. Anon (1810) Downpatrick Assizes. Belfast News-Letter April 3 p. 4.

65. Advertisement in the Belfast News Letter on April 9 1811 p. 3.

66. Conveyance dated 12 August 1811 between William Blacker, Robert Davis and Robert Bateson. There was also a conveyance of Newtownbreda estate dated 8 July 1817 between The Right Honourable Arthur Lord Viscount Dungannon to Robert Bateson Esquire. Copies deposited in Public Records Office, Northern Ireland.

67. Advertisement in Belfast News Letter on Tuesday May 28 1811 p. 3.

68. In Knockbreda Church a number of memorials to the Bateson family can be seen and behind the organ can be glimpsed a memorial to Thomas Bateson of Orangefield who died in 1811 and his wife Elizabeth who died 1810. In the churchyard there is a monument with the following inscription - In memory of THOMAS BATESON of ORANGEFIELD Esq[r] who departed this life the 9th of Oct. 1791 Aged 86 Years. Also MARGARET his Wife, Who died the 31st of July 1775 Aged 38 Years. RICHARD BATESON their Second Son died the 1st July 1783 Aged 28 Years.

69. Abstract of the title of the Right Honourable Robert Wilfrid Baron Deramore to an estate for life in the mansion house and demesne lands of Belvoir. Copy deposited in Public Records Office, Northern Ireland. It is interesting to note that the Bateson family did not initially acquire the entire walled demesne and that in the southwestern part of the demesne there was a second residence, called Derramore or Derrymore. This house was presumably built by members of the Dungannon family. The history of this house lies outside the scope of this publication. For further information see - Valuation of Derrymore House for Sir Robert Bateson (1823), Public Record Office Northern Ireland T3786. Agreement dated 20 August 1823, Sir Robert Bateson with Lawson Annesley, merchant. Copy deposited in Public Records Office, Northern Ireland. Counterpart lease dated 5 March 1824, Sir Robert Bateson with Lawson Annesley, merchant. Copy deposited in Public Records Office, Northern Ireland. See also references to this house in - Molloy, J. and Proctor, E.K. (1983) *Belfast scenery in thirty views.* Published in 1832. Reprinted by Linenhall Library, Belfast with a commentary by Fred Heatley and Hugh Dixon. A detailed map of the Dungannon land around Milltown dated 1827 is in the Public Record Office, Northern Ireland. D/1954/6/17.

70. Lewis, S. (1837) *A topographical dictionary of Ireland.* S. Lewis and Co. London.

71. Anon (1846) *Parliamentary gazetteer of Ireland.* A. Fullarton and Co. Dublin, London, Edinburgh.

72. 'An old fogey' (1923) Belvoir and the Batesons. Northern Whig and Belfast Post. April 4 p. 4.

73. Anon (1860) Rambles by road and rail. *Irish Farmers' Gazette.* **19**: p. 627.

74. For example Robert Bateson was a Vice President of Belfast Academical Institution and a Governor of the Belfast Lunatic Asylum (Belfast News-Letter July 13 1830, March 23 1861)

75. Youatt, W. (1856) *Cattle; their breeds, management and diseases.* R. Baldwin, London. p. 186.

76. Anon (1877) Short horns in the North. *Irish Farmers' Gazette* **36**: p. 75-76.

77. Robert Bateson was a member of the 'Royal Society for the promotion and improvement of the growth of flax in Ireland,' the 'Chemico-Agricultural

Society of Ulster' and the 'Royal Agricultural Society of Ireland.' The Ulster Museum has a silver salver inset with medals awarded to Sir Robert Bateson by the North Eastern Agricultural Society.

78. Anon (1830) Ireland. *Gardener's Magazine.* **6**: 495-496.

79. Day, A. and McWilliams, P. (1991) *Ordnance Survey Memoirs of Ireland.* **7**: Parishes of County Down 11. 1832-4, 1837. Institute of Irish Studies, Belfast.

80. Catalogue of paintings at Belvoir Park, 1865. A copy has been deposited in the Public Record Office, Belfast

81. Anon (1839) Tremendous Hurricane in Belfast. Belfast News-Letter January 8 p. 2.

82. Anon (1839) The late hurricane. Additional intelligence. Belfast News-Letter January 15 p. 1.

83. Robb, C. J. (1955) Site for Ulster Folk Museum? Belfast News-Letter November 14 p. 4.

84. Drummond, J. (1854) Notes on a few country seats in the counties Down and Antrim. *The Scottish Gardener.* **3**: 207-211, 341-345, 379-385.

85. Anon (1863) Death of Sir Robert Bateson, Bart. Belfast News-Letter April 22 p. 3.

86. Anon (1863) Funeral of Sir Robt. Bateson, Bart. Belfast News-Letter April 29 p. 2.

87. Dunlop, D. (1868) *A memoir of the professional life of William Barre Esq.* James Magill, Belfast.

88. Anon (1852) The Lord Lieutenant's visit to the North. Belfast News-Letter September 6 p. 4.

89. Anon (1867) Arrival of Lord Lieutenant in Belfast. Belfast News-Letter October 2 p. 3.

90. Anon (1883) Sir Stafford Northcote's visit. Belfast News-Letter October 3 p. 7.

91. Anon (1885) Viceregal visit to the North. Weekly Northern Whig September 12 p. 5.

92. Anon (1885) Viceregal visit to Belfast. The Belfast News-Letter September 10 p. 8.

93. Anon (1877) Sir Thomas Bateson, BART., M.P. and his tenancy. The Downpatrick Recorder June 2 p. 2

94. Anon (1877) Address to Sir Thomas Bateson. Downpatrick Recorder June 2 p. 2.

95. Anon (1885) Lord Deramore. Belfast News-Letter November 18 p. 5.

96. Anon (1885) Lord and Lady Deramore. The Down Recorder December 5 p. 3.

97. Anon (1890) Death of Lord Deramore. Belfast News-Letter December 3 p. 5.

98. Anon (1890) Funeral of Lord Deramore. Belfast Weekly News December 13 p. 4.

99. 'Chichester' (1966) Belvoir green belt is such a change from city bustle. Belfast Telegraph February 8

100. Deane, C. D. (1976) Demesne spelt death to a village. News Letter February 7 p. 5

101. Deane, C. D. (1977) Save the sanctuary. Newsletter December 31 p. 5.

102. Anon (1900) Advertisement for auction. Belfast News-Letter October 10 p. 1.

103. Lease. The Right Honourable Robert Wilfrid Baron Deramore to Walter Henry Wilson. Mansion House and Demesne of Belvoir County Down. 1st November 1900. Copy deposited in Public Records Office, Northern Ireland.

104. 1901 census. Public Record Office Northern Ireland MIC 354/3/47

105. Anon (1904) Death of Mr Walter H. Wilson. The Belfast News-Letter May 16.

106. Release. The Right Honourable Robert Wilfrid Baron Deramore to John Kinahan and Henry P. Harland. 3rd May 1907. Copy deposited in Public Records Office, Northern Ireland.

107. Anon (1907) Visit to Belvoir Park dairy. Northern Whig. November 1 p. 8.

108. Anon (1907) Model Belfast dairy. Belfast weekly Telegraph November 9 p. 9. The dairy was not listed in *The Belfast Directory* after 1912.

109. Anon (1919) Belvoir Park sold. Belfast Telegraph January 4 p. 6.

110. Mr Jack Agnew (son of David Agnew), Belvoir Park. *pers. comm.* 2004.

111. Mr Eric Wishart (son of James Wishart), Newtownbreda. *pers.comm.* 2004.

112. Suggested sites for houses of parliament. Public Record Office Northern Ireland FIN 18/1/273

113. 'An old fogey' (1923) The Governor's town house. Northern Whig and Belfast Post April 4 p. 4.

114. Cabinet Meeting of 14 August 1923. Public Record Office Northern Ireland CAB/4/85.

115. Belvoir Park. County Down. Proposed residence for Governor of Northern Ireland. National archives, Kew, London. WORK 27/15. Copies of key maps and the lease for James Johnston have been deposited in the Public Records Office, Northern Ireland.

116. Anon (1918) Advertisement for auction. Belfast News-Letter May 21 p1. A catalogue of the 1918 auction is held in the library of Trinity College, Dublin.

117. Anon (1923) Notice of auction at Belvoir Park. Belfast News-Letter October 25 p. 1. A catalogue of the auction is held in the library of Trinity College, Dublin.

118. Anon (1924) Late Sir James Johnston. Northern Whig and Belfast Post May 2 p. 4. His gravestone, to the rear of Knockbreda Church, reads - JOHNSTON In memory of THE RT. HON. SIR JAMES JOHNSTON.WHO DIED 13th APRIL 1924. ALSO HIS WIFE JEANNE, WHO DIED 28th MAY 1942

119. Anon (1925) President entertains members at Belvoir Park. The Northern Whig and Belfast Post. July 27 p. 11.

120. Anon (1925) Belvoir Park. *Proceedings and Annual Report of the Belfast Naturalists' Field Club for 1925* pp. 381-382.

121. Mr Guy Taylor, Ravenhill Park *pers. comm.* 2004 and Silvia Christie, Church Road, Castlereagh *pers. comm.* 2004 remember that Ardnavally house was built by a Miss Duffin. Her niece, Mrs Margaret Hart, was a frequent visitor. Subsequently the house was lived in by Colonel Frank Byers. The house seems to have been used by the American Consul since the 1940s (see reference 37) and was purchased by the American Government as the Consul's residence in 1963. The grounds surrounding the house were sold in the mid 1970s to the Scouts and for the Belfast Indoor Bowls Club.

122. Anon (1929) Golf. Belvoir Park. Belfast Newsletter June 17 p. 3.

123. Indenture dated 7 August 1934 between the Right Hon. Robert Wilfred Baron Deramore to Messrs J & W Stewart (London & Belfast) Limited. Copy deposited in Public Records Office, Northern Ireland.

124. Anon (1934) Growth of Belfast. Belvoir Park Estate. Big scale scheme of development. Belfast Telegraph June 28 p. 3.

125. Anon (1934) Important Belfast development. Northern Whig and Belfast Post. June 27 p. 7.

126. Ernest Wood, Newtownbreda, *pers. comm.* 2003.

127. Dr C. Field, Malone, *pers. comm.* 2003.

128. Mrs Tilly Martin (daughter of Mr Chesney), Newtonbreda. *pers. comm.* 2004.

129. The last person to be buried in the graveyard is thought to have been Lizzie Finlay in 1928 (Berkley Farr, Crossgar *pers. comm.* 2004) or perhaps Micky Taylor, a lock keeper at the second locks, buried at Breda graveyard in about 1925-1927 (Albert Allen of Stranmillis *pers. comm.* 2004).

130. Bigger, F. J. (1925) Old Knock-Breda. Belfast News-Letter April 18 p. 10.

131. Cassidy, W. (1939) The Ulster rector who was tried in a hayloft. Belfast Telegraph August 5. p. 8.

132. Anon (1951) Raid on peer's vault by Belfast thieves. Belfast Telegraph August 13 p. 7. The vault may have previously been broken into during the War. See memories of David Coburn, Chapter 3.

133. Tilly Martin, Newtownbreda. *pers. comm..* 2004

134. Mr Jack Agnew, Belvoir Park. *pers. comm.* 2004

135. Clifford Fairweather, Miltown. *pers. comm.* 2003

136. Dr C. Field *pers. comm.* 2003

137. Anon (1945) *Planning proposals for the Belfast area.* Interim report of the Planning Commission. Cmd. 227. HMSO, Belfast.

138. Belfast Corporation Parks and Cemeteries Committee, 10/1/1946. Public Records Office Northern Ireland LA/7/11AA/6.

139. Belfast Corporation Council meeting 1/2/1946. Public Record Office Northern Ireland LA/7/2EB/171.

140. Anon (1950) Admiralty give up lease of 400-acre Belfast estate. Belfast Telegraph August 25 p. 7.

141. Cecil Kilpatrick *pers. comm.* 2003

142. Clifford Fairweather, Miltown. *pers. comm.* 2003

143. Jim Wishart, Markethill. *pers. comm.* 2004

144. It proved impossible to keep the children out even when an outbreak of typhoid was traced to a stream at Belvoir. See Anon (1954) Typhoid warning in Belfast. Belfast Telegraph July 7 p. 1. and Anon (1955) Typhoid germs in Belvoir Park stream. Newsletter June 9 p. 3.

145. Deane, D. (1956) Belvoir Park must have an 'X' certificate. Belfast Telegraph 26 September p. 4

146. Anon (1953) The lovely grounds of Belvoir may end as another town. Belfast Telegraph December 4 p. 5.

147. Clifford Fairweather, Miltown. *pers. comm.* 2003

148. Anon (1950) Council to take over park. Belfast Telegraph September 18 p. 7.

149. Anon (1952) Belvoir Park as memorial to King. Belfast Telegraph February 11 p. 3.

150. Anon (1952) *Planning proposals for the Belfast area.* Second report of the Planning Commission. Cmd. 302 HMSO Belfast. See also Belfast Telegraph (1952) Map of proposed housing areas outside of Belfast. April 11 p. 4.

151. Anon (1952) Council to acquire Belvoir Park. Belfast Telegraph April 8

152. Anon (1953) £5,000,000 plan for houses at Belvoir Park. Belfast Telegraph May 7.

153. Anon (1954) Housing Trust to build on Belvoir estate. Belfast Telegraph October 12.

154. Anon (1955) Sale of Belvoir Pk. In final stages. Belfast Telegraph January 6 p. 7.

155. Conveyance between J & W Stewart (London and Belfast) Limited, The Right Honourable Stephen Nicholas Baron Deramore and Northern Ireland Housing Trust. 16th April 1955. Copy deposited in Public Records Office, Northern Ireland.

156. Anon (1959) New homes in stately setting. Belfast Telegraph July 27 p3.

157. Anon (1961) Stormont query on Belvoir Park purchase. Belfast Telegraph December 13 p. 8.

158. Anon (1962) Trust tenants take over from the Earl. Belfast Telegraph July 21 p. 6.

159. Anon (1963) New town rises on former estate of an Earl. Belfast Telegraph November 15 p.10.

160. Kennedy, J. (1964) Stewart and Partners to sack their 600 workers. News Letter April 24 p. 1.

161. Anon (1963-1964) *Northern Ireland Housing Trust 19th Annual Report.* p. 13.

162. Andy McFall, Belvoir Park *pers. comm.* 2004. Andy worked as a joiner for Unit Construction at Belvoir.

163. Anon (1954-1955) Northern Ireland Housing Trust 10th Annual Report. pp. 12-13.

164. Anon (1960) Estate plans altered-to save a tree. Belfast Telegraph April 6 p. 8.

165. Bardon, J. (1982) *Belfast an illustrated history.* Blackstaff Press, Belfast p. 268.

166. Maurice Williamson, Boys' Brigade *pers comm* 2003 and information from Belvoir residents.

167. Northern Ireland Housing Trust to Boys' Brigade. Lease dated 11 August 1970. Copy deposited in Public Records Office, Northern Ireland.

168. Cecil Kilpatrick *pers. comm.* 2003.

169. Anon (1960) Estate plans altered – to save a tree. Belfast Telegraph April 6 p. 8.

170. Initially in an indenture dated 6 June 1961 two areas of land were leased, one centred on the house and arboretum, the other in the SW of the demesne. Subsequently the area between these two sites, centred on the Big Meadow, was leased in documents dated 3 November 1978 and 21 December 1979. There is also an additional lease dated 20 November 1983 that concerns the same land as the 1961 lease. Information from Forest Service files.

171. Cecil Kilpatrick *pers. comm.* 2003.

172. Information from Forest Service and Douglas MacAnally, *pers. com*, 2003.

173. Cecil Kilpatrick *pers. comm.* 2004.

174. Information supplied by Forest Service.

175. 'Chichester' (1966) Belvoir green belt is such a change from city bustle. Belfast Telegraph February 8

176. Anon (1976) Down in the forest a tree that promises to sprout gold. *Ulster Commentary.* October p. 7.

177. Forest Service records.

178. Drake, M. (1981) Bonfire lumberjacks for the chop – warning. Belfast Telegraph July 8 p. 3.

179. Hunter-Blair, P. (1995) Belvoir Park Forest: case study of an existing woodland. In: Hodge, S. J. *Creating and managing woodlands around towns.* Forestry Commission handbook 11.

180. Anon (1955) Hopes of an Ulster Folk Museum soon. Belfast News Letter November 11 p. 3

181. Robb, C. J. (1955) Site for Ulster Folk Museum? Belfast News Letter November 14 p. 4.

182. Anon (1956) Second Sacrifice. Belfast Telegraph May 10

183. Anon (1961) Souvenirs of Belvoir. Belfast Telegraph February 21 1961 p. 3.

184. Information from Forest Service

185. Photographs were carried in the Belfast Telegraph February 18 1961 p. 1, February 20 p. 4. Northern Whig and Belfast Post February 20 1961 p. 1. Belfast News-Letter February 20 1961 p. 5, p. 8.

186. Cecil Kilpatrick *pers. comm.* 2003.

187. Anon (1953) N.I. sewerage scheme will cost £275,000. Belfast Telegraph June 25 1953 p. 5. More recently, a fracture in the sewer pipe also gave rise to concern see -Whitsitt, A. (1989) Bailiff urges new body to police Lagan pollution. Belfast Telegraph 20 April.

188. The gate lodge is figured in Anon (1966) *Archaeological Survey of County Down* Government of Northern Ireland HMSO Belfast.

189. Building Design Partnership (1969) *Belfast Urban Area Plan* Volume 1. Ministry of Development. Belfast.

190. Anon (1977) Another Lagan bridge on way? Belfast Telegraph April 5 p. 1.

191. Anon (1978?) *Belfast Urban Area Plan. Review of transportation strategy.* Statement by the Department of the environment for Northern Ireland. HMSO, Belfast. See Appendix 3, Strategic schemes abandoned.

192. Anon (1987) *Belfast Urban Area Plan 2001.* Department of the Environment. HMSO Belfast.

193. Watson, D. (1978) Battle to save forest park from planners. Belfast Telegraph 24 March p. 1.

194. Duffy, G. (1987) Objections to Belvoir proposal growing: RSPB. Belfast Telegraph 23 July p. 2.

195. McDowell, L. (1992) Conservation Campaign: activists fight new road proposal. Belfast Telegraph January 16 p. 10.

196. Anon (1992) Hopes high that this beauty will survive. Belfast Telegraph October 2 p. 16.

197. Wallace, L. (1992) Years of work at Belvoir nature reserve. The Star August 2.

198. McTear, I. (1994) DoE cancels plans for Belvoir road. Belfast Telegraph December 8 p. 7.

199. Northern Ireland Ministry of Health and Local Government (1963) *Belfast regional survey and plan: recommendations and conclusions.* Cmd 451. HMSO, Belfast.

200. Anon (1966) *Report of the Ulster Countryside Committee.* Parliament of Northern Ireland HMSO Belfast. p. 9.

201. Building Design Partnership (1967) *Belfast Urban Area. Lagan Valley Country Park.* Sigma Services, Belfast.

202. Anon (1970*) Report of the Ulster Countryside Committee.* Parliament of Northern Ireland HMSO Belfast. p. 14.

203. Anon (1975) The people and the new park. The Star July 25 p. 4.

204. Indenture dated 9 July 1913 registered 2 August 1913 book 48 no. 180. The Right Hon. Robert Wilfred Baron Deramore and others to The Trustees for the Better Equipment Fund of Queen's University, Belfast. Copy deposited in Public Records Office, Northern Ireland.

205. Conveyance and Assignment dated 4 December 1986 CA. 1644/CQ. Department of the Environment for Northern Ireland to Belfast City Council. Copy deposited in Public Records Office, Northern Ireland.

206. 'The Roamer' (1951) Bird Sanctuaries. Newsletter 27 July p. 4.

207. Joe Furphy *pers. comm.* 2003.

208. Anon (1982) Ulster oak is focus for schools contest. News Letter May 26.

209. Anon (1982) *Seventeenth Report of the Ulster Countryside Committee* HMSO, Belfast.

210. Simon, B. (1999) Carving a woodland future. *Irish Forestry* **56**: 63-68.

211. Department of the Environment Northern Ireland (1993) Lagan Valley Regional Park Local Plan. HMSO, Belfast.

212. Warnock, S. (1996) Lagan Valley Regional Park Management Strategy. Environment and Heritage Service, Belfast.

213. Warnock, S. (1996) Lagan Valley Regional Park Action Programme. Environment and Heritage Service, Belfast.

Chapter Three

1. Wilson, A. (1951) This village had a social service 50 years ago. Belfast Telegraph February 22 p. 4.

2. Anon (1908) *Catalogue of a loan exhibition of Japanese art kindly lent by Mr. Alec Wilson.* Ulster Museum, Belfast.

3. O'Byrne, C. (1946) *As I roved out: a book of the north.* Irish News, Belfast

4. Wilson, A. (1950) *Fragments that remain.* Multiplex Duplicating, Stroud, Gloucester.

Chapter Four

Botanical notes kindly provided by Reg Maxwell, Belfast City Council.

1. Cut leaved beech. *Fagus sylvatica* 'Asplenifolia' This tree has reversions to *sylvatica*, a feature sometimes of the cultivar. It is not very stable. Tree probably planted around 1860s to 1880s.

2. *Abies koreana*

3. *Chamaecyparis lawsoniana* 'Wisselii'

4. *Libocedrus decurrens*, now *Calocedrus decurrens*. From western north America. Introduced 1853.

5. *Chamaecyparis lawsoniana* 'Aureovariegata' This has scattered patches of yellow-cream foliage. *Ca.* 1868.

6. Only observed in spring, before it flowered. It is probably *Rosa longicuspis* or *Rosa filipes* 'Kiftsgate'

7. *Acer pseudoplatanus* 'varigatum' ?

8. *Thuja plicata* 'gracilis'?

9. *Acer pseudoplatanus* 'Simon-Louis Frères'?

10. *Acer platanoides* 'Schwedleri' ?

11. Lawson cypress cultivars including 'Lutea' and 'Pottenii'

12. *Acer pseudoplatanus* 'Leopoldii'

13. *Acer pseudoplatanus* 'Nizetti'?

14. A tall birch with cream to pink bark, on the slope of the hill near the wooden bridge, is *Betula ermanii*

15. Identified by Forest Service as a natural cross between *Chamaecyparis nootkatensis* 'Lutea', Nootka cypress and *Cupressus macrocarpa*, Monterey cypress and is now known as X *Cupressocyparis leylandii* 'Robinson Gold'

Chapter Five

1. Tate, R. (1863) *Flora Belfastiensis: the plants around Belfast with their geographical and geological distribution*. Phillips, Belfast.

2. Stewart, S. A. and Corry, T. H. (1888) *A flora of northeast Ireland*. Macmillan and Bowes, Cambridge.

3. *Proceedings and Annual Report of the Belfast Naturalists' Field Club*. Various years in the second half of the 19th century to mid 20th century describe outings to Belvoir.

Chapter Six

1. Anon (2005) *Champion Trees. A selection of Ireland's great trees.* Tree Council of Ireland. Cabinteely House, Cabinteely, Dublin.

2. Reed, H. (1999) *Veteran Trees. A guide to good management.* English Nature, Peterborough.

3. Loudon, J. C. (1844) *Arboretum et Fruticetum Britannicum.* Longman, Brown, Green and Longmans, London. Volume 1 p. 115, Volume 4 p. 2590.

4. Anon (1889) Belvoir Park. *Annual report and proceedings of the Belfast Naturalists' Field Club* p. 101.

5. Anon (1919) Belvoir Park sold. Belfast Telegraph January 4 p. 6.

Chapter Seven

1. Baillie, M. G. L. (1982) *Tree-Ring Dating and Archaeology.* Croom-Helm London p. 274.

2. Pilcher, J. R., Baillie, M. G. L., Schmidt, B. and Becker, B. (1984) A 7272-Year Tree-Ring Chronology for Western Europe, *Nature* **312**: 150-52.

3. Baillie, M. G. L. and Brown, D. M. (1995) Some Deductions on Ancient Irish Trees from Dendrochronology. In: Pilcher, J. R. and Mac an tSaoir, S. (Eds.) *Wood, Trees and Forests in Ireland.* Proceedings of the Royal Irish Academy, Dublin pp. 35-50.

4. Baillie, M. G. L. (1995) *A Slice through Time: dendrochronology and precision dating.* Routledge, London.

5. Owen, D. J. (1921) *History of Belfast.* W. & G. Baird, Belfast.

6. McCracken, E. (1971) *The Irish woods since Tudor times.* David and Charles, Newton Abbot.

7. Joy, H. (1817) *Historical collections relative to the town of Belfast.* George Berwick, Belfast.

8. Benn, G. (1877) *A history of the town of Belfast.* M. Ward and Co, Belfast

9. Carr, P. (1993) *The Night of the Big Wind.* White Row, Belfast

10. Briffa, K. R. and Matthews, J. A. (2002) Analysis of dendrochronological variability and associated natural climates in Eurasia (ADVANCE 10K). Holocene Special Issue, *The Holocene*, **12**: 6

Chapter Eight

1. Milton, K. (1990) *Our Countryside, Our Concern: The policy and practice of conservation in Northern Ireland.* Northern Ireland Environment Link. Antrim, Northern Ireland.

2. Christie, S. (1996) *Environmental Strategy for Northern Ireland.* Northern Ireland Environmental Link, Belfast.

3. Anon (2000) *Biodiversity in Northern Ireland.* Recommendations to Government for a biodiversity strategy. Northern Ireland Biodiversity Group, HMSO.

4. Brown, D. (1996) *Our Trees, a guide to growing Northern Ireland's native trees from seed.* Conservation Volunteers Northern Ireland. Clandeboye, County Down.

5. Anon (2001) *Handbook of the Convention on Biological Diversity.* Secretariat of the Convention on Biological Diversity. Earthscan, London.

6. Anon (1994) *Biodiversity: The UK Action Plan.* HMSO.

7. Keller, M., Kollmann, J. and Edwards, P. J. (2000) Genetic introgression from distant provenances reduces fitness in local weed populations. *Journal of Applied Ecology*, **37**: 647-659.

8. Worrell, R. (1992) A comparison between European continental and British provenances of some British native trees: Growth, survival and stem form. *Forestry* **65**: 253-279.

9. Doucousso, A., Guyon, J. P., Kremer, A. (1996) Latitudinal and altitudinal variation of bud burst in western populations of sessile oak (*Quercus petraea* (Matt.) Liebl.). *Annales des Sciences Forestieres* **53**: 775-782.

10. Jensen, J. S. (2000) Provenance variation in phenotypic traits in *Quercus robur* and *Quercus petraea* in Danish provenance trials. *Scandanavian Journal of Forest Research* **15**: 297-308.

11. Deans, J. D. and Harvey, F. J. (1996) Frost hardiness of 16 European provenances of sessile oak growing in Scotland. *Forestry* **69**: 5-11.

12. Muir, G., Lowe, A. J., Fleming, C. C. and Vogl, C. (2004) High Nuclear Genetic Diversity, High Levels of Outcrossing and Low Differentiation Among Remnant Populations of *Quercus petraea* at the Margin of its Range in Ireland. *Annals of Botany* **93**: 691-697

13. Kelleher, C. T., Hodkinson, T. R, Kelly, D. L. and Douglas, G. C. (2003) Characterisation of chloroplast DNA haplotypes to reveal the provenance and genetic structure of oaks in Ireland. *Forest Ecology and Management,* **189**:123-131

14. Baillie, M. G. L. and Brown, D. M. (1995) Some deductions on ancient Irish trees from dendrochronology. In: Pilcher J.R. and Mac an tSaoir, S.S. (Eds) 1995. *Wood, trees and forests in Ireland.* 35-50. Royal Irish Academy, Dublin.

15. Mitchell, F. (1990) *Shell Guide to Reading the Irish Lanscape.* Michael Joseph/Country House, Dublin.

16. Pilcher, J. R. (1988) *Paleoecology.* Queen's University of Belfast.

17. Taberlet, P., Fumagalli, L., Wust-Saucy, A., Cossons, J. (1998) Comparative phylogeography and postglacial colonisation routes in Europe. *Molecular Ecology* 7: 453-464.

18. Rackham, O. (1995) Looking for ancient woodland in Ireland. In: Pilcher J. R. and Mac an tSaoir, S. S. (Eds) 1995 *Wood, trees and forests in Ireland.*1-12. Royal Irish Academy. Dublin.

19. Pilcher, J. R. (1973) Pollen analysis and radiocarbon dating of a peat on Slieve Gallion, Co. Tyrone, N. Ireland. *New Phytologist* **72**: 681-689.

20. Cruickshank, J. G. and Cruickshank, M. M. (1981). The development of humus-iron podsol profiles, linked by radiocarbon dating and pollen analysis to vegetation history. *Oikos* **36**: 238-253.

21. McCracken, E. (1971) *The Irish Woods Since Tudor Times.* Queen's University of Belfast. David and Charles.

22. Hall, V.A. (1990) Recent landscape history from a Co. Down lake deposit. *New Phytologist* **115**: 377-383.

23. McCracken, E. (1967) Notes on eighteenth century Irish nurserymen. *Irish Forestry* **24**:39-58

24. Fitzpatrick, H. M. (1966) *The Forests of Ireland.* Society of Irish Foresters.

25. Crawford, W. H. (1964) The woodlands of the manor of Brownlow's-Derry, north Armagh, in the seventeenth and eighteenth centuries. *Ulster Folklife* **10**: 57-63

26. Jones, E. W. (1959) Biological flora of the British Isles. *Quercus* L. *Journal of Ecology* **47**: 169-222.

27. McCauley, D. E. (1995) The use of chloroplast DNA polymorphism in studies of gene flow in plants. *Tree* **10** 198-202.

28. Dumolin, S., Demesure, B., Petit, R. J. (1995) Inheritance of chloroplast and mitochondrial genomes in pedunculate oak investigated with an efficient PCR method. *Theoretical and Applied Genetics* **91**: 1253-1256.

29. Palmer, J. D. (1987) Chloroplast DNA evolution and biosystematic uses of chloroplast DNA variation. *American Naturalist* **130:** 6-29.

30. Schaal, B. A., Hayworth, D. A., Olsen, K. M., Rauscher, J. T., Smith, W. A. (1998) Phylogeographic studies in plants: problems and prospects. *Molecular Ecology* 7: 465-474

31. Petit, R. J., Pineau, E., Demesure, B., Bacilieri, R., Ducousso, A., Kremer, A. (1997) Chloroplast DNA footprints of postglacial recolonisation by oaks. *Proceedings of the Natural Academy of Science USA* **94**: 9996-10001.

32. Cottrell, J. E., Munro, R. C., Tabbener, H. E., Milner, A. D., Forrest, G. I., Lowe, A. J. (2003) Comparison of fine-scale genetic structure using nuclear microsatellites within two British oakwoods differing in population history. *Forest Ecology and Management* **176**: 287-303.

33. Cornuet, J.M., Piry, S., Luikart, G., Estoup, A. and Solignac, M. (1999) New methods employing multilocus genotypes to select or exclude populations as origins of individuals. *Genetics* **153**: 1989-2000.

Chapter Nine

1. Courtecuisse, R. (1999) *Mushrooms of Britain and Europe.* Collins, London.

2. Ainsworth, G. C. (1950) The Belfast Foray, September 11th – 17th, 1948. *Transactions of the British Mycological Society* **33**: 182-188.

3. Anderson, R. (1996) New British records: 134. *Ciboria alni* (Rostr.)Buchw. in *Friesia* 3: 235 (1947). *Mycologist* **10** (4): 155-156 (1 pl.).

4. Anderson, R., Mitchel, D., Shannon, G. & Wright, M. (2004) New or interesting records of Irish fungi. *Irish Naturalists' Journal* (in press).

Chapter Ten

1. Kerney, M. P. (1999) *Atlas of the Land and Freshwater Molluscs of Britain and Ireland.* Harley Books.

2. Anderson, R. (1991) Evidence of recent spread in *Semilimax pyrenaicus* (Férussac) and *Arion owenii* Davies (Mollusca, Gastropoda). *Irish Naturalists' Journal* **23**: 510.

3. Anderson, R. (1986) The land planarians of Ireland (Tricladida, Terricola) a summary of distribution records. *Irish Naturalists' Journal* **22**: 141-146.

4. Anderson, R. (1980) The status of the land nemertine *Argonemertes dendyi* (Dakin) in Ireland. *Irish Naturalists' Journal* **20**: 153-157 (pl).

5. Constantine, B. (1994) A new ecological role for *Gibbium aequinoctiale* Boieldieu (Ptinidae) in Britain. *Coleopterist* **3**: 25-28.

6. Fowles, A. P., Alexander, K. N. A. & Key, R. S. (1999) The Saproxylic Quality Index: evaluating wooded habitats for the conservation of dead wood Coleoptera. *Coleopterist* **8**: 121-141.

7. Anderson, R. (1994) A first Irish record of *Ptinus subpilosus* Sturm (Col., Ptinidae). *Entomologists' monthly Magazine* **130**: 136.

8. Anderson, R. (1977) *Endomychus coccineus* (L.) (Coleoptera: Endomychidae) new to Ireland. *Irish Naturalists' Journal* **19**: 97.

9. Anderson, R. (in press) Insects on oak in Northern Ireland: *Andricus quercusramuli* (L.) (Hymenoptera: Cynipidae) and *Scymnus auritus* Thunberg (Coleoptera: Coccinellidae). *Irish Naturalists' Journal.*

10. Anderson, R. (1990) *Adalia bipunctata* (L.) (Coleoptera, Coccinellidae) in Northern Ireland. *Irish Naturalists' Journal* **23**: 282.

11. Nelson, B., Hughes, M., Nash, R. & Warren, M. (2001) *Leptidea reali* Reissinger 1989: a butterfly new to Britain and Ireland *Entomologists' Record and Journal of Variation* **113**: 97-101.

12. Anderson, R. (1987) Some local woodland hoverflies (Diptera, Syrphidae), including *Parasyrphus lineolus* (Zett.) from the Lagan Valley, Belfast. *Irish Naturalists' Journal* **22**: 258.

13. Anderson, R. (1988) *Parasyrphus annulatus* (Zetterstedt) (Diptera, Syrphidae) in Belvoir Park, Belfast. *Irish Naturalists' Journal* **22**: 455.

14. O'Connor, J. P. & O'Connor, M. A. (1993) *Andricus lignicola* (Hartig) and *A. quercusramuli* (L.) (Hymenoptera: Cynipidae), two gall wasps new to Ireland. *Entomologists' Gazette* **44**: 135-136.

Chapter Eleven

1. Deane, C. D. (1983) Difficult times for a silent watcher at water's edge. News Letter April 2 p. 4.

Chapter Twelve

1. Deane, C. D. (1960) Big house in its last days. Belfast Telegraph August 24 p. 6.

2. Deane, C. D. (1983) *The Ulster Countryside.* Century Books, Belfast.

3. Scott, R. (2004) *Wild Belfast. On Safari in the city.* Blackstaff Press, Belfast

Early advertisements concerning Belvoir Park from some 18th century issues of the Belfast News-Letter

News-Letter 6 March 1739*
Whereas several Wild-Ducks, which were bred in the Gardens belonging to the Hon. *Arthur Hill*, Esq; have of late been shot. Now this to give Notice, that any Person who will discover upon Oath against any who have kill'd or shot at any Time, or shall hereafter shoot at, or kill any Wild-Duck on the *Lagan* Water, betwixt *Shaws-Bridge* and the Bleaching-Green in *Galwally*, shall have five *British* shillings paid to them by the Printer hereof.

News-Letter 24 November 1752
Whereas several Ash-trees have been lately feloniously cut down with saws in the Night-time, and carried off, from the Woods of Ballylenaghan, belonging to the Right Hon Arthur Hill, Esq; particularly three Ash Trees on Monday Night the 20th of this Instant November. Now the said Arthur Hill does hereby promise a Reward of five Guineas to any one who shall discover the Person or Persons, who cut down the said Trees, and were concerned in carrying them away, so as he or they may be brought to Justice and convicted of the same,

Dated this 23d Nov. 1752.

News-Letter 8 December 1752
Mr. Hill, having stock'd his Woods at Belvoir with wild Turkeys and Pheasants, intreats the Favour of his Friends and Neighbours not to Shoot for this Season in his Demesne or Grounds; and if in Sporting they should meet with any of these Birds, he begs they may be spared; which will highly Oblige him.

Dated December 7th, 1752.

News-Letter 14 October 1755
That the Right Honourable Arthur Hill, Esq; begs Leave to acquaint his Neighbours and Friends, That his Woods and Demesne are now in a way of being well stock'd with Pheasants, which in a little Time will probably spread all round the Neighbourhood, if Gentlemen who divert themselves with Sporting; will please to forbear Shooting them for a year or two. These are also some wild Turkeys in the Country, which he intreats may be spared, if they should be by chance met with.

News-Letter 26 September 1758
Whereas several persons have of late made a practice of coming over the Park wall of the right honourable Arthur Hill, Esq; and likewise have past over the Lagan river into his garden, and have made paths and passages through his garden and grounds, greatly to his damage: This is therefore to give notice, that whoever shall be found for the future committing such trespass, shall be prosecuted with the utmost rigour of the law.

News-Letter 27 October 1758
Whereas several Foxes have been of late seen in the demesnes and woods of Belvoir, and the wings and feathers of Pheasants have been found, which are suppos'd to have been kill'd by the said Foxes: This is to give notice, that whoever shall bring one or more Foxes to Belvoir aforesaid, shall receive from the Right Honourable Arthur Hill, Esq. or in his absence from Mr. John Lomas, a Crown reward for each Fox, which shall be prov'd to have been caught, kill'd or unkennell'd in or within three miles of the park or demesnes of Belvoir.

News-Letter 12 January 1762
Whereas several Trees standing and growing in the woods of Breda and Ballylenaghan, have lately been feloniously cut and carried away; and there have also been stolen several pieces of timber and boards lying about the house of Belvoir. Now this is to give notice, that a reward of two guineas will be paid by John Lomas at Belvoir, to the person discovering and prosecuting to conviction the person or persons guilty of said felony, or felonies. And if any one concerned therein shall discover and convict his or her accomplice or accomplices, will not only be paid said reward, but means will be made use of to procure the pardon of the person so discovering.

Dated this 11th January, 1762.

News-Letter 9 November 1762
Whereas many disorderly people have of late made a practice of trespassing upon the fields, plantations and gardens at Belvoir, and have done great damage by cutting down trees in the park and demesne, breaking hedges &c. These are to advise that orders are given to Mr. Trevor's servants to observe all persons who shall hereafter presume to trespass upon his land and park, and immediately proceed to prosecute them at law for the same as also such who shall pass the river into his grounds either with design to take a short cut into the neighbourhood or to walk about his fields or gardens or that shall offer to make use of his avenues or private roads or fields for short passages through the country.

Nov 8 1762

News-Letter 5 April 1771
Whereas of late several audacious and disorderly Persons have made a Practice of getting over the Park Wall, and by other Ways, into the Demesne of Belvoir, and have feloniously cut and carried away, Ash and other Timber-Trees, and done considerable Damage to the Plantations and Improvements: I therefore give Notice, that I am determined to prosecute to the utmost Rigour of the Law, all such; and I do offer a Reward of one Guinea to the Discoverer of any Person, who shall clandestinely come over the Wall of said Park, or into the Demesne; and a further Reward of Five Guineas to the Person who shall within six Months, prosecute to Conviction, Him, Her or Them, who shall commit such Felony as aforesaid. Given under my Hand, Dublin, 12th February, 1771.

LAETITIA TREVOR.

N.B. The Reward to be paid by Edward Brice, Esq; of Belfast.

News-Letter 25 June 1771
Whereas on Saturday Night last the 22d Inst. the Garden at Belvoir was feloniously broken into, by some malicious Person or Persons, and seven Brace of Melons torn up from one of the Melon Beds, and the rest of the Plants destroyed and rendered useless. In order to have such abominable and vicious Offenders brought to condign Punishment, I do hereby offer a Reward of Ten Guineas, to be paid him, her, or them who shall within three Months discover the Person or Persons who committed said Felony, so as they may be convicted thereof. Given under my Hand at Belfast, 24th June, 1771.

EDWARD BRICE

News-Letter 27 September 1771
The Game upon the several Estates of Lord Viscount Dungannon, now a Minor, in the Counties of Down, Antrim and Armagh, having of late been shamefully destroyed, and the Pheasants which the Woods of Belvoir were stocked being mostly killed: Notice is hereby given, that it is the Intention of his Guardian to have the same now preserved. And it is hoped and expected, after this Caution, no Person whatever will come upon any of said Estates in either Counties, with Dogs, Guns, or Nets, as I have received Orders to have all such prosecuted to the Rigour of Law. Dated the 26th of September, 1771.

EDW. BRICE.

News-Letter 7 - 11 February 1774
Whereas on the Nights of either the 3d or 4th Inst. the Dwelling House of Lord Viscount Dungannon at Belvoir, was burglariously broken open and thereout feloniously taken a Quantity of Soap and Candles. These are therefore to offer a Reward of Ten Guineas, to be paid to the Person who will give Information, and prosecute to Conviction the Person or Persons concerned in said burglary and Felony. Given under my Hand, at Belfast, the 6th Day of December, 1773.

EDWARD BRICE

N.B. Some Ash Trees have been lately cut and carried away in the Night out of the Demesne of Belvoir. Mr. Brice will pay the same Reward as above on the Prosecution and Conviction of the Offenders.

News-Letter 30 August – 2 September 1774
Whereas the Gardens of Belvoir have been broke into last Saturday Night, Sunday Night, and last Night, and a vast Quantity of unripe Fruit stolen, and the Trees torn down from the Walls, and much Damage otherwise done: And whereas it has been a Practice for Persons to go over the Park-Wall to the utter Destruction of the same. Now to prevent both which unwarrantable Proceedings, I do give Notice, that from the Date hereof, I shall set Snakes and Fox-Traps in the Gardens, and appoint Persons to watch with Fire-Arms, who have positive Directions that any Persons appearing in the Gardens in the Night-Time, or in the Demesne, and refusing to answer when challenged, shall be fired on without reserve: And the sooner to bring such Villains to Justice, I do offer a Reward of Ten Guineas to any Person who shall discover of their Accomplices. Any Persons that wish to go into the Park to see their Cattle grazing there, are desired to apply to Rodger Woods to be let in at the Gate, but by no Means to presume to go over the Wall. Belvoir, given under my Hand this 1st Day of September.

LAETITIA DUNLUCE

News-Letter 24-27 March 1778
Whereas of late several Persons have made a Practice of passing thro' the Demesne of Belvoir and trespassing thereupon, in Order to have a nearer Way to the County of Antrim: and by a mistaken Indulgence and Inattention, promiscuous People have been permitted to walk into the Improvements, by which Opportunities have been taken of cutting Trees, and committing other Felonies about said Place: This is therefore to give Notice, that no Person will be allowed to have a Road thro' any Part of said Demesne, or to walk in the Improvements: And if after such Notice, any Trespass shall be committed, I have given Orders to have immediate information thereof: and shall take such Steps by Law as will effectually punish the Offenders. Belfast, 25 March, 1778.

ED. BRYCE.

News-Letter 24-27 March 1778
On the night of the 23d inst. there was feloniously stolen out of one of the Offices adjoining the Farm Yard at Belvoir, one Wheel Car, the Property of Lord Viscount Dungannon, painted a dark red, made with four Slats not boarded, broad Wheels, about 26 inches in Height, shod with rose-headed Nails, had an Iron Back-Band and Iron Car-pins, the Work all put together with Iron Nuts and Screws. Whoever shall within the Space of six Months discover on the Person or Persons concerned in said Felony, so that one or more of them shall be convicted thereof, shall be paid by me Ten Guineas as a Reward. Dated Belfast, the 25th March. 1778.

ED. BRYCE.

News-Letter 12 September 1780

Whereas on Wednesday Night the 16th of August last, there was an Ash Tree feloniously cut and carried away, out of the Demesne of Belvoir, and also on or about Friday Night the 8th inst. another Ash Tree was cut and carried away in a like Manner: I do thereby offer a Reward of Ten Guineas to any Person who shall within three Months, give Information of the cutting of either or both said Trees, so as the Person who cut the same be prosecuted in Conviction; and if any Person will give me Information in whose Custody said Trees now are, I will reward them hansomly, and their Names shall not be made publick. Dated 14th Sept. 1780.

EDW. BRICE.

News-Letter 11 April 1783

Whereas several persons have presumed to trespass on the demesne of Lord Dungannon at Belvoir, and have committed various misdemeanours, by getting over the walls and hedges, cutting timber, &c. And of late some people have had the impudence, to pass from Malone, in the county of Antrim, thro' the farm-yard at Belvoir, into the county of Down; and when the gates were locked, had the audacity to get over the rails in the court,- and often in the night at unseasonable hours.

As a caution to all persons, I do hereby give notice, that to prevent such practices for the future, a strict watch will be kept, by men with guns, to detect any who shall be guilty of said offences. And I do further offer a reward of Ten Guineas, to the person who shall give information, and prosecute the first offender to conviction. Given under my hand at Belfast, 2d April, 1783.   EDW. BRICE

*This advertisement appears in the News Letter issue 157, volume 2. The newspaper is dated Tuesday March 6th 1738, but appears to have been printed in 1739.

From an examination of documents held by the Public Records Office and some issues of the Dublin Gazette, the following records relating to Belvoir estate lands were noted. In some of the original records there are errors and spelling mistakes and these have been corrected for clarity.

Note – Balm of Gilead is a North American fir that is no longer planted in Britain, where it is short lived. The Register of Trees and affidavit referred to below are in the Public Records Office Northern Ireland PRONI DOW/7/3/2/1, DOW/7/3/2/2 and DOW/7/3/2/3. A copy of the affidavit for tree planting by Lawson Annesley located during this study has been filed with the Public record Office. For further information about these early schemes for encouraging tree planting and registering trees, see McCracken, E. and D. (1984) A register of trees for County Londonderry, 1768-1911. Public Record Office for Northern Ireland and Tomlinson, R.W. (1996) Tree planting by tenants in County Down during the eighteenth and nineteenth centuries. Irish Geography 29: 83-95.

Dublin Gazette. April 12 1823 p200 and Register of Trees entry 7.
Take Notice, that I have planted, or caused to be planted, within Twelve Calender Months last past, on the Lands of Fort Breda, Townland of Breda, Parish of Knockbreda, Barony of Castlereagh, and County of Down, held under Sir Robert Bateson, Bart. of Belvoir Park, the following Trees, viz. – 600 Larch Fir, 350 Scotch Fir, 125 Spruce do. 105 Silver do. 100 Mountain Ash, 356 Beech, 150 Oak, 60 Birch, 220 Alder, 120 Elm, 75 Willow, 50 Lime, 100 Horse Chestnut, 50 Spanish do. 120 Poplar, 75 Sycamore, 100 Ash- Total 2756; which Trees I intend to register according to Law.- Dated April 9, 1823.
WILLIAM BOYD. Fort Breda, Belfast.
To all whom it may concern.

Dublin Gazette November 11 1824 p814 and Register of Trees entry 31.
Take Notice, that I have planted, or caused to be planted, within Twelve Calendar Months last past, on the Lands of Fort Breda, Townland of Breda, Parish of Knock-Breda, Barony of Castlereagh, and County of Down, held by me under Sir Robert Bateson. Bart. of Belvoir-Park, the following Trees, viz, - 138 Ash, 231 Oak, 285 Beech, 128 Elm, 459 Scotch Fir, 42 Chestnut, 47 Willow, 85 Poplar, 38 Mountain Ash, 98 Alder, 50 Silver Fir, 194 Spruce Fir, 356 Larch Fir, 20 Birch, 158 Sycamore – Total, 2329; which Trees I intend to register according to Law. – Dated this 30th day of October, 1824.
WILLIAM BOYD, Fort Breda, Belfast.

Dublin Gazette August 24 1826 p631 and Register of Trees entry 73.
Take Notice, that I have planted, or caused to be planted, within Twelve Months last past, on the lands of Breda, in the parish of Knock Breda, Barony of Castlereagh, and County of Down, held by me from Sir Robert Bateson, Bart. The following Trees, viz. – 750 Beech, 650 Ash, 1350 Larch, 450 Scotch Fir, 100 Silver Fir, 306 Poplar, 141 Willow, 300 Elm, 110 Mountain Ash, 200 Sycamore, 6 Service, 75 Spruce Fir, 60 Oak – Total 4498 Trees; and that I intend to register the same according to Law. - Dated 18th August, 1826.
WILLIAM BOYD.
To all whom it may concern.

Dublin Gazette. January 11 1831 p42. Copy of affidavit filed with Record Office and Register of Trees, entry 132.
TAKE NOTICE, that I have planted, or caused to be planted, within Twelve Calendar Months last past, on the Lands of Derramore, in the Parish of Drumbo, Barony of Castlereagh, and County of Down, held by me under Sir Robert Bateson, Bart., the following Trees, viz. - 100 Silver Fir, 200 Balm of Gilead, 420 Scotch Fir, 325 Oak, 75 Spanish Chestnut, 75 Horse Chestnut, 175 Sycamore, 75 Willow, 75 Poplar, 475 Beech, 35 Service, 150 Alder, 150 Larch, 50 Ash, 300 Spruce Fir, 10 Lime, and 10 Mountain Ash; which I intend to register pursuant to the Statute in such case made and provided. - 28 December, 1830.
LAWSON ANNESLEY.
To Sir Robert Bateson, Bart; and all whom it may concern.

Register of trees entry 206.
Galwally parish of Knockbreda. Samuel Millikin Gardener to Sir Robert Bateson Baronet his affidavit received 27 Dec 1837 setting forth that he had planted on said lands the following trees viz 38 Lime trees 5 Elm trees and 5 Spruce fir trees.

Dublin Gazette. September 4 1860 p1011 and Register of Trees entry 278.
TAKE NOTICE, that I have planted, or caused to be planted within Twelve Calendar Months last past, on that Farm of Land late in the occupation of Hugh Gray, but now in my possession, situate in the Townland of Ballynavalley, in the Parish of Drumbo, Barony of Castlereagh, and County of Down, the following Trees, viz :- 200 English Oaks, 135 Poplar, 1,642 Larch Fir, 500 Spruce Fir, 200 Silver Fir, and 1,200 Scotch Fir-total, 3,877; and that I purpose registering same pursuant to Act of Parliament.
Dated this 24th day of August, 1860.
ROBT. BATESON.
To The Right Honourable Arthur Hill Trevor, Viscount Dungannon, Brynkinalt, Chirk, Denbighshire; and George Posnett, Esq., J.P., his agent, 57, Upper Arthur-street, Belfast.

TREES OVER 3m GIRTH IN THE AREA OF THE FORMER BELVOIR PARK ESTATE

Location	Tree Tag No.	Eastings	Northings	Species	Girth	Height measured
Belvoir Golf Course	2505	335009.85	369978.15	Horse Chestnut	3.7	1.5
Belvoir Golf Course	2506	335008.91	369950.08	Lime	c. 3	Estimate
Belvoir Golf Course	2507	335008.78	369955.2	Oak	3.2	1.5
Belvoir Golf Course	2508	335002.26	369923.75	Sycamore	3.5	1.5
Belvoir Golf Course	2509	334779.57	369717.77	Oak	6.35	1.5
Belvoir Golf Course	2510	334767.17	369715.63	Oak	5.2	1.5
Belvoir Golf Course	2511	334759.04	369709.95	Oak	3.75	1.5
Belvoir Golf Course	2512	334749.1	369735.13	Oak	4.02	1.5
Belvoir Golf Course	2513	334744	369721	Oak	4.07	1.2
Belvoir Golf Course	2514	334778.21	369678.04	Oak	4.29	0.7
Belvoir Golf Course	2515	334693.46	369752.45	Oak	4.35	1.5
Belvoir Golf Course	2516	334693.72	369744.71	Oak	4.5	1.5
Belvoir Golf Course	2518	334646.01	369769.06	Oak	4.64	1.5
Belvoir Golf Course	2519	334639.19	369781.34	Oak	3.9	1.5
Belvoir Golf Course	2517	334664.9	369773.68	Oak	4.95	1.5
Belvoir Golf Course	2520	334815.62	369863.71	Oak	5.18	1.5
Belvoir Golf Course	2521	334833.87	370016.85	Oak	4.05	1.5
Belvoir Golf Course	2522	334847.55	370020.92	Oak	See note below	
Belvoir Golf Course	2523	334880.91	370028.1	Oak	c. 3.5	Estimate
Belvoir Golf Course	2524	334718.09	369859.22	Beech	4.27	1.5
Belvoir Golf Course	2525	334741.05	369859.3	Beech	4.18	1.5
Belvoir Golf Course	2526	334744.47	369854.6	Beech	3.5	1.5
Belvoir Golf Course	2527	334793.35	369855.91	Beech	4.1	1.5
Belvoir Golf Course	2528	334767.76	369857.72	Beech	4.6	1.5
Belvoir Golf Course	2529	334754.56	369898.45	Beech	4.32	1.5
Belvoir Golf Course	2530	334764.75	369914.63	Oak	3.83	1.5
Belvoir Golf Course	2531	334766.53	369654.51	Oak	3.6	1.5
Belvoir Golf Course	2532	334808.91	369595.46	Beech	3.69	1.5
Belvoir Golf Course	2533	334890	370050	Sycamore	c. 3.6	Estimate
Belvoir Golf Course	2534	334910	370040	Sycamore	3.18	1
Belvoir Golf Course	2535	334785	369760	Sycamore	3.32	1.5
Belvoir Golf Course	2536	334746.27	369595.97	Oak	4.29	1.5
Belvoir Golf Course	2537	334726.72	369557.98	Oak	4.67	0.85
Belvoir Golf Course	2538	334716.27	369529.22	Oak	4.86	1
Belvoir Golf Course	2539	334689.48	369514.01	Oak	5.1	1.5
Belvoir Golf Course	2540	334586.1	369590.58	Oak	4.33	0.9
Belvoir Golf Course	2541	334609.41	369636.42	Oak	3.44	1.5
Belvoir Golf Course	2542	334612.97	369668.3	Oak	3	1.5
Belvoir Golf Course	2543	334405.11	369861.42	Beech	3.3	1.5
Belvoir Golf Course	2544	334418.1	369852.45	Beech	3.28	1.5
Belvoir Golf Course	2545	334470.79	369818.35	Oak	4.35	1.5
Belvoir Golf Course	2546	334586.85	369911.68	Oak	3.27	1.5
Belvoir Golf Course	2547	334570	369880	Sycamore	3.2	1
Belvoir Golf Course	2548	334569.18	369944.86	Oak	See note below	
Belvoir Golf Course	2549	334563.84	369971.54	Oak	See note below	
Belvoir Golf Course	2550	334682.32	369966.03	Oak	3.5	1.5
Belvoir Golf Course	2551	334731.49	369931.91	Oak	3.26	1
Belvoir Golf Course	2552	334535.7	369936.89	Oak	4.36	1.5
Belvoir Golf Course	2553	334487.52	369965.52	Beech	4.85	1.5
Belvoir Golf Course	2554	334510	370010	Beech	3.97	1.5
Belvoir Golf Course	2555	334356.54	369910.8	Oak	5.7	0.1
Belvoir Golf Course	2556	334422.02	369987.03	Ash	4.77	1.5
Belvoir Golf Course	2557	334381.78	370200.87	Beech	4.3	1.5
Belvoir Golf Course	2558	334378.61	370204.6	Beech	4.37	1.5
Belvoir Golf Course	2559	334335.68	370189.61	Sweet Chestnut	3.32	0.5
Belvoir Golf Course	2560	334360.34	370194.36	Beech	3.77	1.5
Belvoir Golf Course	2561	334318.86	370220.49	Beech	5.05	1.5
Belvoir Golf Course	2562	334320	370200	Lime	3.6	1.5
Belvoir Golf Course	2563	334311.01	370259.03	Horse Chestnut	3.7	1.5
Belvoir Golf Course	2564	334319.74	370248.33	Beech	5.08	1.5
Belvoir Golf Course	2565	334327.19	370234	Beech	c. 4.50	Estimate
Belvoir Golf Course	2566	334346.56	370222.46	Oak	3.21	1.5
Belvoir Golf Course	2567	334385	370221.19	Lime	3.73	1.5
Belvoir Golf Course	2568	334389.6	370236.44	Beech	4.87	1.5
Belvoir Golf Course	2569	334592.83	370382.57	Beech	3.13	1.5
Belvoir Golf Course	2570	334604.08	370381.47	Beech	3.03	1.5
Belvoir Golf Course	2571	334595.76	370388.88	Beech	3.18	1.5
Belvoir Golf Course	2572	334554.95	370366.59	Beech	3.36	1.5
Belvoir Golf Course	2573	334660.4	370282.8	Beech	3.43	1.5
Belvoir Golf Course	2574	334666.23	370297.79	Beech	3.72	1.5
Belvoir Golf Course	2575	334663.71	370321.71	Beech	3.68	1.5
Belvoir Golf Course	2576	334661.17	370315.11	Beech	3.05	1.5
Belvoir Golf Course	2577	334840	370300	Beech	3.28	1.5
Belvoir Golf Course	2578	334810	370290	Lime	3.8	0.5
Belvoir Golf Course	2579	334775.95	370165.26	Horse Chestnut	3.81	1.5
Belvoir Golf Course	2580	334773.75	370181.31	Horse Chestnut	3.55	1.5
Belvoir Golf Course	2581	335040	370170	Lime	See note below	
Belvoir Park Forest near big meadow	2461	333474	369470	Oak	3.2	1.5
Belvoir Park Forest near big meadow	2462	333486	369474	Oak	3.26	1.5
Belvoir Park Forest near big meadow	2463	333493	369476	Oak	3.18	1.5
Belvoir Park Forest near big meadow	2464	333513	369480	Oak	4.06	1
Belvoir Park Forest near big meadow	2465	333539	369518	Sycamore	4.84	1.2
Belvoir Park Forest near big meadow	2466	333548	369507	Oak	3.17	1.5

Location	Tree Tag No.	Eastings	Northings	Species	Girth	Height measured
Belvoir Park Forest near big meadow	2467	333559	369496	Oak	4.45	1.5
Belvoir Park Forest near big meadow	2468	333567	369484	Oak	3.2	1.5
Belvoir Park Forest near big meadow	2469	333495	369369	Sycamore	3.2	1.5
Belvoir Park Forest east of big meadow	2450	333603	369392	Oak	c. 4	Estimate
Belvoir Park Forest east of big meadow	2449	333609	369408	Oak	3.9	1
Belvoir Park Forest east of big meadow	2448	333620	369421	Oak	4.3	1.5
Belvoir Park Forest east of big meadow	2451	333628	369391	Oak	4	1
Belvoir Park Forest east of big meadow	2452	333634	369374	Oak	5.4	1
Belvoir Park Forest east of big meadow	2453	333656	369363	Oak	8.8	0.1
Belvoir Park Forest east of big meadow	2454	333647	369384	Oak	3.9	1
Belvoir Park Forest east of big meadow	2458	333676	369286	Ash	4.3	1
Belvoir Park Forest east of big meadow	2455	333736	369389	Oak	3.9	1.5
Belvoir Park Forest east of big meadow	2446	333611	369452	Oak	5.04	1.5
Belvoir Park Forest NE of big meadow	2447	333589	369461	Oak	4.06	1.5
Belvoir Park Forest NE of big meadow	2445	333615	369490	Oak	3.6	1.5
Belvoir Park Forest NE of big meadow	2444	333625	369500	Oak	3	2
Belvoir Park Forest NE of big meadow	2442	333643	369507	Oak	4.84	1.5
Belvoir Park Forest NE of big meadow	2443	333649	369495	Oak	4.4	1.5
Belvoir Park Forest NE of big meadow	2456	333608	369505	Oak	3.16	1.5
Belvoir Park Forest NE of big meadow	2441	333670	369543	Oak	c. 4	Estimate
Belvoir Park Forest NE of big meadow	2440	333678	369545	Oak	3.21	1.5
Belvoir Park Forest North Corbie Wood	2439	333659	369591	Oak	3.4	1.5

Location	Tree Tag No.	Eastings	Northings	Species	Girth	Height measured
Belvoir Park Forest North Corbie Wood	2438	333659	369599	Oak	3.4	1.5
Belvoir Park Forest North Corbie Wood	2437	333654	369621	Oak	3	2
Belvoir Park Forest North Corbie Wood	2435	333664	369650	Oak	3.84	1.5
Belvoir Park Forest North Corbie Wood	2434	333698	369658	Oak	3.46	1.5
Belvoir Park Forest North Corbie Wood	2433	333725	369663	Oak	3.53	1.5
Belvoir Park Forest North Corbie Wood	2432	333726	369622	Oak	3.88	1.5
Belvoir Park Forest North Corbie Wood	2431	333742	369668	Oak	4.46	1.5
Belvoir Park Forest North Corbie Wood	2430	333852	369678	Oak	4.98	1.35
Belvoir Park Forest North Corbie Wood	2429	333877	369675	Oak	3.66	1.5
Belvoir Park Forest North Corbie Wood	2428	333898	369677	Oak	3.4	1.5
Belvoir Park Forest North Corbie Wood	2436	333646	369646	Oak	See note below	
Belvoir Park Forest North Corbie Wood	2586	333750	369613.5	Oak	See note below	
Belvoir Park Forest South Corbie Wood	2585	333868.7	369601.7	Oak	See note below	
Belvoir Park Forest SE of Big Meadow	2457	333757	369466	Beech	3.81	1.5
Belvoir Park Forest SE of Big Meadow	2470	333487	369366	Sycamore	3	1.5
Belvoir Park Forest SE of Big Meadow	2471	333449	369357	Horse Chestnut	4.02	1.5
Belvoir Park Forest SE of Big Meadow	2472	333436	369360	Horse Chestnut	See note below	
Belvoir Park Forest SE of Big Meadow	2473	333432	369362	Horse Chestnut	See note below	
Belvoir Park Forest SE of Big Meadow	2474	333424	369366	Lime	See note below	
S. Belvoir Park Forest nr Housing Estate	2460	333540.3	369022.6	Beech	3.28	1.5
S. Belvoir Park Forest nr Housing Estate	2459	333669.4	368950.8	Beech	3.05	1.5
Belvoir Park Forest near motte	2418	334034	369786	Beech	4.4	1.1

TREES OVER 3m GIRTH IN THE AREA OF THE FORMER BELVOIR PARK ESTATE

Location	Tree Tag No.	Eastings	Northings	Species	Girth	Height measured
Belvoir Park Forest near motte	2419	334014.2	369795.3	Oak	4.44	1.5
Belvoir Park Forest near motte	2420	334019.6	369813.4	Lime	3.45	1.5
Belvoir Park Forest near motte	2421	334013.7	369819.7	Lime	3.38	1.5
Belvoir Park Forest near motte	2422	334007.9	369831.4	Lime	3.07	1.5
Belvoir Park Forest near motte	2423	334035.7	369847.1	Sweet Chestnut	5.32	0.5
Belvoir Park Forest near motte	2424	334063	369797	Oak	See note below	
Belvoir Park Forest Arboretum	2415	334117	369810	Holm Oak	4.5	1.75
Belvoir Park Forest Arboretum	2414	334116	369798	Lucombe Oak	3.02	1.5
Belvoir Park Forest Arboretum	2413	334108	369792	Lucombe Oak	3.38	1.5
Belvoir Park Forest Arboretum	2410	334109	369730	Yew	3.3	0.1
Belvoir Park Forest Arboretum	2411	334116	369761	Yew	3.57	1.4
Belvoir Park Forest Arboretum	2412	334124	369775	Yew	3.47	0.9
Belvoir Park Forest Arboretum	2416	334178	369769	Yew	3.51	0.3
Belvoir Park Forest Arboretum	2417	334164	369820	Yew	3.03	1.5
Belvoir Park Forest Arboretum	2403	334219	369798	Atlas Cedar	5.03	1.5
Belvoir Park Forest Arboretum	2402	334247	369792	Atlas Cedar	4.6	1.5
Belvoir Park Forest Arboretum	2397	334268	369834	Giant Sequoia	7.23	1.5
Belvoir Park Forest Arboretum	2401	334229	369843	Monterey Cypress	c. 3.5	Estimate
Belvoir Park Forest Arboretum	2400	334238	369838	Montery Cypress	c. 3.5	Estimate
Belvoir Park Forest Arboretum	2399	334242.3	369833.9	Monterey Cypress	c. 4.5	Estimate
Belvoir Park Forest Arboretum	2398	334248	369831	Monterey Cypress	4.75	1.5
Belvoir Park Forest Arboretum	2396	334328	369797	Deodar Cedar	3.13	1.5
Belvoir Park Forest						

Location	Tree Tag No.	Eastings	Northings	Species	Girth	Height measured
Arboretum Belvoir Park Forest	2395	334337	369796	Deodar Cedar	3.2	1.5
Arboretum Belvoir Park Forest	2394	334331	369790	Deodar Cedar	4.18	1.5
Arboretum Belvoir Park Forest	2393	334365	369822	Horse Chestnut	3.68	1.5
Arboretum Belvoir Park Forest	2392	334363	369818	Horse Chestnut	3.27	1.5
Arboretum Belvoir Park Forest	2391	334377	369806	Horse Chestnut	3.73	1.5
Arboretum Belvoir Park Forest	2404	334284	369749	Japanese Red Cedar	4.34	0.4
Arboretum Belvoir Park Forest	2425	334268	369741	Mon. Cypress *Lutea*	3.07	1.5
Arboretum Belvoir Park Forest	2405	334327	369672	Ash	3.62	0.5
Arboretum Belvoir Park Forest	2406	334277.5	369682.5	Sycamore	3.1	1.5
Arboretum Belvoir Park Forest	2407	334200	369648	Giant Sequoia	6.3	1.5
Arboretum Belvoir Park Forest	2408	334199	369682	Deodar Cedar	3.2	1.5
Arboretum Belvoir Park Forest	2409	334140	369609	Lucombe Oak	3.9	0.9
Arboretum Belvoir Park Forest	2426	334258	369783	Lime	See note below	
Arboretum	2427	334246	369821	Alder	See note below	
Northeast Belvoir Park Forest	2324	334204.47	370255.96	Sycamore	3.2	1.5
Northeast Belvoir Park Forest	2325	334212.86	370200.51	Sycamore	3.3	1.5
Northeast Belvoir Park Forest	2326	334194.12	370134.44	Horse Chestnut	3.37	1.5
Northeast Belvoir Park Forest	2327	334183.93	370119.61	Horse Chestnut	4.53	1.5
Northeast Belvoir Park Forest	2321	334250.45	370328.87	Lime	c. 5.75	Estimate
Northeast Belvoir Park Forest	2323	334237.53	370305.07	Horse Chestnut	3.43	1.5
Northeast Belvoir Park Forest	2322	334236.77	370307.36	Horse Chestnut	3	1.5
NE Belvoir Park Forest/ Bowling Green Hill	2328	334119.91	370047.6	Sycamore	See note below	
NE Belvoir Park Forest/ Bowling Green Hill	2329	334143.25	370037.13	Oak	4.09	1.5

Location	Tree Tag No.	Eastings	Northings	Species	Girth	Height measured
NE Belvoir Park Forest/ Bowling Green Hill	2330	334133.48	369987.15	Oak	5.72	1
NE Belvoir Park Forest/ Bowling Green Hill	2331	334165.15	369972.12	Oak	3.13	1.5
NE Belvoir Park Forest/ Bowling Green Hill	2332	334169.83	369965.38	Oak	4.05	1.5
SE Belvoir Park Forest (Big Wood)	2333	334400	369798	Oak	c. 4.3	Estimate
SE Belvoir Park Forest (Big Wood)	2334	334437.07	369738.42	Oak	c. 3.10	Estimate
SE Belvoir Park Forest (Big Wood)	2335	334443.98	369734.51	Oak	c. 3.10	Estimate
SE Belvoir Park Forest (Big Wood)	2336	334476.52	369688.91	Oak	4.77	1.5
SE Belvoir Park Forest (Big Wood)	2337	334583.12	369568.01	Horse Chestnut	3.43	1.5
SE Belvoir Park Forest (Big Wood)	2338	334542.4	369539.87	Oak	4.32	1.5
SE Belvoir Park Forest (Big Wood)	2339	334534.34	369543.31	Oak	3.66	1.5
SE Belvoir Park Forest (Big Wood)	2340	334572.44	369529.87	Oak	4.33	1.5
SE Belvoir Park Forest (Big Wood)	2341	334608.07	369531.32	Sycamore	4.19	1.1
SE Belvoir Park Forest (Big Wood)	2342	334622.25	369511.4	Sycamore	3.33	1.5
SE Belvoir Park Forest (Big Wood)	2343	334669.09	369359.99	Oak	3.87	1.5
SE Belvoir Park Forest (Big Wood)	2344	334669.38	369357.94	Oak	3.07	2
SE Belvoir Park Forest (Big Wood)	2345	334654.01	369380.74	Oak	3.4	1.5
SE Belvoir Park Forest (Big Wood)	2356	334339.37	369653.58	Oak	3.18	1.5
SE Belvoir Park Forest (Big Wood)	2355	334444.84	369572.05	Oak	3.1	1.5
SE Belvoir Park Forest (Big Wood)	2354	334375.8	369560.5	Oak	3.85	1.5
SE Belvoir Park Forest (Big Wood)	2353	334434.02	369535.61	Oak	5.01	1
SE Belvoir Park Forest (Big Wood)	2352	334514.37	369509.17	Oak	5.1	1.5
SE Belvoir Park Forest (Big Wood)	2351	334510.75	369509.66	Oak	3.76	2
SE Belvoir Park Forest (Big Wood)	2350	334515.01	369483.91	Oak	3.45	1.5
SE Belvoir Park Forest (Big Wood)	2347	334547.18	369493.28	Oak	4.85	1.5
SE Belvoir Park Forest (Big Wood)	2349	334556.84	369475.02	Oak	3.03	1.5
SE Belvoir Park Forest (Big Wood)	2346	334536.85	369456.53	Oak	4.7	1
S Belvoir Park (S of courtyard)	2587	333981	396464.3	Oak	4.3	1.5
SW Belvoir Park Forest nr River Lagan	2488	333078.5	369111.9	Beech	3.29	1.5
SW Belvoir Park Forest nr River Lagan	2489	333103.9	369110.1	Beech	4.54	1.5
SW Belvoir Park Forest nr River Lagan	2490	333113.2	369114.7	Beech	3.66	1
SW Belvoir Park Forest nr River Lagan	2491	333176.5	369109.2	Beech	3.73	1.5
SW Belvoir Park Forest nr River Lagan	2492	333183	369121.7	Beech	3.77	1.5
SW Belvoir Park Forest nr River Lagan	2493	333225.5	369114.7	Beech	3.06	1.5
SW Belvoir Park Forest nr River Lagan	2494	333294.4	369160.5	Beech	3.25	1.5
SW Belvoir Park Forest nr River Lagan	2495	333280	369189.1	Beech	4.12	1.5
SW Belvoir Park Forest nr River Lagan	2496	333292.1	369226.6	Beech	c. 4	Estimate
SW Belvoir Park Forest nr River Lagan	2499	333252.3	369318.1	Beech	3.03	1.5
SW Belvoir Park Forest nr River Lagan	2500	333235.7	369335.6	Beech	3.7	1.5
SW Belvoir Park Forest nr River Lagan	2501	333217.6	369387.9	Horse Chestnut	3.39	1.5
SW Belvoir Park Forest nr River Lagan	2502	333208.4	369398.5	Horse Chestnut	3.67	0.6
SW Belvoir Park Forest nr River Lagan	2503	333215.8	369450.7	Horse Chestnut	3.94	1.5
SW Belvoir Park Forest nr River Lagan	2504	333252.3	369501.1	Sycamore	c. 3	Estimate
SW Belvoir Park Forest, S of Big Meadow	2497	333348.9	369161.9	Lime	c. 3.5	Estimate
SW Belvoir Park Forest, S of Big Meadow	2498	333334	369176	Lime	See note below	

TREES OVER 3m GIRTH IN THE AREA OF THE FORMER BELVOIR PARK ESTATE

Location	Tree Tag No.	Eastings	Northings	Species	Girth	Height measured
Between Belvoir forest & housing estate	2385	333216.5	368649.7	Oak	3.09	1.5
Between Belvoir forest & housing estate	2384	333183.5	368659.5	Oak	3.56	1.5
Between Belvoir forest & housing estate	2383	333578	369127	Oak	5.83	2
Between Belvoir forest & housing estate	2382	333719	368989	Oak	3.26	1.5
Between Belvoir forest & housing estate	2381	333727	368999	Oak	3.95	1.5
Between Belvoir forest & housing estate	2380	333755	369035	Oak	3.68	1.5
Between Belvoir forest & housing estate	2379	333763	369044	Oak	3.02	1.5
Between Belvoir forest & housing estate	2378	333817	369127.9	Oak	3.6	1.5
Between Belvoir forest & housing estate	2377	333872.8	369136.7	Oak	3.79	1.5
Between Belvoir forest & housing estate	2376	333910	369112.4	Oak	4.72	1.8
Between Belvoir forest & housing estate	2375	333884.2	369206.9	Oak	3.9	1.5
Between Belvoir forest & housing estate	2374	334048.3	369290.6	Oak	3.98	1.2
Between Belvoir forest & housing estate	2373	334061.2	369341.2	Oak	4.44	1.5
Between Belvoir forest & housing estate	2372	334106.2	369328.3	Turkey Oak	3.82	1.5
Between Belvoir forest & housing estate	2371	334129.9	369270.5	Turkey Oak	4.23	1.3
Between Belvoir forest & housing estate	2370	334235.3	369290.6	Oak	3.3	1.5
Between Belvoir forest & housing estate	2369	334207.6	369426.9	Ash	4.13	1.3
Between Belvoir forest & housing estate	2368	334523.7	369400.6	Deodar Cedar	4.02	1.5
Between Belvoir forest & housing estate	2367	334349	369519.8	*Pinus nigra*	3.97	1.5
Between Belvoir forest & housing estate	2366	334373.5	369508.7	Deodar Cedar	3	1.5
Between Belvoir forest & housing estate	2365	334375.8	369462	Lime	4.48	1.5
Between Belvoir forest & housing estate	2364	334383.2	369432.9	Oak	4.1	1.5
Between Belvoir forest & housing estate	2363	334412.3	369404.3	Lime	c. 3.3	Estimate
Between Belvoir forest & housing estate	2362	334508.5	369329.4	Oak	6.92	1
Between Belvoir forest & housing estate	2361	334532.5	369311.4	Oak	5.52	1.5
Between Belvoir forest & housing estate	2360	334546.4	369303.1	Lime	3.73	1.5
Between Belvoir forest & housing estate	2359	334588	369289.2	Oak	4.34	1.5
Between Belvoir forest & housing estate	2358	334504.8	369243.9	Beech	4.27	1.5
Between Belvoir forest & housing estate	2357	334464.6	369255	Sweet Chestnut	3.36	1.5
Belvoir Housing Estate	2388	334019.9	368840.8	Oak	3.77	1.5
Belvoir Housing Estate	2387	334035.4	369012.8	Oak	3.13	1.5
Belvoir Housing Estate	2386	333981.7	369015.4	Turkey Oak	3.78	1.5
Belvoir Housing Estate	2389	334508.4	369172.3	Oak	4.61	1.5
Belvoir Housing Estate	2390	334260	369005	Oak	3.43	1.1
Morelands Meadow	2301	333651.79	369710.16	Oak	3.25	1.5
Morelands Meadow	2302	333687.14	369723.02	Oak	4.18	1.5
Morelands Meadow	2303	333864.6	369740.93	Oak	3.57	1.5
Morelands Meadow	2304	333863.25	369814.51	Oak	4.08	1.5
Morelands Meadow	2305	333769.21	369855.21	Oak	3.15	1.5
Morelands Meadow	2306	333772.73	369882.54	Oak	4.2	1.5
Morelands Meadow	2307	333696.01	369828.76	Oak	3.26	1.5
Morelands Meadow	2308	333697.12	369859.17	Oak	3.78	1.5
Morelands Meadow	2309	333691.74	369772.75	Oak	3.99	1.5
Morelands Meadow	2310	333660.53	369752.2	Oak	3.39	1.5
Morelands Meadow	2311	333632.09	369717.41	Oak	3.24	1.5
Morelands Meadow	2312	333679.34	369743.91	Oak	3.94	1.5
Morelands Meadow	2313	333683.9	369733.02	Oak	3.2	1.5
Morelands Meadow	2314	333707.75	369698.01	Turkey Oak	4.19	1.5
Morelands Meadow	2315	333734.24	369720.34	Lime	3.8	1.1
Morelands Meadow	2316	333949.34	369846.48	Oak	4	0.8
Morelands Meadow	2317	333783.05	369908.65	Atlas Cedar	3.45	2
Morelands Meadow	2318	333780.59	369923.06	Horse Chestnut	3.57	1
Morelands Meadow	2319	333757.02	369897.26	Atlas Cedar	4.12	0.45
Morelands Meadow	2320	333678.55	369797.44	Oak	3.29	1.5
Ardnavally (Scout Centre)	2475	333060	368710	Beech	3.2	1.5
Ardnavally (Scout Centre)	2476	333201.9	368788.9	Monterey pine	3.22	1.5
Ardnavally (Scout Centre)	2477	333009	368822	Irish yew	See note below	
Ardnavally (Scout Centre)	2478	333020.8	368850.8	Sycamore	3.06	1.5
Ardnavally (Scout Centre)	2479	333053.1	368897.5	Monterey pine	3.48	1.5

TREES OVER 3m GIRTH IN THE AREA OF THE FORMER BELVOIR PARK ESTATE

Location	Tree Tag No.	Eastings	Northings	Species	Girth	Height measured
Ardnavally (Scout Centre)	2480	333069.3	368891	Monterey pine	3.47	1.5
Ardnavally (Scout Centre)	2481	333093.8	368874.4	Monterey pine	3.01	1.5
Ardnavally (Scout Centre)	2482	333102.1	368869.3	Beech	3.63	0.1
Ardnavally (Scout Centre)	2483	333049	368881.5	Lime	3.19	1.5
Ardnavally (Scout Centre)	2484	333035	368815	Beech	3	1.5
Ardnavally (Scout Centre)	2485	333036.5	368905.8	Monterey pine	3.58	1.5
Ardnavally (Scout Centre)	2486	332990.3	368928	Monterey pine	3.25	1.5
Ardnavally (Scout Centre)	2487	332966.7	368940	Monterey pine	3.04	1.5
Galwally, at junction with Laurel Wood	2582	334544.5	370477	Horse Chestnut	3.17	1.5
Galwally, garden by north shore of lake	2583	334713	370525.1	Beech	5.06	1.5
Galwally, garden by east shore of lake	2584	334840	370470	Oak	c. 3	Estimate

TREES OVER 3m GIRTH IN LAND AJACENT TO THE FORMER BELVOIR PARK ESTATE

Location	Tree Tag No.	Eastings	Northings	Species	Girth	Height measured
Trees over 3m near Belvoir - Annadale area		334366.8	370833.5	Oak	4.02	1.5
Trees over 3m near Belvoir - Annadale area		334362.9	370814.1	Oak	3.63	1.5
Trees over 3m near Belvoir - Annadale area		334342.3	370789.1	Beech	4.5	1.5
Trees over 3m near Belvoir - Annadale area		334334.7	370782	Beech	3.24	1.5
Trees over 3m near Belvoir - Annadale area		334319.4	370758.2	Horse Chestnut	3.4	1.5
Trees over 3m near Belvoir - Annadale area		334703.5	370770.9	Oak	4.24	1.5
Trees over 3m near Belvoir - Belvoir Road		334759.9	369281.8	Oak	3.25	1.5
Trees over 3m near Belvoir - Belvoir Road		334591.2	369071.5	Oak	c. 3.40	Estimate
Trees over 3m near Belvoir - By towpath, Newforge		333100	369410	Oak	5.9	0.75
Trees over 3m near Belvoir - By towpath, Newforge		333100	369420	Oak	4.69	1.5
Trees over 3m near Belvoir - By towpath, Newforge		333040	369510	Oak	3.42	1.5
Trees over 3m near Belvoir - By towpath, Newforge		333060	369500	Beech	3.26	1.5
Trees over 3m near Belvoir - By towpath, Newforge		333130	369490	Beech	3.17	1.5
Trees over 3m near Belvoir - By towpath, Newforge		333130	369440	Oak	4.18	1.5
Trees over 3m near Belvoir - Tree in field, Newforge		332990	369640	Oak	3.56	1.35
Big trees outside Belvoir - S. Lagan Meadows		333470	369730	Beech	4.15	1.5
Big trees outside Belvoir - S. Lagan Meadows		333450	369740	Beech	4.23	1.5
Big trees outside Belvoir - S. Lagan Meadows		333410	369760	Beech	3.45	1.5
Big trees outside Belvoir - W. Lagan Meadows		333320	369980	Oak	3.35	1.5
Big trees outside Belvoir - W. Lagan Meadows		333300	370000	Beech	3.54	1.5

BIGGEST GIRTH BROADLEAVED TREES NOTED ELSEWHERE IN NORTHERN LAGAN VALLEY

Location	Tree Tag No.	Eastings	Northings	Species	Girth	Height measured
Upper Malone (riding stables): Field by river nr Lagan footbridge.		331661.948	368265.458	Oak	6.5	1.5
Edenderry: In Edenderry UWT nature reserve.		331808.913	368141.844	Sweet Chestnut	5.27	1.5
Upper Malone: Malone Golf Course, near road.		330940	368030	Oak	4.63	1.5
Upper Malone: Dixon Park by main road.		330894	367942.67	Sycamore	5.65	2
Upper Malone: Dixon Park, near fountain.		330509.4	367565.97	Oak	5	1.5
Upper Malone: Dixon Park, near House		330650.18	367542.27	Oak	4.2	1.5
Upper Malone: Barnett Pk, biggest oak near arboretum.		332004.41	368747.37	Oak	5	1
Malone: Barnett Pk, by drive, N of Malone House.		332058.39	369341.78	Sweet Chestnut	4.61	0.9
Malone: Clement Wilson Pk near Malone Rd gate		332282	369516	Oak	4.58	1.5
Malone: Cranmore playing fields in front of ruined house		332583	370965	Sweet Chestnut	7.67	1.5
Malone: Cranmore playing fields in front of ruined house		332586	370967	Sweet Chestnut	4.33	1.7

MULTI-STEMMED & COPPICED TREES OVER 3M GIRTH IN BELVOIR PARK

Oak 2424. At just above ground level the tree has a girth of 28 feet 4 inches (8m 64cm). Near ground level the tree divides into 3 main trunks measuring 2.78m, 3.32m and 4.34m, the latter bough after a short distance dividing into 2 boughs 1.77m and 3.34m.

Lime 2426. At ground level the tree is 3m 48 cm. At just above ground level it divides into two main stems.

Alder 2427. Ivy makes measurement difficult. The girth at about 30cm height is c. 3m 80 cm. There are two main trunks from near ground level and one of these divides into two trunks at a height of about 1.5m

Sycamore 2328. An impressive tree, measured at 50cm the tree has a girth of 6m 05cm. There are two trunks from close to the ground. One is 2m 90cm in girth, the second is aprox. 4min girth. The latter bough divides into four big branches at a height of 1.5-2m.

Oak 2436. A tree at the corner of path, on stream bank. At ground level the trunk is c. 5m girth. A short distance above ground the tree divides into three upwards growing trunks

Horse chestnut 2472. A hollow stump only c.30cm high out of which a number of young shoots are growing. The stump is 3m 90cm in circumference at ground level

Horse Chestnut 2473. A hollow stump only c. 20cm high out of which a number of young branches are growing. The stump is c. 5m 74cm at a height of c. 10cm.

Lime 2474. An extraordinary tree with numerous tall thin branches growing closely together, originating from a roughly circular area c. 8m in circumference at ground level.

Irish Yew 2477. A typical Irish yew, with numerous thin branches growing from a roughly circular base. At a height of 10 cm this tree has a girth of 4m 70cm.

Lime 2498. Multi stem tree 4m 70cm in girth at ground level with numerous thin upwards growing branches.

Oak 2548. Multi stem tree. 4m 40cm at 10cm. Six branches grow from base, largest has a girth of under 2m.

Oak 2549. Multi stem tree. 4m 90cm at 10cm. Five main branches, the largest stem has a girth of less than 1.50m

Oak 2522. Multi stem tree. 5m.80cm at near ground level. Two trunks from just above ground level, the largest trunk has a girth of 3m 60cm, the other 2.96cm at 1.5m height.

Lime 2581. Multi stem tree 3m 60cm at a height of 25cm. Five trunks under 2m in circumference.

Oak 2585. Tree was felled a number of years ago, leaving c. 2.5m high standing trunk remaining. The trunk is 5m 80cm at a height of 1m 80cm. It is hollow and has produced a number of small, upwards growing stems (the largest is c.50cm in circumference) and a dense growth of twigs from the trunk.

Oak 2586. Tree was felled a number of years ago, leaving c.1m high standing trunk remaining. It has a girth of 4m 80cm at a height of 80cm. The trunk has resprouted, with a single tall, thin, upward growing stem c. 45cm in circumference.

Note about tree 2453. As this tree is the largest girthed tree in Belvoir it is worth stating that girth was measured at just above ground level because above this height this tree has completely decayed on one side and so girth measurements at greater heights are underestimates (at 1m the tree has a girth of 8.07m at 1.5m it has a girth of 7.93m).

METHODOLOGY FOR THE TREE SURVEY

The survey was undertaken using the methodology promoted by the Veteran Trees Initiative (Treework Environmental Consultancy). However it was felt to be more appropriate to measure girth at a height of 1.5m, as used in the Tree Record of Ireland (TROI) survey, which has recently surveyed thousands of trees throughout Ireland, rather than 1.3m as suggested by the Veteran Tree Initiative. For trees with irregular shaped trunks, girth was measured at the most appropriate height and as the height at which measurements were taken was recorded for each tree, any future survey will have no difficulty in checking measurements and determining growth rates.

Following TROI, where trees were growing on sloping ground the height at which girth was measured was taken from ground level on the upper side of the slope.

There is no standard way of measuring the girth of multi-stem trees and as only a small number of such trees were encountered in this study, it was decided to measure girth at near ground level and to give a brief description of the number and girths of the main stems at their widest point.

In the spreadsheet, no figure is entered in the girth column for multi-stem trees but information about the tree is noted at the end of the end of the last page of the spreadsheet.

Only large multi-stem trees were recorded, for example multi-stem hazel trees and some small multi stem birch in the golf course near Galwally Lake were excluded.

Where it was not clear if several stems growing close together were trunks of the same tree or a group of closely growing trees, they were excluded from the study.

An earlier survey of trees of parts of Belvoir Park Forest was undertaken by Norman Taylor was incorporated into the present study, though as Norman did not give the height that girth was measured, the circumference of these trees at 1.5m was determined and recorded.

A few trees could not be accurately measured due to excessive ivy, fencing, access issues etc, and the girth of these trees was estimated, this being clearly noted in the Excel database.

A very small number of trees in private land (the American Consul's home at Ardnavally, one large garden on Galwally Avenue) could not be visited though an oak on the eastern shore of Galwally lake which when viewed from a distance appears to be quite large was entered in the spreadsheet, with an estimated girth of 3m.

Location	Tree Tag No.	Grid Reference Eastings	Grid Reference Northings	Species	Girth	No. of dead wood units	When/ how tree fell
Bowling Green Hill	0001	3334151.70	370057.96	Oak	3m	0	L. F
Bowling Green Hill	0002	334132.97	370053.98	Sweet Chestnut	7m	1	L. F
Bowling Green Hill	0003	334122.5	370056.4	?	3.5m	1	L. F
Bowling Green Hill	0004	334112.60	370057.08	Oak	4.5m	1	L. F
Bowling Green Hill	0005	334140.46	370039.05	Oak	4.5m	0	L. F
Bowling Green Hill	0006	334200.61	370028.95	Yew	3m	4	L. U
Big Wood	0007	334727.9	369482.8	Oak	4m	6	R. U
Big Wood	0008	334743.9	369468.7	Beech	4m	0	L. F
Big Wood	0009	334324.99	369511.04	Oak	4.5m	8	R. U
Arboretum	0010	334103.08	369817.92	?	4m	0	L. F
Arboretum	0011a	334253.77	369834.33	Monterey Cypress?	3m	3	R. S
Arboretum	0011b	334177	369723	Cedar	3m	12m	R. U
Arboretum	0011c	334224	369767	?	3m	0	L. ?
Between forest & estate	0012	334174.58	369406.52	Turkey Oak	5m	5	R. F
South Corbie Wood	0013	333976.9	369587.2	Oak	4m	5	L. F
South Corbie Wood	0014	333938.65	369609.74	Oak	4.5m	6	L. F
South Corbie Wood	0015	333864.3	369560.6	Oak	4.5m	2	L. F
South Corbie Wood	0016	333818.96	369570.25	Oak	3.5m	1	L. F
South Corbie Wood	0017	333770.6	369593.7	Oak	3.5m	2	L. F
NE Big Meadow	0018	333623.40	369486.09	Oak	3.5m	1	L. S
NE Big Meadow	0019	333622.0	369514.7	Oak?	3.5m	0	L. ?
NE Big Meadow	0020	333647.4	369534.1	Oak	3.5m	0	L. ?
N Corbie Wood nr Lagan	0021	333663.12	369561.53	Oak	3.5m	1	L. F
N Corbie Wood nr Lagan	0022	333660.77	369567.89	Oak	4m	1	L. F
N Corbie Wood nr Lagan	0023	333656.77	369611.06	Oak	3m	6	R. U
N Corbie Wood nr Lagan	0024	333681.09	369629.76	Oak	8.5m?	3	L. ?
N Corbie Wood nr Lagan	0025	333673.09	369589.25	Oak	3.5m	16	R. S
N Corbie Wood nr Lagan	0026	333749.36	369637.23	Oak	4m	8	L. F
N Corbie Wood nr Lagan	0027	333781.8	369604.3	Oak	3m	3	L. F
N Corbie Wood nr Lagan	0028	333805.4	369609.0	Oak	4.5m	8	L. F
N Corbie Wood nr Lagan	0029	333805.4	369637.9	Oak	3m	16	L. F
N Corbie Wood nr Lagan	0030	333782.4	369671.5	Oak	3m	2	L. F
N Corbie Wood nr Lagan	0031	333829.39	369633.02	Oak	3m	3	L. F
N Corbie Wood nr Lagan	0032	333806.6	369666.2	Oak	4m	0	L. ?
N Corbie Wood nr Lagan	0033	333802.4	369674.4	Oak?	3m	0	L. ?
N Corbie Wood nr Lagan	0034	333828.57	369616.83	Oak	3m	5	L. F
N Corbie Wood nr Lagan	0035	333866.1	369668.5	Oak	3m	4	L. F
N Corbie Wood nr Lagan	0036	333894.81	369620.03	Oak	6.5m	3	L. F
N Corbie Wood nr Lagan	0037	333892.08	369647.91	Oak	4m	2	L. F
N Corbie Wood nr Lagan	0038	333915.63	369672.47	Oak	3.5m	2	L. ?
N Corbie Wood nr Lagan	0039	333927.11	369675.23	Oak	4m	0	L. F
N Corbie Wood nr Lagan	0040	333942.1	369650.8	Oak?	4m	6	L. F
N Corbie Wood nr Lagan	0041	333941.09	369661.82	Oak	3.5m	0	L. F
East of Big Meadow	0042	333620.9	369370.2	Oak	4m	4	L. F
East of Big Meadow	0043	333627.3	369343.1	Oak	4m	25	R. S
SW Belvoir near Lagan	0044	333300.2	369226.4	Beech?	4m	4	L. S
SW Belvoir near Lagan	0045	333283.7	369156.8	Beech	4m	7	L. S
SW Belvoir near Lagan	0046	333147.5	369107.9	Beech?	3m	0	L. ?
SW Belvoir near Lagan	0047	333177.66	369120.62	Beech	3m	11	R. S
SW Belvoir near Lagan	0048	333244.2	369103.2	Beech	3m	0	L. ?
Ardnavally	0049	332998.4	368924.6	Monterey pine	3m	9	L. S
Ardnavally	0050	333022.5	368911.6	Monterey pine	4m	0	L. F
Morelands Meadow	0051	333643.3	369709.2	Beech	3m	20	R. U
Morelands Meadow	0052	333619.7	369683.3	Beech?	4m	0	L. F
Morelands Meadow	0053	333813.6	369871.3	Oak	4.5m	40	R. S

Area surveyed

The woodlands, Housing Executive open space and Morelands Meadow were surveyed. The golf course was excluded from the survey because fallen trees and stumps are quickly removed in this area.

Girth

The girth of dead trees 3m in circumference or greater were measured to the nearest 50cm.

Dead wood units

The methodology of the Veteran Trees Initiative (Treework environmental consultancy) was used:
Trunk and branches at least 1m long and over 15cm diameter were identified.
Each 1m length counted as one unit and total number of units recorded.

When fell

L = Long dead, no bark or small branches remain. No obvious gap in woodland canopy.

R = Recently died. (c. 20 years or less). Some bark and small branches remain, there is often a gap in the woodland canopy.

How fell

U = Uprooted
S = Trunk snapped, rootplate *in situ*.
F = Felled, sawn face visible, rootplate *in situ*.
? = Probably felled, rootplate *in situ* but too rotten for sawn face to be clearly seen.

Table 1. Allocation of individual trees to genetic groupings based on microsatellite data. For grid references of trees see Appendix 3.

Tree number and location	Tree girth (m)	DNA grouping	Notes
2354 SE Belvoir Park Forest (Big Wood)	3.85	3	
2301 Morelands Meadow	3.25	3	
2516 Belvoir Golf Course	4.50	4	
2539 Belvoir Golf Course	5.10	4	
2549 Belvoir Golf Course	4.90	4	
2451 Belvoir park forest east of big meadow	4.00	4	
2338 SE Belvoir Park Forest (Big Wood)	4.32	4	
2307 Morelands Meadow	3.26	4	
2510 Belvoir Golf Course	5.20	5	
2383 Between Belvoir Park Forest & housing estate	5.83	5	
2352 SE Belvoir Park Forest (Big Wood)	5.10	5	
2362 Between Belvoir Park Forest & housing estate	6.92	5	
2302 Morelands Meadow	4.18	5	
2303 Morelands Meadow	3.57	5	
2306 Morelands Meadow	4.20	5	
2520 Belvoir Golf Course	5.18	6	
2467 Belvoir Park Forest near big meadow	4.45	6	
2453 Belvoir Park Forest east of big meadow	8.80	6	
2446 Belvoir Park Forest east of big meadow	5.04	6	
2447 Belvoir Park Forest NE of big meadow	4.06	6	
2305 Morelands Meadow	3.15	6	
2514 Belvoir Golf Course	4.29	7	
2536 Belvoir Golf Course	4.29	7	
2537 Belvoir Golf Course	4.67	7	
2430 Belvoir Park Forest Corbie Wood nr lagan	4.98	7	
2353 SE Belvoir Park Forest (Big Wood)	5.01	7	
2346 SE Belvoir Park Forest (Big Wood)	4.70	7	
2376 Between Belvoir Park Forest & housing estate	4.72	7	
bpl Upper Malone	5.00	7	outside Belvoir
2507 Belvoir Golf Course	3.20	8	
2456 Belvoir Park Forest NE of big meadow	3.16	8	
2435 Belvoir Park Forest Corbie Wood nr lagan	3.84	8	
2332 NE Belvoir Park Forest/Bowling Green Hill	4.05	9	
2304 Morelands Meadow	4.08	9	
2309 Morelands Meadow	3.99	9	
2310 Morelands Meadow	3.39	9	
305 Annadale	4.24	9	outside Belvoir
2454 Belvoir Park Forest east of big meadow	3.95	10	
2452 Belvoir Park Forest east of big meadow	5.40	10	
300 Annadale	4.02	10	outside Belvoir
2509 Belvoir Golf Course	6.35	11	
2545 Belvoir Golf Course	4.35	11	
2440 Belvoir Park Forest NE of big meadow	3.21	11	
2364 Between Belvoir Park Forest & housing estate	4.10	11	
2308 Morelands Meadow	3.78	11	
eb1 Upper Malone	6.50	11	outside Belvoir
2521 Belvoir Golf Course	4.05	12	
2329 NE Belvoir Park Forest/Bowling Green Hill	4.09	12	
2339 SE Belvoir Park Forest (Big Wood)	3.66	12	
stl Upper Malone	5.00	12	outside Belvoir
st3 Upper Malone	4.20	12	outside Belvoir

DNA Extraction

DNA was extracted from 0.1g of clean leaf material with no obvious signs of disease (in order to minimise DNA contamination from other organisms, which might affect ISSR results) using the Nucleon Phytopure kit (Amersham) according to the manufacturers instructions. The DNA pellet was resuspended in 200µl of deionised water and left at 4°C overnight before being visualised by running 4µl on a 1.2% agarose gel stained with ethidium bromide. DNA concentration was assessed by comparing with a standard, in this case Low DNA Mass Ladder (Invitrogen) and quantifying the DNA using Phoretix 1D Advanced gel analysis software.

Microsatellites

Microsatellites, or their synonyms, simple sequences and short tandem repeats, are tandemly repeated short sequence motifs ranging from 1-6 bp. Depending on the length of the repeat unit, microsatellites are classified as mono-, di-, tri-, tetra-, penta- and hexa-nucleotide repeats. Microsatellites are embedded in single copy DNA, which allows the specific PCR amplification of a single microsatellite locus. A classic microsatellite consists of a single repeat type only, which can be repeated up to a hundred times. For several plants, the most abundant dinucleotide microsatellite is $(AT/TA)_n$, followed by $(AG/TC)_n$ and then $(AC/TG)_n$.

Microsatellites provide a huge reservoir of polymorphic genetic markers because their alleles differ in repeat number. When microsatellites are individually amplified by PCR using a pair of flanking unique oligonucleotides as primers, they usually show high levels of polymorphism as a result of this variation in repeat units. Their high variability, codominance and distribution over the euchromatic genome (in contrast to other classes of repetitive DNA e.g. minisatellites) make microsatellites a useful marker for the construction of genetic maps, paternity testing, forensics, relatedness estimates, population genetics and phylogenetic reconstruction of closely related species.

It has been shown that microsatellites are a useful marker for the discrimination of closely related species,[1] therefore microsatellite analysis was used to address the question of the genetic relationships among Belvoir *Q. robur* and *Q. petraea*.

Microsatellite loci were amplified following standard protocols.[2] Briefly, fluorescent labelled PCR primers were used in a 10 µL reaction volume (1.5 mM $MgCl_2$, 200 µM, dNTPs, 1 µM of each primer, 20-100 ng template DNA and 0.5 U *Taq* polymerase). The cycling profile consisted of an initial denaturation step of 3 min followed by 35 cycles of 60 seconds at 94°C, 60 seconds at 45-60°C (depending on the primer combination) and 1 min at 72°C. A final extension at 72°C for 45 min was used to assure a quantitative terminal transferase activity of the *Taq* polymerase. PCR products were then separated and quantified on an automated DNA sequencer.

Table 2. Microsatellite primer sequences and repeat motif for each locus

Locus	Repeat motif [#]	Forward primer (5'-3')	Reverse primer (5'-3')
ZAG 1/5	$(GT)_5(GA)_9$	GCT TGA GAG TTG AGA TTT GT	GCA ACA CCC TTT AAC TAC CA
ZAG 1/2	$(AG)_{16}$	TCC TCC GCT CAC TCA CCA TT	AAA CCT CCA CCA AAA CAT TC
ZAG 7	$(AG)_{13}(AAAG)_3$	CGC ACG ACC GAC CTA GGT A	CTTATA GGA GAC ATG CCC AG
ZAG 9	$(AG)_{12}$	GCA ATT ACA GGC TAG GCT GG	GTC TGG ACC TAG CCC TCA TG
ZAG 15	$(AG)_{23}$	CGA TTT GAT AAT GAC ACT ATG G	CAT CGA CTC ATT GTT AAG CAC
ZAG 16	$(AG)_{21}$	CTT CAC TGG CTT TTC CTC CT	TGA AGC CCT TGT CAA CAT GC
ZAG 46	$(AG)_{13}$	CCC CTA TTG AAG TCC TAG CCG	TCT CCC ATG TAA GTA GCT CTG
ZAG 110	$(AG)_{15}$	GGA GGC TTC CTT CAA CCT ACT	GAT CTC TTG TGT GCT GTA TTT
ZAG 119	$(GA)_{24}$	GAT CAG TGA TAG TGC CTC TC	GAT CAA CAA GCC CAA GGC AC
ZAG *7	$(TC)_{17}$	CAA CTT GGT GTT CGG ATC AA	GTG CAT TTC TTT TAT AGC ATT CAC
ZAG 20	$(TC)_{18}$	CCA TTA AAA GAA GCA GTA TTT TGT	GCA ACA CTC AGC CTA TAT CTA GAA
ZAG 31	$(GA)_{31}$	CTT AGT TTG GTT GGG AAG AT	GCA ACC AAA CAA ATG AAA T
ZAG 87	$(TC)_{20}$	TCC CAC CAC TTT GGT CTC TCA	GTT GTC AGC AGT GGG ATG GGT A
ZAG 96	$(TC)_{20}$	CCC AGT CAC ATC CAC TAC TGT CC	GGT TGG GAA AAG GAG ATC AGA
ZAG 101	$(TC)_{20}(AC)_{15}$	CCT GCA CAA TCA AAT CCT TCA CTT	GCC ATG AAC AAC GGA GGT ATC TAG
ZAG 108	$(GA)_{19}(GGGA)_3$	AAG AGA GCA AAT TTA GAG TGA TGT	GAA CCT TGA TCA TAC GTG GAG A
ZAG 112	$(GA)_{32}$	TTC TTG CTT TGG TGC GCG	GTG GTC AGA GAC TCG GTA AGT ATT C
ZAGM 36	$(AG)_{19}$	GAT CAA AAT TTG GAA TAT TAA	TCG TGG AGG TTA GTC CCN TTT
ZAGM 58	$(GA)_{34}$	AAT TGA GAG TGA CAG AAA GAG	TTC TTT TTC CTA ATC TCA ACT
ZAGM 102	$(AG)_5AA(AG)_{13}$	AAG CTT TCC AAT TGC ATA AAC	ATG TAC AAT GTG TTG ACT ACT

[#] Repeat unit of cloned allele after Steinkellner *et al.* 1997 ; Kampfer *et al.* 1998.[3-5]

Inter -Simple Sequence Repeats

The marker system know as Inter - Simple Sequence Repeats (ISSR) was developed by Zietkiewicz *et al*[6] as an anonymous, RAPD – like approach that can be used to assess variation in microsatellite regions distributed throughout the genome. It shares many of the advantages and disadvantages of RAPDs (Randomly Amplified Polymorphine DNAs), a technique independently developed by Williams *et al.*[7] and Welsh and McClelland in 1990.[8] Like RAPDs, ISSRs are dominant markers, require no prior knowledge of the genome under study and use a single primer for forward and reverse PCR reactions producing multi-band 'fingerprints'. ISSRs, like RAPDs have problems with reproducibility, but are considered more stringent due to the generally longer primers being used.[9] The list of primers screened is given in Table 3. For oaks, primers were chosen that fulfilled two criteria, namely they produced clear, reproducible banding patterns and included polymorphic loci.

Table 3. Oak ISSR primers used in study of Belvoir oaks

Primer Name	Primer Sequence (5'-3')
(CT)8RG	CTCTCTCTCTCTCTCTRG
(CT)8RA	CTCTCTCTCTCTCTCTRA
(CT)8RC	CTCTCTCTCTCTCTCTRC
(CT)8TG	CTCTCTCTCTCTCTCTTG
(GAG)4RC	GAGGAGGAGGAGRC
(GT)6YR	GTGTGTGTGTGTYR
(CA)6YR	CACACACACACAYR
(CA)6RG	CACACACACACARG
(GT)6AY	GTGTGTGTGTGTAY
(GT)6RG	GTGTGTGTGTGTRG
(CA)7YG	CACACACACACACAYG
GGGC(GA)8	GGGCGAGAGAGAGAGAGA
(GA)7RG	GAGAGAGAGAGAGARG
(GTG)4RC	GTGGTGGTGGTGRC
(CTC)4RC	CTCCTCCTCCTCRC
(CAC)4RC	CACCACCACCACRC
(GT)7TG	GTGTGTGTGTGTGTTG
CAA(GA)5	CAAGAGAGAGAGA
(CT)8RG	CTCTCTCTCTCTCTCTRG
(CT)8TG	CTCTCTCTCTCTCTCTTG

The PCR conditions for all ISSR reactions were the same. A 20µl reaction was prepared with 50ng of genomic DNA, 1.5mM MgCl2, 1mM dNTPs, 1µM of each primer and 1 unit Taq polymerase. Cycling conditions consisted of an initial denaturing step of 5 minutes, followed by 40 cycles of 45 seconds at 94°C, 40 seconds at 48°C and 1 minute 30 seconds at 72°C. A final elongation step of 7 minutes at 72°C was included. The amplifications were performed on a ThermoHybaid PCR Express thermal cycler (Hybaid). All ISSR reactions were carried out in duplicate so that unstable products could be identified and eliminated from the analysis. All ISSR reactions included a negative control.

Visualising ISSR Products
After PCR amplification, 8µl of each reaction was loaded onto a 2% agarose gel. The gel was run at a constant 80 volts and 120mA for approximately 60 minutes to allow good separation of PCR products. The bands were visualised under UV light using a transilluminator (UVP) and digitally captured on computer using GrabIt (Annotating Grabber version 2.59).

ISSR Gel Analysis
Banding patterns were assessed using the gel analysis software Phoretix 1D and from this, matrices denoting the presence (1) or absence (0) of each band were constructed. Bands that did not appear in both replicates were ignored.

Chloroplast DNA Experiments
Chloroplast analysis was performed using a combination of DNA sequencing and restriction enzyme digestion of PCR products.[10] The primers of Taberlet et al.[11] amplifying the trnL intron and the trnF-trnT intergenic spacer were used in this study as they have been found to be polymorphic in oak.[12,13] The sequences of the primers amplifying the trnL intron were: (forward) CGA AAT CGG TAG ACG CTA CG and (reverse) GGG GAT AGA GGG ACT TGA AC. The primers amplifying the IGS were: (forward) GGT TCA AGT CCC TCT ATC CC and (reverse) ATT TGA ACT GGT GAC ACG AG. A 25µl volume reaction was prepared with 100ng of genomic DNA, 1.5 mM MgCl2, 200µM dNTPs, 1µM of each primer and 1 unit of Taq polymerase. Reaction conditions consisted of an initial denaturing step of 94°C for 5 minutes followed by 37 cycles of 94°C for 30 seconds, 55°C for 30 seconds and 72°C for 45 seconds, and a final extension stage of 72°C for 7 minutes.

PCR products were purified using GenElute PCR Clean Up kits (Sigma) according to the manufacturers instructions. The amount of purified fragment was quantified by running it on a 1.2% agarose gel against Low DNA Mass Ladder (Invitrogen) prior to sequencing. Sequencing reactions were performed using BigDye Terminator Kit Version 3 (ABI) according to the manufacturer's instructions, followed by ethanol precipitation of the product. Sequencing was carried out on a ABI 2100 Genetic Analyser. Sequences were edited using Contig Express (InforMax).

APPENDIX 5: GENETIC ANALYSIS OF BELVOIR OAKS: TECHNICAL INFORMATION

References

1. Harr, B., Kauer, M., Schlotterer, C. (2002) Hitchhiking mapping: A population-based fine-mapping strategy for adaptive mutations in *Drosophila melanogaster. Proceedings of the National Academy of Sciences of the United States of America* **99**: 12949-12954.

2. Schlötterer, C. (1998) Microsatellites. In: Hoelzal, R. A (Ed) 1998. *Molecular Genetic Analysis of Populations: a practical approach.* Oxford University Press. Oxford.

3. Steinkellner, H., Lexer, C., Turetschek, E. and Glossl, J. (1997a) Conservation of GA microsatellite loci between *Quercus* species. *Molecular Ecology* **6**: 1189-1194.

4. Steinkellner, H., Fluch, S., Turetschek, E., Lexer, C., Streiff, R., Kremer, A., Burg, K. and Glossl, J. (1997b) Identification and characterisation of ga/ct microsatellite loci from *Quercus petraea. Plant Molecular Biology* **33**: 1093-1096.

5. Kampfer, S., Lexer, C., Glössl, J. and Steinkellner, H. (1998) Characterisation of $(GA)_n$ microsatellite loci from *Quercus robur. Hereditas* **129**: 183-186.

6. Zietkiewicz, E., Rafalski, A., Labuda, D. (1994) Genomic fingerprinting by simple sequence repeat (SSR)-anchored polymerase chain reaction amplification. *Genomics* **20**: 176-183.

7. Williams, J. G. K., Kubelik, A. R., Livak, K. J., Rafalski, J. A. and Tingey, S. V. (1990) DNA polymorphisms amplified by arbitrary primers are useful as genetic markers. *Nucleic Acids Research* **18**: 6531-6535.

8. Welsh, J and McClelland, M. (1990) Fingerprinting genomes using PCR with arbitrary primers. *Nucleic Acids Research* **18**: 7213-7218.

9. Godwin, I. D., Aitken, E. A. B. and Smith, L. W. (1997) Application of inter simple sequence repeat (ISSR) markers to plant genetics. *Electrophoresis* **18**: 1524- 1528.

10. Kelleher**,** C. T., Hodkinson, T. R., Kelly, D. L. and Douglas, G. C. (2003) Characterisation of chloroplast DNA haplotypes to reveal the provenance and genetic structure of oaks in Ireland**.** *Forest Ecology and Management*, **189**: 123-131.

11. Taberlet, P., Gielly, L., Pautou, G., Bouvet, J. (1991) Universal primers for amplification of three non-coding regions of chloroplast DNA. *Plant Molecular Biology* **17**: 1105-1109.

12. Ferris, C., Oliver, R. P., Davy, A. J. and Hewitt, G. M. (1993) Native oak chloroplasts reveal an ancient divide across Europe. *Molecular Ecology* **2**: 337-344.

13. Ferris, C., King, R. A., Vainola, R., Hewitt, G. M. (1998) Chloroplast DNA recognises three refugial sources of European oaks and suggests independent eastern and western immigrations to Finland. *Heredity* **80**: 584-593.

Ascomycetes - cup fungi

Anthracobia melaloma		J337697	29-Jan-92	In several dense clusters on charcoal from burning tree branches the previous summer.
Arecophila muroiana	[First European record]	J344694	02-Jun-01	On dead stems of bamboo, *Pseudosalsa japonica*.
Ascobolus albidus		J331691	13-Dec-00	Sparse on rabbit dung in needle litter under spruce.
Ascobolus roseopurpurascens		J332692	09-Feb-01	On rabbit pellets in litter under grey alder.
Ascocoryne sarcoides		J345695	30-Sep-97	On peeling bark of a felled sycamore.
Berlesiella nigerrima		J347695	11-Feb-04	On *Eutypella leprosa* on dead box branches.
Bisporella citrina		J344695	26-Nov-94	On beech branches in litter.
Botryotinia calthae		J333694	18-May-96	On last year's rotting stem of marsh marigold; grey alder wood.
Bulgaria inquinans	Black Bulgar	J344697	30-Jun-90	A few erumpent on fallen horse chestnut boughs.
Capitotricha bicolor		J345695	14-Apr-01	On oak twigs still attached to large half-fallen tree.
Catinella olivacea		J332692	30-Sep-94	On bark of a very rotten alder branch with the bark separated and peeling.
Cheilymenia coprinaria		J331691	13-Dec-00	One, on rabbit dung in needle litter under spruce.
Cheilymenia fimicola		J331688	07-Apr-98	Growing on algaed rabbit pellets on a wet, wooded lawn.
Cheilymenia granulata		J337697	28-Jan-95	On cow dung under trees.
Cheilymenia rubra		J337698	30-Jan-98	On old cow dung with leaves under a Lebanon Cedar in pasture.
Cheilymenia stercorea		J337697	29-Jan-92	Extremely abundant on cow dung over the whole meadow.
Ciboria caucus	Alder Goblet	J330692	10-Mar-94	Frequent on female alder catkins.
Ciboria juncorum	Rush Goblet	J335695	26-Apr-01	On seeds of Juncus in litter.
Ciboria lentiformis	Alder Seed Goblet	J332692	19-Mar-96	On free seeds and seeds still in female cones of native alder in wet carr.
Ciboria viridifusca		J338700	16-May-96	Several apothecia on an old female cone of grey alder; riverbank.
Colpoma quercinum		J345695	14-Apr-01	On oak twigs still attached to large half-fallen tree.
Coprotus albidus		J331691	13-Dec-00	Abundant on rabbit dung in needle litter under spruce.
Cordyceps militaris	Scarlet Caterpillar Fungus	J334693	06-Oct-83	On caterpillars of *Mamestra* in litter under grass.
Cordyceps ophioglossoides		J332692	03-Sep-89	On *Elaphomyces granulatus* under beech.
Coronophora gregaria		J342697	29-May-03	On dying branches of rowan.
Cudoniella acicularis		J339696	24-Oct-03	On humus material on old oak stump.
Cudoniella clavus		J340696	09-Mar-96	Several on an alder stick in very wet litter.
Cudoniella clavus var. grandis		J346694	23-Feb-99	In wet alder/willow swamp.
Daldinia loculata	Cramp Ball	J344695	28-Nov-90	On burnt branch of living birch.
Dasyscyphus pulveraceus		J334693	26-Apr-01	On fallen branches in blackthorn thicket.
Dermea cerasi		J343697	12-Sep-97	Conidial stage on fallen cherry branch.
Diaporthe eres		J342696	05-Jun-01	On dead stem of *Berberis darwinii*.
Diaporthe hederae		J345694	02-Jun-01	On 1cm ivy branches on the ground under ash.
Diaporthe leiphaemia		J345695	14-Apr-01	On oak twigs still attached to large half-fallen tree.
Diatrype stigma		J332691	26-Nov-91	On dead hawthorn branches in a wet alder wood.
Diatrypella quercina		J345695	11-Feb-94	Frequent on fallen oak twigs.
Elaphomyces granulatus		J332692	03-Sep-89	At the roots of beech in mossy litter.
Eutypa leprosa		J347695	11-Feb-04	On dead standing branches of box.
Eutypella prunastri		J334693	26-Apr-01	On fallen branches in blackthorn thicket.
Eutypella sorbi		J342697	06-Feb-04	On dead attached branch of rowan.
Fimaria cervaria		J332692	09-Feb-01	On rabbit pellets in litter under grey alder.
Geoglossum fallax		J344693	22-Nov-97	Growing on mossy slopes of mown grass.
Gloniopsis praelonga		J334693	26-Apr-01	On fallen branches in blackthorn thicket.
Helvella lacunosa		J332692	04-Nov-83	Occasional at the roots of beech by a gravel path.
Humaria hemisphaerica		J342696	27-Aug-99	In moss on stones under oak.
Hyaloscypha aureliella		J335695	26-Apr-01	On bark of felled Japanese larch.
Hyaloscypha leuconica		J331688	13-Mar-98	On cones of hybrid larch; plantation.
Hymenoscyphus calyculus		J332692	30-Sep-94	On the cut end of an alder branch in litter.
Hymenoscyphus fagineus		J332691	03-Sep-99	On cupules in a seepage under beech.
Hymenoscyphus lutescens		J339697	13-Apr-98	On Scots pine cones in damp litter.
Hypoxylon fuscum		J345695	31-Dec-91	Frequent on hazel twigs lying by a stream.
Hypoxylon intermedium		J335695	26-Apr-01	On fallen dead ash branches on a tree; scarce.
Hypoxylon petriniae		J343696	27-Nov-04	On fallen ash branches.
Hysterographium fraxini		J342694	15-Apr-04	On bark of dead standing twig on sapling ash.
Iodophanus carneus		J331688	07-Apr-98	Growing on algaed badger dung on a lawn.
Lachnellula occidentalis		J331691	02-Mar-94	On larch branches in grass by a spruce/larch block.
Lachnellula willkommii		J331691	13-Dec-00	On fallen twigs of hybrid larch in spruce planting.
Lachnum niveum		J346694	23-Mar-96	On dead oak wood in wet, mixed woods with laurel.
Leotia lubrica	Jelly Babies	J332692	06-Nov-91	On a bare clay pathside bank under beech.
Melanconis alni		J346694	02-Jun-01	On 0.5cm twigs of felled alder branches by path.
Melanconis stilbostoma		J344694	02-Mar-04	On small branches and twigs of a sapling birch.

Melanomma fuscidulum		J346694	16-Apr-04	On dead fallen stems of honeysuckle.
Mollisia cinerella		J335695	26-Apr-01	On bark of felled Japanese larch.
Mollisia discolor		J340696	11-Oct-97	Erumpent on clusters on oak branches in long grass.
Mollisia fallax		J339697	13-Apr-98	On Scots pine cones in damp litter.
Mollisia ventosa		J345695	14-Apr-01	On de-barked oak twig still attached to fallen tree.
Mytilinidion gemmigenum		J335695	26-Apr-01	On bark of felled larch log; scarce.
Nectria cinnabarina	Common Coral Spot	J345695	30-Sep-97	On peeling bark of a felled sycamore.
Nectria coccinea		J343694	15-Apr-04	On heartwood of dead elm sapling.
Nectria episphaeria		J345695	14-Apr-01	On *Trematosphaeria* on ash branches.
Nectria fuckeliana		J331691	21-May-01	On fallen branches of Norway spruce in needle litter.
Nectria hederae		J334693	26-Apr-01	On twigs among fallen branches of ivy [conidial stage only - no spores present].
Nectria magnusiana		J333689	21-May-01	On branch of sycamore in litter.
Nectria peziza		J343694	15-Apr-04	On dead heartwood of standing *Ulmus procera* sapling.
Nectria punicea		J334693	28-Apr-01	On dead branch of living tree.
Nectria ralfsii	Ralfs' Coral Spot	J345695	30-Sep-97	On peeling bark of a felled sycamore.
Nectria sinopica		J345694	02-Jun-01	On 1cm ivy branches on the ground under ash.
Orbilia comma		J343694	15-Apr-04	Inside peeling bark of dead sapling *Ulmus procera*.
Orbilia sarraziniana		J333694	08-Sep-99	On grey alder branches sunk in mud of a dried out woodland pool.
Otidea alutacea		J338696	24-Oct-03	In litter under silver fir.
Otthia spiraeae		J347694	14-Apr-01	On sycamore branches lying on the ground.
Pachyella babingtonii		J332691	26-Nov-91	On rotting alder branches.
Pezicula houghtonii		J347694	26-Oct-97	On branch of Portuguese laurel still with wilting leaves; wood very fresh.
Pezicula sporulosa		J342696	11-Oct-97	On fallen twig of *Cryptomeria japonica*.
Peziza flavida	Yellow Elfcup	J347694	26-Oct-97	On coarse sycamore wood shavings.
Peziza varia	Variable Elfcup	J337697	29-Jan-92	Emerging from bark on long-dead oak trees.
Pezizella alniella		J333694	18-May-96	On grey alder female cone in wet woodland.
Phaeohelotium flexuosum		J346694	16-Apr-04	Underside of log; gravelly streambank.
Phaeohelotium monticola		J333694	27-Nov-91	On bark of a decaying branch of horse chestnut in carr.
Phaeohelotium subcarneum		J347694	25-Oct-97	On oak twigs in a black woodland sheugh.
Pithyella erythrostigma		J342697	05-Jun-01	On *Eutypella leprosa*.
Plicaria leiocarpa		J341698	21-Feb-98	Among *Funaria* on burn site.
Polydesmia pruinosa		J340694	11-Sep-97	Parasitic on *Diatrypella quercina* on oak twigs.
Propolomyces farinosus		J342697	06-Apr-01	On fallen hazel branches.
Pseudovalsa lanciformis		J344696	08-Oct-97	In slits of bark on fallen birch branches in a ditch.

Pyrenopeziza revincta		J343696	17-Mar-98	Near base of stem in common figwort; open, wet area of woodland.
Rhytisma acerinum		J347696	10-Oct-03	On leaves of standing *Salix caprea*.
Rosellinia britannica		J334693	28-Apr-01	On fallen ivy stems.
Rosellinia sublimbata		J344694	02-Jun-01	On dead stems of bamboo, *Pseudosalsa japonica*.
Roussoella intermedia	[First European record]	J344694	02-Jun-01	On dead stems of bamboo, *Pseudosalsa japonica*.
Saccobolus depauperatus		J331691	13-Dec-00	Abundant on some rabbit dung in needle litter under spruce.
Sarcoscypha austriaca	Scarlet Elfcup	J340696	09-Mar-96	Several on alder sticks in very wet litter by the main path.
Scutellinia scutellata	Common Eye-lash Fungus	J332692	13-Oct-97	Erumpent from decaying bark of a rotted beech branch.
Scutellinia superba		J344696	11-Oct-97	On very wet clay under logs.
Tapesia fusca		J345694	21-Jan-99	On bare wood of very rotten stump of oak.
Tapesia rosae var. prunicola		J334693	28-Apr-01	On fallen branches in a blackthorn thicket.
Trematosphaeria pertusa		J345695	14-Apr-01	On ash twigs still attached to fallen trees.
Trichophaea hemisphaeroides		J341698	21-Feb-98	Among *Funaria* on burn site.
Velutarina rufo-olivacea		J331691	13-Dec-00	Erumpent in groups on lime twigs in litter.
Xylaria polymorpha	Dead Man's Fingers	J333692	04-Feb-94	Occasional on dead beech.

Phragmobasidiomycetes – jelly fungi

Auricularia mesenterica	Tripe Fungus	J337698	28-Jan-91	Clustered abundantly on a hollow oak log in a cattle-grazed water meadow.
Calocera cornea		J337697	11-Nov-91	On stumps and bare heartwood of various trees in cattle-grazed water meadows.
Exidia glandulosa	Witches Butter	J344699	10-Oct-03	On fallen branch under oak 2536.
Exidia thuretiana		J334694	30-Dec-91	On the branches with bark of a dead elm.
Exidia truncata		J343695	22-Nov-97	On an oak branch in wet grass; arboretum.
Hirneola auricula-judae	Jew's Ear	J345695	30-Sep-97	On peeling bark of a felled sycamore.
Tremella foliacea		J345695	22-Nov-97	Festooning old, dead branches of laurel.
Tremella globospora		J342697	05-Jun-01	On *Eutypella leprosa* on sycamore.
Tremella mesenterica	Yellow Brain Fungus	J344697	10-Oct-03	On dead branch on young oak nr. 2541.

Aphyllophorales – bracket fungi

Species	Common name	Grid ref	Date	Notes
Abortiporus biennis		J344693	16-Nov-96	Growing on buried wood where a tree had been felled on a mown lawn.
Athelia neuhoffii		J346695	19-Jan-99	On fresh fallen rotten bough of gale-blown oak.
Bjerkandera fumosa		J345694	25-Dec-91	Covering a large section of cut trunk of a felled oak dumped in open parkland.
Cerocorticium confluens		J340694	11-Sep-97	On fallen branches under young oak.
Clavulinopsis helvola		J344693	22-Nov-97	Growing on mossy slopes on extensive mown grass.
Daedalea quercina		J339697	28-Sep-96	On fallen dead trunk of oak among conifers.
Fistulina hepatica	Beefsteak Fungus	J342697	14-Nov-88	Several very small specimens on a long dead oak stump.
Ganoderma adspersum		J345694	25-Dec-91	Imbricate on a section of oak trunk on the ground.
Ganoderma resinaceum		J344696	10-Oct-03	At base of oak 2540 in grass.
Grandinia barba-jovis		J334695	26-Nov-94	Underside of alder branches lying in litter.
Grifola frondosa		J347696	10-Oct-03	At base of oak 2510.
Hymenochaete cinnamomea		J339697	30-May-99	On hazel branches in litter.
Hymenochaete rubiginosa		J345695	22-Nov-97	On very old de-barked oak log in litter.
Inonotus radiatus		J331691	05-Nov-90	On decaying upright alder in wet riverbank alder woods.
Laetiporus sulphureus	Chicken of the Woods	J337695	09-Sep-97	Young fruiting body on dead oak stump in mixed woods.
Macrotyphula fistulosa var. contorta		J332692	04-Nov-83	Abundant on twigs and branches of alder in wet riverbank woods.
Mycoacia uda		J344696	08-Oct-97	Underside of a felled ash branch in litter.
Peniophora cinerea		J342697	06-Apr-01	On fallen oak branches.
Peniophora lycii		J334692	05-Feb-92	On twigs of grey alder.
Peniophora quercina		J344697	10-Oct-03	On dead branch on young oak nr. 2541.
Phellinus ferreus		J344695	07-Jan-92	On the underside of an oak branch, wet woodland.
Phlebia livida		J337697	28-Nov-90	In moss on an oak log in pasture.
Phlebia merismoides		J332691	25-Nov-91	Patches on an alder log; riverine carr.
Piptoporus betulinus	Birch polypore	J347703	10-Oct-03	On fallen birches in planting.
Pseudotrametes gibbosa		J337697	10-Nov-90	Abundant on cut sycamore stumps, parkland.
Ramaria stricta		J343697	09-Sep-99	In litter and bare soil under Monterey cypress.
Schizopora paradoxa		J342697	02-Sep-97	Underside of felled Portuguese laurel logs.
Skeletocutis nivea		J345695	31-Dec-91	On hazel twigs by a boggy stream in mixed wet woodland.
Stereum gausapatum		J344695	28-Nov-90	Abundant on bare heartwood of a young, damaged oak.
Stereum hirsutum		J344695	28-Nov-90	Large patches on bare heartwood of a young oak.
Stereum ochraceo-flavum		J344695	26-Jan-95	On alder twigs in dense, wet undergrowth.
Stereum rugosum		J345695	31-Dec-91	Abundant on living or half-dead mature laurel in mixed woods.
Stereum sanguinolentum		J330692	26-Nov-90	Abundant on cut ends of thinned Scots pine and larch.
Trametes versicolor		J345694	25-Dec-91	Oak stump in parkland.
Trichaptum abietinum		J338700	30-Nov-90	Common on larger wind blown boughs of Scots pine.
Typhula erythropus		J344695	26-Nov-94	On petiole of Alnus leaf in litter.
Typhula phacorrhiza		J332692	04-Nov-83	Abundant in alder litter; wet riverbank wood.
Typhula setipes		J331691	05-Nov-01	On sclerotia poking through bark of a small ash branch.
Vuilleminia comedens		J344697	10-Oct-03	On dead branches on young oak nr. 2541.

Agaricales – mushrooms

Species	Common name	Grid ref	Date	Notes
Agaricus silvicola	Wood Mushroom	J343697	25-Aug-99	In litter and bare soil under Monterey cypress.
Amanita fulva	Tawny Grisette	J342697	29-Aug-00	In litter under oak.
Amanita inaurata	Snakeskin Agaric	J342697	26-Aug-99	In litter under young oak.
Amanita muscaria	Fly Agaric	J344700	10-Oct-03	In grass under birch nr. oak on 7th fairway.
Armillaria ostoyae	Honey Fungus	J345697	10-Oct-03	In grass under oak 2516.
Boletus porosporus		J341696	25-Aug-99	In grass under oak.
Calyptella capula		J347694	25-Oct-97	On rotting nettle stem in black woodland sheugh.
Clitocybe bresadoliana		J343697	25-Aug-99	In litter and bare soil under Monterey cypress.
Clitopilus prunulus	The Miller	J344698	10-Oct-03	In grass under small oak nr. 2542.
Cortinarius purpurascens		J343696	24-Aug-92	Under beech and oak in an arboretum.
Crepidotus variabilis		J334694	30-Dec-91	On the branches of a fallen, dead elm.
Hygrocybe psittacina	Parrot Waxcap	J344693	16-Nov-96	Growing on extensive mown grass.
Hygrocybe virginea		J344693	22-Nov-97	Growing on extensive mown grass.
Hygrophoropsis aurantiaca	False Chanterelle	J331689	27-Aug-99	In litter under planted European spruce.
Hypholoma fasciculare	Sulphur Tuft	J347697	10-Oct-03	On fallen limb of oak 2513.
Inocybe geophylla var. lilacina		J346701	10-Oct-03	Under large beech.
Laccaria laccata	Deceiver	J346701	10-Oct-03	Under large beech.
Lactarius acris		J343696	24-Aug-92	Under beech in a grassy arboretum.
Lactarius glyciosmus		J340696	12-Oct-03	In grass under birch.
Lactarius quietus	Oak Milkcap	J345698	10-Oct-03	In grass under oak 2517.
Lactarius subdulcis		J333693	06-Nov-91	Under beech; in deep litter.
Lactarius torminosus		J340696	12-Oct-03	In grass under birch.
Leccinum roseofracta		J346694	02-Sep-00	Under downy birch in scrub.
Leccinum scabrum		J340696	25-Aug-99	In grass under birch.
Lepista inversa		J335696	10-Nov-90	On a pathside bank under alder.

Lepista nuda	Wood Blewit	J337698	16-Nov-95	In nettles etc. in the shade of parkland oaks.
Leucopaxillus giganteus	Giant Funnel Cap	J345698	10-Oct-03	In grass cuttings/midden under oak 2515.
Mycena galericulata	Bonnet Mycena	J337698	16-Nov-95	Tufted in crevices of a fallen oak limb.
Mycena inclinata		J339696	24-Oct-03	On old oak stump.
Mycena leucogala		J339696	24-Oct-03	On humus material on old oak stump.
Paxillus involutus	Roll Rim	J344700	10-Oct-03	In grass under birch nr. oak on 7th fairway.
Pholiota squarrosa	Shaggy Pholiota	J346701	10-Oct-03	At base of dying cherry.
Resupinatus applicatus		J346695	19-Jan-99	On fresh fallen rotten bough of gale-blown oak.
Russula aeruginea	Birch Brittlegill	J342697	31-Aug-00	Under downy birch in arboretum.
Russula albonigra		J342697	26-Aug-99	In litter under young oak.
Russula anatina		J344697	10-Oct-03	In grass under young oak nr 2541.
Russula atropurpurea		J342696	27-Aug-99	In litter under parkland oak.
Russula chloroides	Blue-line Brittlegill	J342697	29-Aug-00	In litter under oak.
Russula claroflava	Blackening Swamp Brittlegill	J344700	10-Oct-03	In grass under birch nr. oak on 7th fairway.
Russula cyanoxantha		J332691	03-Sep-99	In grassy litter under beech.
Russula cyanoxantha var. peltereaui		J332691	03-Sep-99	In grassy litter under beech.
Russula farinipes		J342697	26-Aug-99	In litter under young oak.
Russula fellea		J332692	23-Sep-87	Frequent under beech in mixed woods.
Russula fragilis		J342697	26-Aug-99	In litter under young oak.
Russula graveolens		J345694	Sep-90	Frequent in mown grass under oak.
Russula heterophylla		J331692	25-Jul-00	In dryish litter under beech.
Russula mairei	Beechwood Sickener	J331692	25-Jul-00	In dryish litter under beech.
Russula nigricans	Blackening Brittlegill	J342697	25-Aug-99	In litter under young oak.
Russula nitida		J340696	25-Aug-99	In grass under birch.
Russula ochroleuca	Common Brittlegill	J346701	10-Oct-03	Under large beech.
Russula parazurea		J339695	11-Sep-97	In litter and bare soil under a mature oak.
Russula pectinatoides		J342697	30-Aug-00	In litter under oak.
Russula sericatula		J330692	25-Jul-00	In dryish litter under beech.
Russula velenovzkyi	Coral Brittlegill	J347696	10-Oct-03	In grass at base of oak 2510.
Suillus aeruginascens		J340696	26-Aug-99	In grass under one hybrid larch.
Suillus grevillei	Larch Bolete	J340696	25-Aug-99	In grass under larch.
Tricholomopsis rutilans	Prunes and Custard	J331689	27-Aug-99	On spruce stumps under planted European spruce.

Gasteromycetes – puffball fungi

Geastrum striatum	Striate Earthstar	J342695	12-Dec-95	In litter under a large, old Monterey cypress; arboretum.
Langermannia gigantea	Giant Puffball	J333692	12-Sep-78	1, 30cm in diameter, on previously burnt grassy ground.
Lycoperdon perlatum	Puffball	J340694	16-Nov-96	Around felled conifers in mossy grass.
Lycoperdon pyriforme	Stump Puffball	J344699	10-Oct-03	On dead roots under oak 2536.
Mutinus caninus	Dog Stinkhorn	J333694	24-Sep-78	In litter under hybrid larch.
Phallus impudicus	Stinkhorn			
Scleroderma areolatum	Leopard-spotted Earthball	J344696	10-Oct-03	Erupting from dry sods at base of oak 2540.
Scleroderma verrucosum	Scaly Earthball	J342695	24-Aug-92	In litter and bare soil under evergreen oak.

GROUP	Grid Ref	Date	Habitat
Tricladida – flatworms			
Arthurdendyus triangulatus	J337698	24-Apr-91	Under fallen oak branches in wet riverine meadowland.
Kontikia andersoni	J332691	17-Apr-81	Under rotting alder branches in a wet alder wood.
Microplana terrestris	J333693	24-Jan-84	Under rubble, deciduous scrub on streambank.
Nemertea – nemertine worms			
Argonemertes dendyi	J322691	29-Dec-89	Under moss and alder branches; wet carr.
Mollusca – slugs and snails			
Aegopinella nitidula	J335693	27-Mar-91	In litter, herb-rich grey alder planting.
Aegopinella pura	J344695	26-Nov-94	In litter under isolated oaks.
Anisus vortex	J337697	28-Jan-95	In sparsely vegetated margins of R. Lagan.
Arion ater	J342704	12-Dec-95	In fairly deep sycamore leaf litter.
Arion circumscriptus	J335693	27-Mar-91	In litter, herb-rich grey alder planting.
Arion distinctus	J335693	27-Mar-91	Under dead wood grey alder planting.
Arion intermedius	J332692	30-Sep-94	In mossy leaf litter.
Arion lusitanicus (= vulgaris)	J332696	01-May-05	Under dead wood on lawn in the arboretum.
Arion owenii	J335693	27-Mar-91	Under dead wood in a mainly grey alder plantation.
Arion subfuscus	J335693	27-Mar-91	In litter, herb-rich grey alder planting.
Bithynia tentaculata	J337697	28-Jan-95	In sparsely vegetated margins of R. Lagan.
Carychium minimum	J335693	27-Mar-91	In litter of herb-rich grey alder planting.
Carychium tridentatum	J344695	26-Nov-94	Under branches in wet mixed wood on clay soils.
Clausilia bidentata	J342704	12-Dec-95	In fairly deep sycamore leaf litter.
Cochlicopa lubrica	J335693	27-Mar-91	In litter, herb-rich grey alder planting.
Cochlicopa lubricella	J335693	27-Mar-91	In litter, herb-rich grey alder planting.
Columella aspera	J332692	14-Feb-96	On branches in litter under beech; beech/alder/ash growths.
Columella edentula	J335693	27-Mar-91	On branches, riverine grey alder wood.
Deroceras panormitanum	J335693	27-Mar-91	Under dead wood.
Deroceras reticulatum	J335693	27-Mar-91	Under dead wood.
Discus rotundatus	J342704	12-Dec-95	In fairly deep sycamore leaf litter.
Euconulus alderi	J335693	27-Mar-91	In litter, herb-rich grey alder planting.
Euconulus fulvus	J335693	27-Mar-91	In litter, herb-rich grey alder planting.
Gyraulus albus	J338698	09-Apr-00	Shallow 'scrape' pond on the banks of the River Lagan.
Lehmannia marginata	J335693	27-Mar-91	Under dead wood.
Limacus maculatus	J335693	27-Mar-91	Under dead wood.
Limax maximus	J335693	27-Mar-91	Under dead wood.
Lymnaea fusca	J338698	09-Apr-00	Shallow 'scrape' pond on the banks of the River Lagan.
Lymnaea stagnalis	J337697	28-Jan-95	In sparsely vegetated margins of R. Lagan.
Nesovitrea hammonis	J332692	14-Feb-96	On branches and in litter.
Oxychilus alliarius	J335693	27-Mar-91	In litter, herb-rich grey alder planting.
Oxychilus cellarius	J335693	27-Mar-91	In litter, herb-rich grey alder planting.
Physa fontinalis	J338698	09-Apr-00	Shallow 'scrape' pond on the banks of the River Lagan.
Planorbarius corneus	J337697	28-Jan-95	In sparsely vegetated margins of R. Lagan.
Planorbis carinatus	J337697	28-Jan-95	In sparsely vegetated margins of R. Lagan.
Potamopyrgus antipodarum	J338698	09-Apr-00	Shallow 'scrape' pond on the banks of the River Lagan.
Radix balthica	J337697	28-Jan-95	In sparsely vegetated margins of R. Lagan.
Semilimax pyrenaicus	J332691	29-Dec-89	Under alder branches and leaf litter.
Spermodea lamellata	J344695	26-Nov-94	In litter under isolated oaks in mixed woods, clay soil.
Trichia hispida	J342704	12-Dec-95	In fairly deep sycamore leaf litter.
Trichia striolata	J342704	27-Dec-95	Under a stone in deep litter.
Vitrea contracta	J332692	14-Feb-96	On branches in litter under beech.
Diplopoda – millipedes			
Anamastigona pulchellum	J338696	14-Apr-04	In wet litter under alder.
Boreoiulus tenuis	J342695	28-Apr-95	Trapped with fish-baited pitfall in rabbit's burrow.
Brachydesmus superus	J344695	26-Nov-94	In wet sycamore litter on clay, under laurel; streambank.
Craspedosoma rawlinsi	J333694	08-Sep-99	Under grey alder branches; dried out woodland pool.
Cylindroiulus britannicus	J332692	30-Sep-94	Under bark of well-rotted alder branches.
Cylindroiulus punctatus	J332692	30-Sep-94	Under bark of well-rotted alder branches in litter.
Glomeris marginata	J342704	12-Dec-95	In fairly deep sycamore leaf litter.
Leptoiulus belgicus	J342704	12-Dec-95	In fairly deep sycamore leaf litter.
Melogona scutellare	J344695	26-Nov-94	In deep leaf litter under Quercus or sycamore.
Nanogona polydesmoides	J345695	26-Nov-94	Underside of alder branch in litter; mixed wood.
Ommatoiulus sabulosus	J339697	30-May-99	On hazel branches in litter.
Ophyiulus pilosus	J332692	30-Sep-94	In mossy litter and under bark of well-rotted alder branches.
Polydesmus angustus	J345695	26-Nov-94	Underside of alder branch in litter; mixed wood.
Proteroiulus fuscus	J332692	30-Sep-94	Under bark of well-rotted alder branches in litter.
Tachypodoiulus niger	J344695	26-Nov-94	Scarce; in deep leaf litter under oak/sycamore.
Chilopoda – centipedes			
Brachygeophilus truncorum	J346694	23-Apr-98	Under bark of mature felled sycamore lying on the ground.
Lithobius borealis	J346694	17-Mar-98	Underside of log in leaf litter.
Lithobius melanops	J346694	17-Mar-98	Underside of log in leaf litter.
Lithobius microps	J339695	09-Mar-96	Under dead wood beneath oak; old hedgerow.
Lithobius variegatus	J344695	16-Dec-95	Under bark of oak branch under isolated oaks.

Crustacea – woodlice or slaters [land]

Androniscus dentiger	J337697	09-May-91	Under a boulder by an old wall; riverine pasture.
Haplophthalmus danicus	J332692	30-Sep-94	Under bark of well-rotted alder branches in litter.
Oniscus asellus	J342704	12-Dec-95	In fairly deep sycamore leaf litter.
Philoscia muscorum	J342704	12-Dec-95	In fairly deep sycamore leaf litter.
Porcellio scaber	J336695	25-Nov-92	Under flaking bark on an old sycamore; wet meadow.
Trichoniscus pusillus	J342704	12-Dec-95	In fairly deep sycamore leaf litter.

Crustacea – slaters/shrimps [freshwater]

Asellus aquaticus	J337697	28-Jan-95	In sparsely vegetated margins of R. Lagan.
Crangonyx pseudogracilis	J338698	09-Apr-00	Shallow 'scrape' pond on the banks of the River Lagan.
Gammarus pulex	J337697	28-Jan-95	In sparsely vegetated margins of R. Lagan.

Coleoptera – beetles
Carabidae – ground beetles

Agonum fuliginosum	J337698	19-Apr-91	In or under fallen oak stems or stones.
Agonum marginatum	J333694	04-Jun-82	On wet litter by a woodland pool.
Anchomenus dorsalis	J337698	19-Apr-91	In or under fallen oak stems or stones.
Asaphidion curtum	J333693	24-May-84	*Alnus* carr on the banks of the River Lagan.
Bembidion bruxellense	J333694	04-Jun-82	On wet litter by a woodland pool.
Bembidion dentellum	J339697	22-May-04	running on muddy rivermargin.
Bembidion guttula	J333694	04-Jun-82	On wet litter by a woodland pool.
Bembidion mannerheimi	J333694	04-Jun-82	On wet litter by a woodland pool.
Bembidion tetracolum	J339697	22-May-04	Running on muddy rivermargin.
Bradycellus harpalinus	J334690	19-Feb-84	In grass tussocks.
Clivina fossor	J337698	19-Apr-91	In or under fallen oak stems or stones.
Cychrus caraboides	J337698	19-Apr-91	In or under fallen oak stems or stones.
Elaphrus riparius	J333694	04-Jun-82	On damp sand under dense vegetation.
Laemostenus terricola	J342695	28-Apr-95	Trapped with fish-baited pitfall; rabbit burrow.
Leistus fulvibarbis	J333694	04-Jun-82	On damp sand under dense vegetation.
Loricera pilicornis	J346694	16-Apr-04	Running on muddy streambank.
Nebria brevicollis	J337698	19-Apr-91	In or under fallen oak stems or stones.
Ocys harpaloides	J3469	03-Jul-86	Under bark of *Pinus* logs.
Platynus albipes	J333693	24-May-84	Caught in *Alnus* carr on the banks of the River Lagan.
Platynus assimilis	J337698	19-Apr-91	In or under fallen oak stems or stones.
Platynus obscurus	J337698	19-Apr-91	In or under fallen oak stems or stones.
Pterostichus diligens	J337698	19-Apr-91	In or under fallen oak stems or stones.
Pterostichus melanarius	J337698	19-Apr-91	In or under fallen oak stems or stones.
Pterostichus strenuus	J3469	03-Jul-86	In fresh hay.
Trechus obtusus	J337698	19-Apr-91	In or under fallen oak stems or stones.

Dytiscidae – water beetles

Hydroporus erythrocephalus	J338698	09-Apr-00	Shallow 'scrape' pond on the banks of the River Lagan.

Hydrophilidae – water margin beetles

Megasternum obscurum	J331688	07-Apr-98	Crawling on algaed rabbit pellets on a wet, wooded lawn.

Ptiliidae – feather-wing beetles

Acrotrichis atomaria	J3469	03-Jul-86	In fresh hay.
Acrotrichis thoracica	J332692	27-Sep-93	In cap cuticle of foetid *Russula nigricans* under beech.
Ptenidium pusillum	J3469	03-Jul-86	In fresh hay.
Leptinidae - nest beetles			
Leptinus testaceus	J342695	28-Apr-95	Trapped with fish-baited pitfall; rabbit's burrow.

Leiodidae – round fungus beetles

Agathidium nigripenne	J346694	23-Apr-98	Under bark of mature felled sycamore lying on the ground.
Agathidium varians	J343696	24-Feb-99	Underside of alder log in litter; arboretum.
Leiodes polita	J346694	26-Jul-93	Swept from an oak tree, lower branches; woodland edge.

Staphylinidae – rove beetles

Aloconota gregaria	J343694	25-Apr-04	On dandelions.
Aloconota insecta	J346694	16-Apr-04	Under stone on gravelly streambank.
Anomognathus cuspidatus	J337697	18-Nov-92	Under peeling bark of large beech logs in riverine pasture.
Anotylus inustus	J339698	22-May-04	On *Rumex obtusifolius*.
Anotylus rugosus	J346694	16-Apr-04	In moss on logs; gravelly streambank.
Anotylus sculpturatus	J331688	14-Mar-98	Crawling on rabbit pellets on a short, mossy lawn.
Anthobium unicolor	J342695	28-Apr-95	Trapped with fish-baited pitfall; rabbit's burrow.
Atheta britanniae	J339696	09-Sep-97	In rotting *Boletus* under oak.
Atheta castanoptera	J331691	06-Sep-97	In fresh *Russula* sp. under spruce.
Atheta crassicornis	J335694	12-Oct-03	In rotted *Fistulina* on oak.
Atheta hepatica	J3469	03-Jul-86	By general sweeping.
Autalia impressa	J332692	27-Sep-93	In 6 blackened *Russula nigricans* under beech.
Bessobia fungivora	J346694	16-Apr-04	In *iptoporus betulinus* on birch.
Bessobia occulta	J335694	12-Oct-03	In rotted *Fistulina* on oak .
Bolitochara obliqua	J337697	18-Nov-92	Under bark of beech branch in a wet meadow.
Coryphium angusticolle	J341695	12-Apr-95	Under bark of 1 year-fallen large Scots pine.
Creophilus maxillosus	J343692	30-May-99	Under a stone by a small, artificial pool.
Datomicra zosterae	J335694	12-Oct-03	In rotted *Fistulina* on oak .
Deleaster dichrous	J346694	16-Apr-04	Under stones/wood; gravelly streambank.
Gabrius appendiculatus	J346694	16-Apr-04	In moss on log; gravelly streambank.
Gyrophaena gentilis	J332692	27-Oct-93	In *Clitocybe geotropa* in litter under beech.
Gyrophaena minima	J345695	01-Sep-97	Beaten from *Stereum hirsutum* on a laurel log.
Gyrophaena pulchella	J332692	27-Oct-93	In *Clitocybe geotropa* in litter under beech.
Homalota plana	J337697	18-Nov-92	Under peeling bark of large beech logs in riverine pasture.
Lathrobium brunnipes	J346694	16-Apr-04	In moss on sycamore trunk.

Species	Grid ref	Date	Notes
Lordithon exoletus	J331691	03-Sep-97	On fresh *Russula* sp. under spruce.
Lordithon lunulatus	J332692	27-Sep-93	In 6 blackened *Russula nigricans* under beech.
Lordithon thoracicus	J337695	28-Sep-96	Beaten from *Collybia butyracea* under young beech.
Lordithon trinotatus	J333691	28-Sep-96	Beaten from *Clitocybe geotropa* under larch.
Mniusa incrassata	J346694	16-Apr-04	In moss on sycamore trunk.
Mocyta fungi	J3469	03-Jul-86	In fresh hay.
Mocyta orbata	J335694	12-Oct-03	In rotted *Fistulina* on oak.
Ocypus brunnipes	J343696	16-Apr-04	Under stone in the old cemetery.
Oligota pusillima	J345693	28-Sep-96	In dried out, mildewed sulphur tuft at the base of a large oak.
Olophrum piceum	J345694	15-Apr-04	In grass tussock under sapling oak.
Omalium italicum	J346694	11-Oct-97	In *Hypholoma fasciculare* on cut alder logs.
Oxypoda alternans	J332693	27-Sep-93	In the gills of honey fungus under beech.
Oxypoda elongatula	J346694	16-Apr-04	In moss on log; gravelly streambank.
Philonthus decorus	J334694	09-Mar-99	Underside of fallen larch log in grass.
Philonthus rotundicollis	J338695	09-Sep-95	Inside a decaying *Fistulina* on oak log.
Philorinum sordidum	J347693	10-May-04	On flowering *Cytisus scoparius*.
Phloeonomus pusillus	J341695	12-Apr-95	Under bark of 1 year-fallen large Scots pine.
Phloeopora testacea	J341695	12-Apr-95	Under bark of dead, wind-blown pine.
Phyllodrepa ioptera	J336696	22-May-04	Hawthorn flowers.
Phyllodrepa vilis	J337697	15-Apr-04	Under bark of fallen oak.
Proteinus brachypterus	J332692	27-Sep-93	In blackened *Russula nigricans* under beech.
Proteinus ovalis	J339696	09-Sep-97	In rotting *Boletus* under oak.
Stenus flavipes	J346694	27-Aug-93	In long grass under a parkland lime.
Stenus impressus	J3469	03-Jul-86	By general sweeping.
Stenus picipes	J339697	10-Aug-93	Swept off leguminosae; cleared riverbank.
Tachinus humeralis	J332692	27-Sep-93	In blackened *Russula nigricans* under beech.
Tachinus laticollis	J342695	28-Apr-95	Trapped with fish-baited pitfall; rabbit's burrow.
Tachinus pallipes	J332692	27-Sep-93	In blackened *Russula nigricans* under beech.
Tachinus signatus	J3469	03-Jul-86	In fresh hay.
Tachyporus chrysomelinus	J3469	03-Jul-86	In fresh hay.
Scarabaeidae – dung and flower beetles			
Aphodius sphacelatus	J331688	07-Apr-98	Crawling on algaed rabbit pellets on a wet lawn.
Melolontha melolontha	J346694	31-May-04	From lower branches of a large oak.
Scirtidae – marsh beetles			
Cyphon coarctatus	J339697	10-Aug-93	Swept off leguminosae, riverbank.
Elateridae – click beetles			
Aplotarsus incanus	J346694	10-May-04	On ungrazed grassy area.
Athous haemorrhoidalis	J3469	03-Jul-86	On *Pinus* log.
Ctenicera cuprea	J347693	10-May-04	On flowering *Cytisus scoparius*.
Dalopius marginatus	J346694	10-May-04	On sapling oak *Quercus*.
Hemicrepidius hirtus	J343695	14-Jun-04	General sweeping in the Arboretum.
Cantharidae – soldier beetles			
Cantharis figurata	J343695	14-Jun-04	General sweeping in the Arboretum.
Cantharis nigra	J343695	14-Jun-04	General sweeping in Arboretum.
Cantharis nigricans	J336696	22-May-04	Hawthorn flowers or on oak foliage.
Cantharis pallida	J343695	14-Jun-04	General sweeping in Arboretum.
Cantharis rufa	J345694	31-May-04	Mainly on willow or oak.
Malthinus flaveolus	J346694	05-Jul-93	Swept off the lower branches of young *Quercus robur*.
Malthodes guttifer	J346694	04-Jul-93	Swept at evening along a scrubby woodland edge.
Rhagonycha fulva	J346694	05-Jul-93	By general sweeping, meadowland.
Rhagonycha lignosa	J3469	03-Jul-86	General sweeping.
Rhagonycha limbata	J346694	04-Jul-93	Swept off *Quercus robur*.
Ptinidae – spider beetles			
Ptinus subpilosus	J336695	25-Nov-92	Under flaking bark on an old sycamore; wet meadow.
Kateretidae – marsh pollen beetles			
Kateretes rufilabris	J339697	22-May-04	On *Alnus glutinosa*
Nitidulidae – pollen beetles			
Brachypterus glaber	J343695	14-Jun-04	Beaten off rose flowers.
Brachypterus urticae	J346694	04-Jul-93	Swept off stinging nettle.
Cychramus luteus	J332693	27-Sep-93	In the ring of a honey fungus stipe under beech.
Epuraea aestiva	J336696	22-May-04	Hawthorn flowers.
Epuraea melanocephala	J346694	18-Apr-94	On flowers of *Salix caprea*.
Meligethes aeneus	J337697	26-May-04	Hawthorn blossom.
Meligethes flavimanus	J346694	10-May-04	On crab apple flowers.
Meligethes pedicularius	J337697	26-May-04	Hawthorn blossom.
Omosita discoidea	J331691	03-Sep-97	On cattle spine bones under spruce.
Rhizophagidae – narrow bark beetles			
Rhizophagus dispar	J337697	18-Nov-92	Under peeling bark of large beech logs.
Cryptophagidae – silken fungus beetles			
Atomaria atricapilla	J3469	03-Jul-86	In fresh hay.
Cryptophagus dentatus	J337697	18-Nov-92	Under bark of a beech branch; wet meadow.
Cryptophagus pseudodentatus	J337697	18-Nov-92	Under bark of a beech branch; wet meadow.
Cryptophagus ruficornis	J335694	12-Oct-03	In rotted *Fistulina* on oak .
Cryptophagus scanicus	J336695	25-Nov-92	Under flaking bark of an old sycamore; wet meadow.
Cryptophagus setulosus	J331691	03-Sep-97	In gills of *Pholiota* on a deciduous log.
Micrambe vini	J347693	10-May-04	On flowering *Cytisus scoparius*.
Byturidae – raspberry beetles			
Byturus tomentosus	J3469	03-Jul-86	On raspberry.
Erotylidae – shiny fungus beetles			
Dacne bipustulata	J342694	23-Apr-04	Decaying *Bjerkandera adusta* on oak.
Coccinellidae – ladybirds			
Adalia bipunctata	J343695	14-Jun-04	General sweeping in arboretum.
Adalia decempunctata	J346694	26-Jul-93	Swept off long grass, meadowland.
Coccinella septempunctata	J346694	26-Jul-93	Swept off long grass, meadowland.
Calvia quattuordecimguttata	J339697	22-May-04	On *Salix caprea*.
Halyzia sedecimpunctata	J345694	22-May-04	On sycamore.
Propylea 14-punctata	J346694	04-Jul-93	Swept off *Quercus robur*.
Scymnus auritus	J346694	31-May-04	On one large oak near the Belvoir carriageway.

Endomychidae – false ladybirds

Endomychus coccineus	J337697	01-Nov-92	Under bark of shattered, fired beech stump on a riverbank.

Latridiidae – mould beetles

Aridius bifasciatus	J345693	28-Sep-96	Beaten from dried out sulphur tuft; large parkland oak.
Aridius nodifer	J334693	09-Sep-95	In fairly fresh Collybia in mossy litter under alder.
Cortinicara gibbosa	J347693	10-May-04	On flowering Cytisus scoparius.
Stephostethus lardarius	J346694	27-Aug-93	Swept off Salix caprea.

Ciidae – small fungus beetles

Cis bidentatus	J332691	01-Apr-81	Under bark of a dead upright oak tree.
Cis bilamellatus	J342694	15-Apr-04	In Bjerkandera adusta on oak stump.
Cis boleti	J341700	16-Dec-93	In decayed Trametes suaveolens brackets on beech.
Cis festivus	J337697	15-Apr-04	Under Stereum hirsutum brackets on oak.
Cis nitidus	J341700	16-Dec-93	In decayed Trametes suaveolens brackets on beech.
Octotemnus glabriculus	J342694	23-Apr-04	Decaying Bjerkandera adusta on oak.

Scraptiidae – tumbling flower beetles

Anaspis maculata	J3469	03-Jul-86	On Cotoneaster blossom.
Anaspis regimbarti	J336696	22-May-04	Hawthorn flowers.
Anaspis rufilabris	J3469	03-Jul-86	On Cotoneaster blossom.

Cerambycidae – longhorn beetles

Rhagium bifasciatum	J337698	19-Apr-91	1, in pupal chamber in a small, rotted oak log; pasture.
Grammoptera ruficornis	J3469	03-Jul-86	On Cotoneaster blossom.

Chrysomelidae – leaf beetles

Bruchidius villosus	J347693	10-May-04	On flowering Cytisus scoparius.
Bruchus atomarius	J343694	10-May-04	On Vicia sepium by path.
Cassida rubiginosa	J336696	19-Jun-85	On Cirsium; rubbishy field margin.
Chalcoides fulvicornis	J346694	04-Jul-93	On Salix caprea scrub, woodland edge.
Galerucella calmariensis	J346694	04-Jul-93	On Salix caprea scrub.
Gastrophysa viridula	J3469	03-Jul-86	On docks.
Hydrothassa marginella	J339698	22-May-04	On Ranunculus repens; riverbank.
Phaedon tumidulus	J3469	03-Jul-86	On Heracleum spondylium.
Phratora vitellinae	J346694	05-Jul-93	Swept off Salix caprea scrub.
Phratora vulgatissima	J338700	16-May-96	On low herbs in a grey alder plantation.
Pyrrhalta viburni	J340697	09-Sep-97	On planted guelder rose below the main carpark.

Apionidae – seed or snout weevils

Apion apricans	J339697	10-Aug-93	Swept off planted red clover; riverbank.
Apion curtirostre	J346694	05-Jul-93	Swept off leguminosae.
Apion ervi	J346694	05-Jul-93	Swept off Trifolium pratense, woodland edge.
Apion fulvipes	J339697	10-Aug-93	Swept off planted red clover.
Apion gibbirostre	J342693	13-Aug-94	On Cirsium arvense; rough grass.
Apion haematodes	J346694	31-May-04	On Rumex acetosa.
Apion hydrolapathi	J339698	22-May-04	On Rumex obtusifolius.
Apion loti	J345694	31-May-04	Swept off Lotus uliginosus.

Apion subulatum	J346694	27-Aug-93	Swept from Lotus uliginosus in rough grassland.
Apion violaceum	J339698	22-May-04	On Rumex obtusifolius.
Apion virens	J339697	15-Aug-93	Swept off planted Trifolium pratense.
Apion vorax	J345694	15-Apr-04	In grass tussock under sapling oak.

Curculionidae – weevils

Acalles misellus	J346694	27-Aug-93	Swept from Salix caprea bush; rough grassland.
Anthonomus rubi	J345694	31-May-04	Swept; overgrown meadow.
Archarias pyrrhoceras	J346694	04-Jul-93	On Quercus robur, mainly young trees.
Archarias salicivorus	J346694	27-Aug-93	Swept from Salix caprea.
Barypeithes pellucidus	J3469	03-Jul-86	General sweeping.
Cidnorhinus quadrimaculatus	J346694	04-Jul-93	Swept off stinging nettle.
Dorytomus rufatus	J346694	11-Aug-93	Swept off Salix caprea.
Dorytomus taeniatus	J345694	31-May-04	On Salix caprea.
Limnobaris dolorosa	J339697	10-Aug-93	Swept off leguminosae; cleared riverbank.
Orchestes fagi	J3469	03-Jul-86	On Fagus leaves.
Orchestes quercus	J346694	26-Jul-93	Swept off lower branches of mature Quercus robur
Orchestes rusci	J346694	11-Aug-93	Swept off Betula pubescens.
Otiorhynchus singularis	J345694	31-May-04	On Salix caprea.
Phyllobius argentatus	J345694	31-May-04	On oak and birch.
Phyllobius viridiaeris	J336696	22-May-04	Hawthorn flowers.
Polydrusus pterygomalis	J346694	04-Jul-93	Mainly on willows.
Rhamphus pulicarius	J346694	05-Jul-93	Swept off Salix caprea.
Rhinoncus castor	J346694	31-May-04	On Rumex acetosa.
Rhopalomesites tardyi	J337697	18-Nov-92	Under peeling bark of large beech logs in riverine pasture.
Sitona regensteinensis	J347693	10-May-04	On flowering Cytisus scoparius.
Strophosoma melanogrammum	J346694	05-Jul-93	Swept off oak/hazel.
Tychius picirostris	J345694	31-May-04	Swept; meadow.

Scolytidae – bark or ambrosia beetles

Hylastes brunneus	J3469	03-Jul-86	Under bark of Pinus logs.
Hylurgops palliatus	J333692	16-Dec-93	Under peeling bark of a year-dead, felled spruce.
Pityogenes bidentatus	J340699	16-May-96	Galleries under bark of dis-masted, dead larch.
Tomicus piniperda	J342702	10-May-02	Infesting living Scots Pine by R. Lagan.
Xyloterus domesticus	J337697	18-Nov-92	Under peeling bark of large beech logs in riverine pasture.

Diptera:Syrphidae – hoverflies

Cheilosia illustrata	J334695	18-Jul-86	On umbels, hay meadow.
Chrysotoxum bicinctum	J334694	30-Jun-86	On Potentilla erecta in hay meadow.
Criorhina berberina	J337696	14-Jun-87	On Heracleum and Symphoricarpos by forest path.
Criorhina floccosa	J340697	04-Jun-86	On rowan flowers near the carpark at Belvoir.
Dasysyrphus albostriatus	J340697	04-Jun-86	On Cotoneaster in carpark.
Dasysyrphus tricinctus	J335696	22-Jul-87	On Potentilla erecta; hay meadow.

Dasysyrphus venustus	J337696	16-Jun-87	On *Ranunculus* at pathside.
Didea fasciata	J341697	08-Jun-86	On *Heracleum mantegazzianum* under pines.
Epistrophe eligans	J340696	08-Jul-86	On Viburnum in the carpark.
Episyrphus balteatus	J340697	08-Jul-86	On Viburnum in the carpark.
Eristalis arbustorum	J334695	18-Jul-86	On umbels, hay meadow.
Eristalis arbustorum	J340697	08-Jul-86	On Viburnum in the carpark.
Eristalis intricarius	J334695	18-Jul-86	On umbels, hay meadow.
Eristalis nemorum	J334695	18-Jul-86	On umbels, hay meadow.
Eristalis pertinax	J334695	18-Jul-86	On umbels, hay meadow.
Eristalis tenax	J334695	18-Jul-86	On umbels, hay meadow.
Eupeodes luniger	J334694	16-Jun-87	On *Leontodon*, hay field.
Helophilus hybridus	J334695	29-Sep-85	On ragwort; hay meadow.
Helophilus pendulus	J447982	26-May-94	On hawthorn flowers.
Helophilus pendulus	J335695	01-Jul-86	On ground elder; pathside.
Leucozona glaucia	J335695	01-Jul-86	On ground elder (*Aegopodium*) on pathside.
Leucozona laternaria	J335695	01-Jul-86	On ground elder (*Aegopodium*) on pathside.
Leucozona lucorum	J335695	01-Jul-86	On *Symphoricarpos*, pathside.
Melangyna lasiophthalma	J335694	01-May-86	On *Ranunculus* in mixed, mainly alder, plantation.
Melanostoma mellinum	J340697	08-Jul-86	On Viburnum in the carpark.
Meliscaeva auricollis	J334694	30-Jun-87	On *Potentilla erecta* in hay meadow.
Meliscaeva cinctella	J397745	05-Sep-94	On *Heracleum*; woodland edge.
Metasyrphus latifasciatus	J334694	16-Jun-87	On *Leontodon*; hay field.
Myathropa florea	J340697	08-Jul-86	On Viburnum at carpark.
Parasyrphus annulatus	J333694	30-Jun-87	On *Potentilla erecta* in larch planting.
Parasyrphus lineolus	J334694	10-Aug-84	One on *Chenopodium* by path.
Platycheirus albimanus	J335696	01-May-86	On *Ranunculus*; alder planting.
Platycheirus scambus	J334697	26-Jul-84	On umbels; alder planting.
Sphaerophoria menthastri	J333693	16-Jun-87	On *Ranunculus*; hay meadow.
Syritta pipiens	J340697	08-Jul-86	On *Viburnum* in the carpark.
Syrphus ribesii	J340697	08-Jul-86	On *Viburnum* in the carpark.
Syrphus vitripennis	J333694	30-Jun-87	On *Potentilla erecta*; hay meadow.
Volucella bombylans	J335695	01-Jul-86	Feeding at *Symphoricarpos*.
Xylota segnis	J340697	08-Jul-86	On *Viburnum* in the carpark.

Hemiptera – true bugs

Acanthosoma haemorrhoidale	J345694	10-May-04	Beaten off hawthorn.
Pentatoma rufipes	J346694	31-May-04	From lower branches of a large oak.
Troilus luridus	J335695	02-Jun-90	Feeding on caterpillar on shrubs.

Hymenoptera – bees and wasps

Andricus fecundator	J346694	12-Aug-04	On buds of *Quercus robur*.
Andricus quercusramuli	J346694	05-Jun-04	On male flowers of mature *Quercus robur*.
Andricus quercuscalicis	J346694	10-Oct-03	On acorns of *Quercus robur*.
Biorhiza pallida	J346694	05-Jun-05	On shoots of *Quercus robur*.
Neuroterus quercusbaccarum	J346694	05-Jun-04	On male flowers and leaves of *Quercus robur*.

Lepidoptera – butterflies

Aglais urticae	J339697	8-Jul-86	Caravan park.
Anthocaris cardamines	J334695	10-May-86	Flying, Sculpture Meadow.
Aphantopus hyperantus	J334695	18-Jul-86	Flying, Sculpture Meadow.
Leptidea reali	J333693	16-Jun-87	On grasses; hay meadow.
Lycaena phlaeas	J334695	15-Jun-86	Flying, Sculpture Meadow.
Maniola jurtina	J334695	18-Jul-86	Flying, Sculpture Meadow.
Pararge aegeria	J333694	30-Jun-87	Margins of larch plantation.
Pieris brassicae	J339697	8-Jul-86	Caravan park.
Pieris napi	J334695	18-Jul-86	Flying, Sculpture Meadow.
Pieris rapae	J339697	8-Jul-86	Caravan Park.
Polyommatus icarus	J333694	30-Jun-87	Around *Lotus;* margins of larch planting.

Picture Credits

Cover picture by Jonathan Fisher is from a private collection. Photograph: photographic Survey, Courtauld Institute of Art. Photograph of Belvoir entrance in the introductory page is from the Forest Service archive.

Chapter 1. Page 11. Picture of a shoot presented to Forest Service by Miss Byers. Page 12. Morelands Meadow by Mark Hamilton, Forest Service. Page 13. Arboretum by Roy Anderson. Page 15. Oak near the motte by Carol Baird for Forest of Belfast. Page 16. Painting by Hugh Frazer. Reproduced by kind permission of the trustees of the museums and galleries of Northern Ireland.

Chapter 2. Page 17. Motte by Ben Simon. Page 18. The Dungannon family by Philip Mercier from a private collection. Photograph: photographic Survey, Courtauld Institute of Art. Pages 19, 20, 21. Paintings by Jonathan Fisher from a private collection. Photograph: photographic Survey, Courtauld Institute of Art. Page 22. Dungannon plaque by Esler Crawford Photography. Page 23. Belvoir by Lord Mark Kerr reproduced by kind permission of Hector McDonnell of Glenarm. Page 24. Hill-Trevor boundary marker (precise location unknown) from the Douglas Deane collection, which is currently housed in the RSPB offices at Belvoir Park. Page 25. Photograph of the Belvoir gate lodge kindly provided by Dixie Dean. Scale drawing of the ink pot gatelodges at Belvoir from The Archaeological Survey of County Down (1966), HMSO, Belfast. Page 26. Engraving of Robert Bateson reproduced by kind permission of the trustees of the museums and galleries of Northern Ireland. Ulster Museum reference III/BATESON,R. Page 27. Painting by Hugh Frazer reproduced with the kind permission of the Trustees of the museums and galleries of Northern Ireland. Ulster Museum reference IIa5/D/6b. Robert Bateson plaque by Esler Crawford Photography. Page 29. Thomas Bateson by Spy reproduced from Vanity Fair, January 28 1882. Bateson crest on Belvoir House from Douglas Deane Collection. Page 30. Photograph of the Farr family kindly lent by Berkley Farr. Page 31. Directors of Harland and Wolff by Robert Welsh. Reproduced by kind permission of the Trustees of the museums and galleries of Northern

Ireland. Ulster Museum reference IIIB/HARLAND. Page 32. The hall at Belvoir by Robert Welsh. Reproduced with the kind permission of the Trustees of the museums and galleries of Northern Ireland. Ulster Museum reference W05/23/5. Page 33. The interior of Belvoir are from the file 'Belvoir Park. County Down. Proposed residence for Governor of Northern Ireland'. National archives, Kew, London. Reference WORK 27/15. Page 34. Dungannon Vault. Left – photograph given by Miss Byers, daughter of a gamekeeper at Belvoir, to Forest Service. The Forest Service archive is currently housed in their offices at Belvoir Park Forest. Middle – Douglas Deane collection. Right – by Roy Anderson. Page 36. Belvoir House from Douglas Deane collection. Page 37. Belvoir housing estate by Roy Anderson. Belvoir sign is a slide in Forest Service archive, Belvoir. Page 38. Operation Lusty programme from Belvoir Park files, Forest Service. Page 39. This picture was published by The Belfast Telegraph on the day of demolition. Copy kindly provided by a Milltown resident. Page 40. Three photographs of the Belvoir Tree Fair kindly provided by Kevin Collins, Forest Service, Dublin. Kingfisher sculpture by Ben Simon. Page 41. Ulster Wildlife Trust picture. Visitors to Belvoir by Ben Simon, 2003.

Chapter 3. Page 44. Estate map reproduced by kind permission of Noel Witchell and family. Page 47. Photographs reproduced by kind permission of Noel Witchell and family. Page 49. Photograph from Douglas Deane collection. Page 50. Photograph of Lily Dobbin by kind permission of Dorin Bell. Page 51. Gate lodge from an album of photographs of gate lodges presented to Built Heritage, Environment and Heritage Service. Page 52. Photograph of Dobbin family by kind permission of Dorin Bell. Page 57. Belvoir House by Deirdre Crone. Reproduced by kind permission of the artist.

Chapter 4. Photograph of a detail of the old Belvoir Garden sundial by Aurora Photography for The Forest of Belfast. Photographs numbered 1, 4, 5, 6, 8 and 9 are among a number of photographs of Belvoir Park presented to Forest Service by Miss Byers in the 1970s. It is not known if she took the pictures, though details indicate that they were not all taken at the same time. They seem to be from the late Victorian to Edwardian period. Miss Byers was the daughter of the gamekeeper at Belvoir Park. Hugh Byers, gamekeeper, was named in the 1901 census at which time he was 28 years old, single and living in a house owned by Walter Wilson. Photographs 2, 3 and 10 are by Robert Welch from the Ulster Museum collection. References 23/3, 23/4, 23/6. Reproduced with the kind permission of the Trustees of the museums and galleries of Northern Ireland. Most of the photographs taken by Robert Welch (1859-1936) are not dated. However, he was known by the Wilson family (he took photographs at Harland and Wolff and was a guest at the wedding of Alec Wilson, to whom he gave a album of photos as a present (see Northern Whig July 30 1915 p.9). It seems most likely that the Welch photographs of Belvoir date from the time when the Wilson family leased Belvoir and before 1909 when they were reproduced in the book by R. M. Young, *Belfast and the Province of Ulster*. W. T. Pike, Brighton. Photograph 7 of the stream is from the Douglas Deane collection and is undated. The slide mount is annotated 'Belvoir Park Rock Garden, Belfast.1st years growth'. Photograph 11 by Alexander Hogg (1870-1939), a lantern slide from his series 'River Lagan from source to sea' thought to date from around the turn of the last century. Reproduced with the kind permission of the Trustees of the museums and galleries of Northern Ireland.

Chapter 5. Page 68. Air Photograph from the Ordnance Survey of Northern Ireland archive. Reference H frame 29908 Run 46. Pages 69-75. Slides kindly provided by Roy Anderson. Page 76. Photograph by Ben Simon.

Chapter 6. Page 77. Photograph taken for Forest of Belfast. Pages 82, 83. Photographs by Ben Simon. Page 84. Illustration by Carol Baird for the Forest of Belfast. The Deramore Oak by Robert Welch. Reproduced with the kind permission of the Trustees of the museums and galleries of Northern Ireland. Ulster Museum reference 23/7.

Chapter 7. Page 85. Tree rings by Esler Crawford Photography. Page 87. Illustrations by Carol Baird for the Forest of Belfast. Page 88. Photograph by Ben Simon. Page 92 and 93. Illustrations by Carol Baird for the Forest of Belfast. Page 96. Photographs by Mike Baillie.

Chapter 8. Page 102. Illustrations of oak leaves by Carol Baird for the Forest of Belfast.

Chapter 9. All pictures by Roy Anderson

Chapter 10. All pictures by Roy Anderson

Chapter 11. Page 127. Picture kindly provided by the Lagan Valley Regional Park. Page 128. Pictures by Mark Hamilton, Forest Service. Page 129. Pictures kindly provided by Davy McAllister, Forest Service. Page 130. Pictures kindly provided by Davy McAllister, Forest Service. Page 131. Pictures of crows by Peter Cush and swans by Ben Simon.

Chapter 12. Page 133. Badgers from the Douglas Deane Collection. Page 134. Red squirrel by Mark Hamilton, Forest Service. Illustrations by Carol Baird for the Forest of Belfast. Author and family by Aurora Photographic for the Forest of Belfast. Page141. Illustration by Carol Baird for the Forest of Belfast.

Back Cover illustration from Taylor and Skinner's maps of the roads of Ireland, surveyed 1777. Published for the authors, sold by G. Nicol, 1778.